PARENT WORK CASEBOOK

Parent Work Casebook

Edited by:
Kerry Kelly Novick, Jack Novick,
Denia Barrett and Thomas Barrett

IPBOOKS.net
International Psychoanalytic Books

International Psychoanalytic Books (IPBooks)
New York • http://www.IPBooks.net

Published by IPBooks
Queens, New York
Online at: www.IPBooks.net

Cover design by Blackthorn Studio (BlackthornStudio.com)

ISBN: 978-1949093-46-9

To our parents and grandparents
To the parents of our grandchildren
To the parents we've worked with and learned from

ACKNOWLEDGEMENTS

We gratefully acknowledge the efforts of all our contributors, the creativity of their thinking, and their generosity in participating in this volume. We thank the American Psychoanalytic Association and the International Psychoanalytic Association for making space for innovative discourse on this topic.

TABLE OF CONTENTS

CONTRIBUTORS

Anne Alvarez, Ph.D., M.A.C.P

Consultant Child and Adolescent Psychotherapist (and retired Co-Convener of the Autism Service, Child and Family Dept., Tavistock Clinic, London). Author of *Live Company: Psychotherapy with Autistic, Borderline, Deprived and Abused Children;* Editor with Susan Reid, *Autism and Personality: Findings from the Tavistock Autism Workshop.* A book in her honor, edited by Judith Edwards, titled *Being Alive: Building on the Work of Anne Alvarez,* was published in 2002. Visiting Professor at the San Francisco Psychoanalytic Society in November 2005 and Honorary Member of the Psychoanalytic Center of California. Her latest book, *The Thinking Heart: Three Levels of Psychoanalytic Therapy with Disturbed Children*, was published in April 2012 by Routledge.

Denia Barrett, M.S.W. (Editor)

Child and Adolescent Supervising Analyst on the faculty of The Chicago Psychoanalytic Institute. Formerly a member of the faculty of the Hanna Perkins Center and editor of *Child Analysis:*

Clinical, Theoretical, and Applied. Member of the editorial boards of *The Psychoanalytic Study of the Child* and *Psychoanalytic Social Work*. Presenter and author of papers on clinical work, theory, supervision, and ethics in work with children and parents. Past President of the Association for Child Psychoanalysis.

Thomas Barrett, Ph.D. (Editor)

Child and Adolescent Supervising Analyst on the faculty of the Chicago Psychoanalytic Institute and adjunct Professor in Infant and Early Childhood Mental Health (IECMH) at Chicago's Erikson Institute. Executive and Clinical Director of the Hanna Perkins Center in Cleveland, OH from 1990—2010. Writes extensively and presents regularly, both nationally and internationally, on topics related to work with children, adolescents and their parents. President-elect of the Association for Child Psychoanalysis.

Janis A. Baeuerlen, M.D.

Child and adult psychoanalyst in private practice in Berkeley, CA. Child and Adolescent Supervising Analyst, child faculty member and former chair of the Child Analysis training program of The San Francisco Center for Psychoanalysis. Adult faculty member SFCP.

B. James Bennett, M.D.

Child, Adolescent and Adult Psychoanalyst and Psychiatrist in private practice. Clinical Professor, Dept. of Psychiatry, University of Texas Southwestern Medical School Dallas; Faculty, Dallas Psychoanalytic Center and Center for Psychoanalytic Studies—Houston.

Sarah Rabb Bennett, M.S.W.

Child, adolescent and adult psychoanalyst on the faculty of the Dallas Psychoanalytic Center. Graduate of Smith College School for Social Work with a fellowship at the Yale Child Study Center, the Anna Freud Centre in London, and the Dallas Psychoanalytic Center.

Peter Bruendl, Ph.D.

Psychoanalyst in private practice for children, adolescents and adults in Munich, Germany. Member of ACP, DGPT, MAP, VAKJP. Training and Supervising Analyst of Münchner Arbeitsgruppe für Psychoanalyse (MAP). Numerous publications on adolescence, migration, trauma, the impact of Nazi terrorism on first, second, and third generations, male development, and parenthood.

Enrico DeVito, M.D.

Psychiatrist and Psychoanalyst, Member of the Italian Psychoanalytic Society and of the International Psychoanalytical Association with a private practice in Milan, Italy. Founded and directed Progetto A, Center for Consultation and Psychotherapy of Adolescents. Formerly President of the International Society of Adolescent Psychiatry and Psychology (ISAPP).

Joshua Ehrlich, Ph.D.

Clinical psychologist and psychoanalyst in private practice in Ann Arbor, Michigan. Faculty, Michigan Psychoanalytic Institute and Department of Psychiatry, University of Michigan. Author of *Divorce and Loss: Helping Adults and Children Mourn When a Marriage Comes Apart* published in 2014.

Theodore Fallon, Jr., M.D., M.P.H., FAACAP, FABP
Board certified in Internal Medicine, Psychiatry, Child Psychiatry, and both Child and Adult Psychoanalysis. Former Chair of the Child Psychoanalytic Training Program at the Psychoanalytic Center of Philadelphia, and Clinical Associate Professor at Drexel College of Medicine and St. Elizabeth's Hospital in Washington, DC. Active in research, teaching and clinical practice and has published numerous papers, articles, book chapters, and a book, *Disordered Thought and Development: From Chaos to Organization in the Moment.* Private practice in child and adult psychoanalysis, psychotherapy and forensics in Philadelphia, and consultant to Center for Families in Malvern, PA.

Philip Herschenfeld, M.D.
Training and Supervising Analyst at the New York Psychoanalytic Institute, certified in Child and Adult Psychoanalysis. Former Dean of the NYPSI and teacher of numerous courses. Previously on the faculties of Albert Einstein and Mt. Sinai Schools of Medicine.

James Herzog, M.D.
Adult and child psychiatrist and psychoanalyst. Previously did clinical work and research at Children's Hospital and the Beth Israel Hospital in Boston. Supervisory and Training Analyst for adults and children at Boston Psychoanalytic Society and Institute, and a supervisory analyst at the Sigmund Freud Institute in Zurich, Switzerland. Has written extensively on fatherhood and psychoanalytic technique.

Leon Hoffman, M.D.
Co-Director Pacella Research Center and Training and Supervising Child, Adolescent, and Adult Analyst, The New York Psychoanalytic Society and Institute. A widely published researcher as well as clinician, he has written about Regulation-Focused Psychotherapy for Children.

Claudia Lament, Ph.D.
Training and Supervising Analyst at The Psychoanalytic Association of New York, an affiliate of The New York University Langone School of Medicine. Editor-in-Chief of *The Psychoanalytic Study of the Child* and President of The Anna Freud Foundation.

Jacqueline Langley, Ph.D.
Psychologist and child and adolescent psychoanalyst in private practice for over thirty-five years in the St. Louis area. Serves on the faculties of the St. Louis and Michigan Psychoanalytic institutes teaching candidates and advanced psychodynamic psychotherapists about psychological development and psychoanalytic work with adolescents and children and concurrent work with parents. Speaks widely to schools and parents regarding these topics.

Marsha Levy-Warren, Ph.D.
Training and Supervising psychoanalyst at The Contemporary Freudian Society, the International Psychoanalytical Association, and the Confederation of Independent Societies. Faculty and Clinical Consultant at the NYU Postdoctoral Program in Psychotherapy and Psychoanalysis. Private practice in New York City where she sees adolescents, adults, and parents, and is the author of *The Adolescent*

Journey (2004) and numerous articles on development, culture, clinical theory and treatment.

Norka T. Malberg, Psy.D.

Certified Child and Adolescent Psychoanalyst, Adult Psychoanalyst; Assistant Clinical Professor, Yale Child Study Center, School of Medicine; Private Practice in New Haven, CT; Member of the Contemporary Freudian Society and the Western New England Psychoanalytic Society. Has written extensively, with numerous volumes on emotion, psychotherapy, and mentalization.

Mali Mann, M.D.

Training and Supervising Analyst, Geographic Supervising Child Analyst at the San Francisco Center for Psychoanalysis. Clinical Professor at the Department of Psychiatry and Behavioral Science at Stanford University School of Medicine. Has written on immigration and assisted reproductive technology.

Anna Migliozzi, Dottore

Supervising Child and Adolescent Analyst for the Italian Psychoanalytical Society and head of an evaluation and referral service for children and adolescents in Milan, Italy.

Jill M. Miller, Ph.D.

Graduate of the Anna Freud Centre, Child, Adolescent, and Adult Training and Supervising Analyst at the Washington Baltimore Psychoanalytic Center, and past President of the Association for Child Psychoanalysis. Teaches and supervises candidates in psychoanalysis both locally and nationally, and has written on a variety of topics related to children and adolescents. Private practice in Washington DC.

Viviane Sprinz Mondrzak, M.D.

Full member and Training Analyst of the Porto Alegre Psychoanalytic Society, past President of the Porto Alegre Psychoanalytic Society, Chair of the Study Group on Psychoanalytic Epistemology of the Porto Alegre Psychoanalytic Society, Brazil.

Elissa Baldwin Murphy, Ph.D.

Clinical social worker in private practice with children, adolescents, and adults in Chapel Hill, NC. Child analyst and advanced adult candidate at the Psychoanalytic Center of the Carolinas (PCC). Faculty of the PCC and Lecturer and Research Advisor at the Smith College School for Social Work.

Jack Novick, M.A., Ph.D. (Editor)

Adult, Adolescent and Child Training and Supervising Psychoanalyst. Co-author of a book and numerous articles on concurrent parent work, as well as five other books and many papers on termination, sadomasochism, child and adult technique. Co-founder: Allen Creek Preschool, MPI Child Analysis and Integrated Training program, Alliance for Psychoanalytic Schools. President, Association for Child Psychoanalysis, and former IPA Board and Executive Committee member.

Kerry Kelly Novick, FIPA (Editor)

Child, Adolescent, and Adult Training and Supervising Psychoanalyst on the faculties of numerous psychoanalytic centers in the United States and the IPA. Formerly Chair, IPA Committee on Child and Adolescent Psychoanalysis, and President, Association for Child Psychoanalysis. Founder, Allen Creek Preschool. Editorial Board of the *Journal of the American Psychoanalytic Association*. Has co-authored six books and many articles on various topics.

Deborah W. Paris, M.S.W., BCD
Child Psychoanalyst who has worked with children and parents for
45 years. She has been a school consultant, teacher and supervisor
and at The Hanna Perkins Center for Child Development she has
led numerous parent groups.

Felecia Powell-Williams, Ed.D.
Child, adolescent and adult psychoanalyst in private practice.
President of the Board of Directors, and on the faculty of the
Center for Psychoanalytic Studies - Texas. Registered Play Therapist
Supervisor and provides clinical supervision for the State of Texas
licensing board. Teaches on a collegiate level and provides clinical
consultation and professional training with many preschools and state
and local agencies on recognizing the need of mental health services
for children, adults, and families.

Ruth Axelrod Praes, Ph.D.
Clinical psychologist at the National Autonomous University
of Mexico, where she was awarded the Gabino Barreda Medal.
Psychoanalyst who has served on the IPA Board and as past co-chair
of the IPA Committee on Women and Psychoanalysis. Past President
of the Mexican Psychoanalytic Association (APM), director of the
APM Institute and Postgraduate Study Center. Author of articles
and several books on adoption, divorce, children of divorce, gender,
trauma and betrayal. Private practice in Mexico City.

Justine Kalas Reeves, M.S.W., D.Psych.
Child, adolescent and adult psychoanalyst in Washington, DC.
Trained at the Anna Freud Centre and the Contemporary Freudian

Society (CFS). Currently Secretary of the Association for Child Psychoanalysis and is on the curriculum committee of CFS-DC. Helped initiate the integrated training track at CFS-DC, and has written about the history of child analysis, toddlers, the diagnostic profile, and the developmental point of view in psychoanalysis.

Timothy Rice, M.D.
Associate Professor of Psychiatry at the Icahn School of Medicine at Mount Sinai in New York, NY. Chief of Child and Adolescent Inpatient Services for the Mount Sinai Health System, and Director for Medical Student Education in Psychiatry at Mount Sinai St. Luke's-West. Senior candidate in child and adult psychoanalysis at the Columbia University Center for Psychoanalytic Training and Research.

Donald Rosenblitt, M.D., FABP
Adult Training and Supervising and Child and Adolescent Supervising Analyst with the Psychoanalytic Center of the Carolinas. Founding Clinical/Executive Director of the Lucy Daniels Center (1991–2019). Widely published in professional journals and popular newspapers and magazines.

Samuel C. Roth, Ph.D.
Child and adult psychoanalyst in private practice in Newton, Massachusetts. Teaches at the Boston Psychoanalytic Society and Institute, the Massachusetts Institute for Psychoanalysis and the Massachusetts Mental Health Center.

Majlis Winberg Salomonsson
Swedish training and child psychoanalyst in private practice and at the Mama Mia Child Health Centre, Stockholm. Lecturer at the Faculty of Psychology, University of Stockholm and a researcher at the Karolinska Institutet, Stockholm, and author of several papers and books on psychoanalysis with children and adolescents.

Caroline Sehon, M.D., FABP
Director, International Psychotherapy Institute (IPI); former Chair and Supervising Analyst, The International Institute for Psychoanalytic Training (IIPT) at IPI; Member, The International Psychoanalytic Association's Committee on Child and Adolescent Psychoanalysis; Clinical Associate Professor of Psychiatry, Georgetown University; Member of the American Psychoanalytic Association and the International Psychoanalytical Association; author of articles and book chapters on ethics; child, couple and family therapy; and teleanalysis. Child and adult analyst working with individuals, couples and families in Bethesda, MD.

William Singletary, M.D.
Child and adult psychiatrist and psychoanalyst on the faculty of the Psychoanalytic Center of Philadelphia and President of the Board of the Margaret S. Mahler Child Development Foundation. Private practice near Philadelphia, PA.

Michael Slevin, M.S.W.
Sees adults and adolescents in his private practice and in hospitals. Co-editor with Beverly Stoute, M.D., of two volumes forthcoming by Routledge, *Psychoanalysis and the Trauma of Racism: Lessons from*

the Therapeutic Encounter, and *Psychoanalysis and Racism beyond the Consulting Room.*

Donna Roth Smith, M.S.W., FIPA

Child, adolescent and adult psychoanalyst. Private practice in NYC working with infants through young adults and their families, adults and couples, and consultant to private and public schools, research and therapeutic nurseries. Training and Supervising Analyst (Child, Adolescent, and Adult) and faculty at the Institute of The Contemporary Freudian Society; supervisor and faculty at the Institute for Psychoanalytic Training and Research and the Anni Bergman Parent-Infant Program. Formerly faculty at Bank Street Graduate School Infant and Parent Development and Early Intervention Program and The Institute for the Clinical Study of Infants, Toddlers and Parents at JBFCS.

Ann Smolen, Ph.D.

Training and Supervising Analyst and Director of Child and Adolescent Training at The Psychoanalytic Center of Philadelphia. Private practice in Ardmore, PA where she sees children, adolescents and adults in psychoanalysis and psychotherapy. Has written and edited a number of books on child treatment and the development of homeless children.

Alan Sugarman, Ph.D.

Training and Supervising Child, Adolescent, and Adult Psychoanalyst at the San Diego Psychoanalytic Center. Clinical Professor of Psychiatry at the University of California, San Diego and the Head of the APsaA Department of Psychoanalytic Education. Author of many frequently cited articles, he is also on the editorial boards of the *Journal of the American Psychoanalytic Association*, the *Psychoanalytic Quarterly*, and *Psychoanalytic Psychology*.

Frances Thomson-Salo, Ph.D.
Adult and child psychoanalyst who has also specialized in working with infants and parents. Has written and edited numerous books on femininity and infancy and is a former President of the Australian Psychoanalytic Society.

Kenneth Winarick, Ph.D.
Director of Academic Affairs, Training and Supervising Analyst, The American Institute for Psychoanalysis (AIP). Faculty and member of the Steering Committee of the Integrated Training Track of Adult, Child and Adolescent Psychoanalysis of The Institute for Psychoanalytic Training and Research (IPTAR).

CHAPTER ONE

INTRODUCTION: ASSUMPTIONS AND RATIONALE

Fundamental Assumptions

The contributors to this volume are all psychoanalysts specializing in work with children, adolescents, emerging adults, parents and families. We live in different places around the world and work in various kinds of settings, with many populations, and use a wide variety of treatment modalities. Our training traditions are heterogeneous and draw on a wide spectrum of psychoanalytic thought.

And yet we share some fundamental assumptions that shape the discourse. All of us see development as central to life and to psychoanalytic understanding and technique. Concepts of development inform our ideas about how children grow into adults and how adults help that process, while themselves engaged in change. We have an epigenetic, life-cycle perspective, assuming that development is taking place at all stages of life, influenced from within and without in a complex and evolving interaction.

That holistic view of development implies that we are interested in the whole person, that is, all aspects of a person's development, not just pathology. When we think about clinical technique, we

1

assume that we will engage with strengths and vulnerabilities, progressive and regressive forces in the personality, linear and non-linear growth.

All child and adolescent therapists have to engage with their patients' parents, since children do not bring themselves alone to treatment. But how we deal with that fact gives rise to many different views and practices. In this volume we see a range of ideas about whether and how to work with parents, as well as variations related to age and stage of the child, and family configuration.

Many of the contributions are drawn from the proceedings of the Parent Work Discussion Group at the Annual Meetings of the American Psychoanalytic Association, while others come from different conferences and meetings. The convenors of that discussion group and editors of this book sought to make available a space for consideration of an evolving model of parent work, previously described in a book (Novick, K.K. & Novick, J. 2005) and in papers published and presented earlier and subsequently.

The model asserts that parent work is substantive and legitimate and makes use of the full repertoire of psychoanalytic interventions. Progression through the phases of the child's treatment affects and is dynamically affected by interaction with the parent work. Parental consolidation in the phase of parenthood may also be profoundly impacted by the child's forward developmental movement.

Working with Parents

The main reason for working with parents is pragmatic, since we can demonstrate that it helps people enter treatment, stay and do the necessary work, and leave in a timely fashion, maintaining the benefits of the work (Novick, K. K. and Novick, J. 2005).

Parents are a big part of the child's world. They are also part of the child's troubles, either primarily as contributing to the cause, or secondarily as affected by the impact of disturbance. Parents or other caretaking adults are integral to assessment and treatment of young people. Children continue to live in and will return to their family and environment. Adaptive growth in parents supports child change; parental pathology can destroy child treatment gains. Current neurological research demonstrates the importance of close attachment and communication between parents and children. The ongoing plasticity of the child's brain through late adolescence and into emerging adulthood offers hope that deep and long-lasting change can be effected in the bonds of the family.

We assume that the center of most treatments will be the individual, hopefully intensive, work with the child or adolescent. But, if we restrict the idea of child analysis only to the individual child, then we would be denying the knowledge that psychoanalysis offers about the complexity of development and the relationships that foster both health and pathology. If we focus only on a child's symptoms, that is not a psychoanalytic approach. From the beginning of an evaluation, we assume and communicate to child and parents that the child's troubles are part of a larger parent-child history, embedded in a community, in society, in culture. For full understanding and therapeutic change, we say that both individual and family aspects will need attention. Differences of opinion arise within the field, however, as to how to structure that attention.

There have historically also been many areas of resistance within analysts to doing parent work at all, including social-historical, theoretical, political, and psychodynamic concerns that can interfere with effective clinical work. We have included in this volume commentaries from analysts who represent theories that exclude parent work and also from those who accept parent work but think that in certain cases parent work should be done by someone other than the therapist. We hope in this way to present a view of child and adolescent psychoanalysis which includes the controversies. Different chapters in this volume will illustrate some effects of such resistances.

Difficulties can also arise from many sources within the therapeutic process. It is hard for analysts, faced with child and parent distress, not to want to start treatment of the child immediately. But, without a foundation of a beginning alliance with parents, many treatments will fail. A salient factor can be the mindset or self-state of analysts, conceptualizing themselves only as the therapist of the child. In that traditional role parents are seen as other adults who respect the expertise of the analyst, and are there to bring the child, pay, deal with logistics and support the work. Parents are rarely perceived as people with multiple needs as they deal with shame, guilt, resentment, the practical burdens of supporting a child or adolescent in treatment, marital pressures and tensions and so forth. Here too we hope that this book will illuminate these complexities.

Why a Casebook?

Psychoanalysts work with individuals. In our professional lifetimes, as Winnicott observed, "one analyst cannot have enough cases to cover all contingencies..." (1958, p. 123). He was referring to the fact that we each have a relatively small number of cases at any one time or even over a lifetime. When we share our work, however, we expand our experience and are pushed by the examples of others to think about our choices in how we set up treatments, articulate goals, make interventions, and know when the work is done. By understanding more about each unique therapeutic relationship and situation, we arrive at general ideas and approaches, and begin to develop models and theories.

Models and theories can offer a rough map of the unknown terrain to be traversed in the journey of a treatment. But they may feel too removed from the experience of the work, and even risk setting up an idealized image of how it 'should' be done, which can constrain therapists or make them feel they are somehow falling short when the case doesn't fit the model.

Our goal in this book has been to collect clinical vignettes as examples of actual work with parents, to demonstrate the reality of doing parent work, how hard it is, what the challenges are, how people try to meet them, what sometimes succeeds and the rewards and pleasures that come with effective work, what doesn't work even with massive effort, pitfalls, techniques and their rationales, and the impact on analysts, patients, and parents when they do or don't work together. Rather than think about these issues from the vantage point of theory, tradition, or opinion, we have tried to gather actual data about parent work as a substantive contribution to a pragmatic and effective child and adolescent psychoanalysis.

We know there is a very wide range of opinions and practices in relation to the rapidly changing dimension of parent work concurrent with the individual treatment of a child or adolescent. In an effort to encompass that range and gather a useful set of ideas and attitudes, we then sought commentaries on each clinical vignette from practicing colleagues. Just as it sometimes breaks an impasse or illuminates a problem when we discuss a case with a trusted colleague, our hope is that the varied perspectives of the commentators can spark thoughtful consideration of the technical choices and challenges facing each therapist, giving the reader a sense of possibilities in addressing dilemmas and difficulties. Each chapter consists of a clinical vignette, some commentaries, and editorial reflections highlighting points arising from the chapter. We also hope that a volume like this, which brings together the voices of forty child psychoanalysts, working all over the world, can be useful in clinical teaching, offering examples from real-life practice and assuring students and trainees that we all grapple with similar predicaments.

A further aim of this book is to build on the experiences of working child analysts to contribute to the ongoing evolution of a model of parent work. We seek to expand and elaborate our knowledge and understanding of basic ideas, adjust what experience shows needs alteration, add to our repertoire of techniques—ultimately to make child and adolescent psychoanalysis more accessible, practical, available, and effective.

Here, in the introductory chapter, we will describe a few of those basic ideas as we formulated them coming into this project. At the end of the book there is a summary chapter, where we reexamine these ideas in the light of what we have gleaned from the various chapters, identify themes common to the experience of the Contributors, and discuss our conclusions and suggestions for future directions.

Some aspects of the working model of concurrent dynamic parent work

A developmental approach is essential
The parent-child relationship is fundamental

Parents constitute a major primary environmental influence in ongoing ways throughout the child's development.

❖ The first determinant of any current behavior is likely to be found in the parent/child relationship, as early as infancy and in some cases in prenatal development, especially in the pleasure/pain economy and in the fantasies that accompany that relationship.

❖ Behavior evolves through phases in which current levels of psychological and biological functioning influence and are influenced by previous phases, forward and backward along the time dimension. Fantasies and expectations regarding future development by children, parents, siblings, teachers, peers and many others can have a powerful effect on the course of development and the understanding of the past.

❖ Transformation is the main characteristic of this epigenetic evolution.

❖ No one phase has more importance than any other and developmental transformations continue throughout the life span.

❖ Each phase brings something unique to the mix, which may compensate for earlier difficulties or raise prior dormant issues to problematic intensity (Nachträglichkeit, après-coup, or deferred action).

The therapeutic alliance determines outcome
Establishing multiple alliances

Research in psychoanalysis and adjoining fields finds that the quality of the therapeutic or working alliance is a critical factor in predicting treatment outcome. We see building an alliance as primarily the responsibility of the therapist; the alliance is one dimension of the whole therapeutic relationship. A relationship has to be established with all parties to the treatment if we hope for a good outcome.

Dual goals for every treatment

Anna Freud defined the goal of child therapy and analysis as restoration of the child to the path of progressive development (1970). Taking into account the principle of epigenesis we have extended this idea to the parent-child relationship to include a second goal:

- ❖ Restoration of the child to the path of progressive development
- ❖ Restoration of the parent-child relationship to a life-long constructive resource for both

Parent Work throughout the treatment
Using the full range of interventions

Parents have therapeutic alliance tasks throughout treatment, so it is important to maintain a relationship to address new anxieties and concerns as they arise. Regularly scheduled meetings create a strong and safe relationship that is better able to withstand inevitable crises and pressures.

Most parents hear echoes of their own development as their children traverse those same phases. If trauma was endured or conflicts occurred which remain unresolved during a particular period, related emotions may press forward from repression and appear in the parents' attitudes and defenses. These may color their interactions with various members of the family. Some parents may, as a result, become less amenable to the work, while for others, it can provide a "window of opportunity" for reparative work and mastery. Maintaining the alliance by means of regular meetings throughout treatment helps everyone weather these fluctuations.

In addition to the traditional use of education, support, validation, modeling, facilitating and so forth that have been staples of parent guidance, we incorporate in parent work the interventions traditionally labeled as dynamic therapy. These include analysis of defenses, verbalization, insight, reconstruction, interpretation, and the use of transference and countertransference for understanding and technique. We can use criteria for termination developed in psychoanalytic treatment of children and adults (Novick, J. and Novick, K.K. 2006).

We have suggested that one of the dual goals of treatment is the shift of the parent-child relationship from a predominantly closed-system power struggle to an open-system relationship of cooperation, mutuality, respect, and love. This will provide children with sturdier capacities to face the unknown future with resilience, flexibility, and creativity, and offer parents increased possibilities to change along with their children. This derives from our experience that dynamic change in children and their parents occurs throughout the work, with each affecting the other, and the effects persisting over time, after termination of treatment.

Differentiating privacy and secrecy

Maintaining confidentiality and preserving the therapeutic relationship are legitimate major concerns for therapists. These goals are most often cited as a reason not to do parent work. Our experience has demonstrated that, when we differentiate privacy and secrecy, it helps us define confidentiality more precisely. We talk with parents and youngsters about the intrinsic privacy of thoughts and feelings, but state that actions are public. Safety is the paramount clinical requirement and it will be destructive of the treatment, and perhaps dangerous to the child or adolescent, if unsafe actions are concealed.

Confidentiality should be maintained in support of privacy, but not as a reflexive collusion with secrecy. Our clinical goal is to make secrecy an object of therapeutic exploration and insight, so that patients and their parents can begin to take pleasure in fruitful sharing and communication.

Devising this book

Writing about parent work brings an additional dimension of challenge. Conveying the dynamics of complex interactions among several people means describing material and relationships in detail; for the clinical examples to be meaningful and useful, they have to be somewhat specific. Yet we have a clinical, moral, and ethical duty to protect the privacy of children and families and the confidentiality of their clinical material.

As Editors of this volume, we have addressed this in two ways. One is by asking contributors to take all possible precautions in their descriptions, including those where permission has been obtained. And the second has been to make the clinical vignettes and commentaries anonymous. Contributors have generously agreed to this provision, in the effort to add a further layer of confidentiality.[1] Thus readers will see everyone's names and affiliations in the List of Contributors, but not attached to their particular contribution.

We hope that readers find this volume useful and welcome feedback and ideas.

---

1 This approach was recently endorsed by the International Psychoanalytic Association as a sound ethical practice (2019).

CHAPTER TWO

TREATMENT VIA THE PARENTS FOR GENDER DYSPHORIA

Preschool

Clinical Vignette

George's parents called seeking an evaluation because their four-year-old son wanted to dress up in his older sister's clothes. When I returned their call and could spend some time on the phone with them both, they said that George had been doing this for a year, but they had been advised by their pediatrician to ignore the behavior, as he would "grow out of it." The telephone call now was prompted by the concern expressed at George's nursery school, where the teachers noted that he avoided playing with the boys and was beginning to be teased by classmates. The parents were confused and anxious, not knowing how to respond or what to make of the "feminine" behavior.

The parents had taken George to a number of psychological and medical specialists without any definitive answers. Endocrinologists had assured them there was no underlying physiological disorder. George had told his parents that he wanted to be a girl and that he dressed up because it made him feel "so good." George's parents wanted me to evaluate the reasons, to see George and tell them, as they put it, "whether George was a boy pretending to be a girl or a girl in a boy's body."

Rather than jump to diagnostic conclusions, for instance, to considering questions of transgender identity or body dysmorphic concerns, I suggested that parents and I first meet to explore George's history and see whether we could together begin to make some sense of the mystery. "Perhaps," I said, "you will be able to help George through this confusion yourselves if we understand what it means to you all."

George's parents were clearly very anxious and his father particularly pressured me to see George immediately. They reiterated their concern about his being teased at preschool and said they were terribly worried about what would happen when he started elementary school. They had been told that the problem was probably psychological; they had been given my name as an expert, even though my office was over an hour away from where they lived. Surely it would be more convenient, they said, if they could all come together and I would see them with George.

This was rather hard, as I both understood their practical challenges of distance and time, and also felt internal pressure to respond to their distress by giving them what they felt would relieve it. Stepping back from that feeling, however, I responded that I generally find that it's helpful to work together with parents as a team, pooling our knowledge and perceptions. I said that my experience had been that these situations generate a lot of strong feelings and worry, but that parents often know more about what is going on than they realize. In the process of getting to know one another and learning more about George's story, things would likely start to make more sense. After a moment's pause, I could hear the mother begin softly crying; father said that he got the idea and we arranged to meet in the evening two days later. My thought was that my crediting them with knowledge, combined with offering them assurance that we could sort things out, relieved the mom and calmed the dad. Perhaps they didn't then feel so helpless and mystified, even though we still had no idea what the issue was.

When we met, the parents thanked me for seeing them so soon and for insisting that we meet first without George. They thought there was probably a lot to go over after all. They started by telling me that they had a conversation with George that day, in which he had said clearly that he knew he was a boy but felt it would "be safer" to be a girl. I said that this was why it could be useful for us to work together initially, since they had just provided a crucial clue. We could wonder what might possibly feel dangerous to George about being a boy.

They began to speculate about possible sources of such a worry, imagining that a little boy might get scared if a male relative died, and so forth, but they were drawing a blank. Father was a large man who still looked like the athlete he had been and he noted that his work did not entail any physical risks. They looked at me for an answer. I had some generic ideas, but I held back and asked them to let their minds explore more what might feel dangerous to a little boy.

After a short silence, the mother began to cry hard; her husband hugged her and apologized. I said that this was a safe place to share feelings and that, when she is ready, we will be able to put words to the tears. Again, stopping myself internally from supplying hypotheses, knowing the answers, I pushed myself to just sit, repeated that it was all right and passed the mother the tissues. In a moment, the parents told me that George had undergone a series of three major surgeries to address a cranial/sacral fusion, starting at the age of nine months, with a further operation projected for age nine. This information made it clear that there was a great deal to process together; we then met weekly for six months without my meeting George.

In the first few meetings, I provided a space for them to express their intense sadness and anxiety. They said they had never been able to talk about these issues with the many medical personnel who had taken care of their son. I struggled with my anger at these professionals who had left parents and child without crucial support in times of crisis, as well as a sense of impotence about child analysts not being able to better educate pediatric medical professionals. I also had to contain my surge of empathic worry, helplessness, and imagination of how awful the first couple of years must have been and use it instead to explore the experience with them.

The operations themselves had been frightening, and, after each one, they had to restrain George and prevent any gross motor activity. Both parents worried about George's future, and his father, who had been a star high school wrestler and football player, said with great sorrow that George would never be able to play contact sports. I wondered aloud why he focused on contact sports, when there were many non-contact sports, such as swimming, fencing, or tennis, which George could enjoy if he wanted to. Father began to engage with this issue and realized that he equated contact sports with masculinity, as his own father had done. He recalled his father and brothers calling non-contact sports "pussy games." "That's crazy," he said and then began to bring into the discussion the increasing evidence of the long-term dangers of contact sports to all boys, not only his son.

This work led quickly to the realization that they believed and conveyed to George that being a boy exposed him to serious danger, since boys are drawn to rough sports. As they understood this, they became able more easily to separate this idea from their love for him as the boy he was. They talked to George about how they would work together with the doctors to help him stay safe from injury. They noted that he would be able to do all sorts of things that big boys liked, such as running, swimming and tennis.

Clarifying the history of the medical interventions and the prognosis with me gave the parents practice in how to talk with George about the scary things that happened when he was a baby and how to give him appropriate explanations of his condition. George then told them that he could remember being held down and restrained. He recalled his frustration, terror and rage and revealed that he felt as if he was being punished for being a bad boy. When I wondered if George might be making any additional connections between the surgeries and the dangers of being a boy, the parents remembered that his six-year-old sister, out of her own terror, had told George that girls never needed that kind of operation.

The final piece of work related to George's pleasures in masturbation and his oedipally tinged conclusion that having boy feelings in his penis for his mother and sister would bring further medical trauma upon him. The parents themselves had been traumatized, first by having a damaged child and then by unsupported medical experiences. After months of sharing, sorrow, and reliving of their panic and distress, they worked together with each other and me effectively in George's behalf. George responded within weeks.

Work with the parents on George's guilt and his belief that the operations were punishment for oedipal wishes and masturbation allowed me to engage with the mother's own guilt for producing a damaged child. She had continued to react with great intensity to the memories of the three surgeries and with panic to the thought of the next one, when George turned nine. I used George's guilt as an interpretation in displacement to describe how we are all prone to react when faced with something that makes us feel helpless. We talked about how guilt conveys a sense of responsibility. If we imagine that we did some bad thing that made the danger happen, then we think we can fix it, and then we won't be overwhelmed with helplessness, that is, we won't be traumatized and immobilized. If George attributed his operations to touching his penis, he could use his guilt to deny his masculinity and its accompanying urges and thereby forestall being anaesthetized, cut into, and restrained. He was operating with the magical thought that being a girl and dressing in his sister's clothes would prevent trauma. As the light dawned in the mother's eyes, I differentiated such guilt from useable concern and talked about the real things she and her husband could do and encourage George to do in the realm where they aren't helpless. They could find the best surgeon, talk to George about how they and the doctors will work to make it be as good as possible, and express their confidence that this feeling will really help before and after.

After six months of working with the parents, George was functioning in an age-appropriate masculine way at home and school. He played with both boys and girls, loved fire trucks, stopped talking about wanting to be a girl, and still loved ballet. The case was closed for the time being, with the parents understanding that the medical situation left George vulnerable to finding magical solutions at times of stress. They felt equipped to help him more effectively and also knew how well they could make use of professional assistance to enhance their parenting in good times and bad. They talked about coming back for help when George reached adolescence.

They never did return but sent me a letter after George recovered from his operation at nine. They had used what they had learned from our work to George's benefit and theirs. The mother added a note that she had begun to panic and feel guilty and overwhelmed, but had stopped herself, with the internal reminder "That won't help! What will?" She then went about giving George (and herself) the realistic reassurance that most likely all would be well.

Finally, a card came when George was about fifteen, telling me that they were moving to another state for work. George was on his high school swim team and a "darn good tennis player."

Commentary 1

George was lucky. His parents got help from a therapist to understand and work with their worries and anxieties—and to help their son with his. But let us start from the beginning.

The parents searched for help since George had a symptom and later on also had problems in relation to his preschool classmates, who teased him. Already in the first telephone call, the therapist was put under pressure to meet with George for an evaluation. The therapist wanted to see the parents first, which is often the case in child therapeutic work (Blake 2008). He/she managed to convey to them his/her point of view in a convincing way. In conversation with the parents, the therapist showed a great capacity to contain the parents' anxiety and keep his/her own thinking clear. He/she also possessed a "negative capability," as Bion defines it (1970), the capacity of not knowing in advance and thus refrain from giving advice or opinions.

The basis of the professional role with parents is that they come to the therapist with the welfare of their child as the focus. They have not come as "patients." The therapist tried to give the parents the feeling that they were in charge, that they had knowledge about what was going on without fully realizing it at the moment. Many authors have focused on therapeutic work with parents (Jacobs 2006; Novick, K.K.

and Novick, J. 2005). They emphasize that the therapist can provide a holding environment, explore the parents' concerns, encourage their curiosity about dynamic processes, enhance their self-esteem, and develop greater reflective capacities (Fonagy and Target 1996; Fonagy and Target 1997).

Returning to the case, two days after the phone call the therapist met the parents. It was soon after their first talk over the phone and the parents were thankful for it. This meeting started in the same way as the phone call; the parents kept pushing for answers. Once again, the therapist needed to hold back and wait. Now the parents revealed the story of several surgeries on the little boy and it was evident that the whole family had suffered from traumatic events. The parents had been traumatized both by having a "damaged" child and also by not being fully supported by medical and psychological professionals. The child's trauma was physical, being operated on and restricted from gross motor activities, as well as psychological with all the pertaining fears and anxieties.

The parents started talking about their sadness and anxiety. Feelings of guilt often appear when parents view their child's problems as a reflection of their own failures. The therapist was able to help the parents process their trauma. He/she also traced some of their fears back to their own history. There are particular technical issues related to work with parents' own childhood histories that are different from how one might work in individual therapy with a parent (Whitefield and Midgley 2015). One could ask if there is a way of working with the unconscious of the parents in the service specifically of coming to terms with their relationship with the child (Altman 2004). In this case, the therapist helped the parents to examine and work through these childhood histories in order to understand their own as well as George's inner state of mind. In this situation he/she apparently also worked with his/her own countertransference, feelings of helplessness and anger at the other professionals' treatment in the traumatic situations in connection to the surgery. In that way he/she could help the parents to examine what had happened and their reactions to this. The therapy went on with the parents and there were no meetings with the boy.

There seems to be a paradigm shift emphasizing parent-focused work. The parent-child relationship is considered to comprise the child's internal representations, both of self and other (Jacobs 2006). Parent work thus strives to reconfigure relational patterns through an alteration of projections and introjections, which in turn, alters the child's self-experience (Jacobs 2006). This relational perspective is further developed by attachment theorists (Bowlby 1969; Ainsworth 1985; Ainsworth 1991; Ainsworth et al. 1991) who propose that parent-child interactions become internalized as psychic structures and eventually organize the psychological and interpersonal life of the child.

What about George? The symptoms vanished after some time. However, as analysts we assume he had an internal world of his own with its unconscious phantasies. Klein got as far as stating that the child "can be immensely helped in childhood by the love and understanding of those around him, but the deep problems can neither be solved for him nor abolished" (1937, p. 316n). Could you really work with the boy's trauma solely through the parents? When is it possible to work through the parents only? And how can you do it? The therapist used interpretation in his/her work with both mother and father. In an indirect way he/she also made use of interpretations concerning George. The boy had his first traumatic experience at the age of nine months. Later the symptoms emerged at an age when oedipal wishes were stronger as well as the guilt feelings. Here the therapist conveyed his interpretations to the parents, who thereby could better understand and address their child. During six months of treatment with the parents alone it turned out to be feasible to help them all. But what if the boy's symptoms remained? We could think of many reasons for that. Possibly, the therapist would then meet the boy in order to find out how deeply internalized his conflicts were. If he/she then would have taken the boy in therapy is another question.

Commentary 2

Working with parents is an essential component of child treatment, especially with young children. It is not unusual to work exclusively with the parents. This clinical vignette illustrates key aspects of listening, assessment and clinical choices when working with parents.

How we begin our work with parents influences the goals and outcome of the treatment, the growth and development of both the child and the parents, and the parent–child relationship. Parents often come to us with a sense of urgency, confused and anxious, wanting us to give them answers quickly and to meet with their child immediately. George's parents presented in just this way during the first phone call to the analyst. During the call, the analyst listened and responded to the parents' anxiety and practical considerations, while also conveying conviction that it would be more effective initially to meet the parents without their child present. The analyst recognized the parents' sense of urgency and vulnerability, and credited the parents with knowing more than they realized about their son.

The analyst accomplished a great deal during the initial phone call and consultation session. During the consultation George's parents quickly expressed appreciation for the analyst's approach and acknowledged that there was a "lot to go over after all." The analyst was listening and learning, not only about the situation at hand but also about what the parents can tolerate and bear in the face of intense affect. Assessment of the parents' capacities guides the analyst's approach through the initial consultation sessions.

During the two days between the phone call and the initial consultation the parents had a conversation with their son. The analyst had already imparted that there was more to learn and that it was possible to involve George in this process without having him in the office. These parents wanted very much to understand and be responsive to their son. Four-year-old George wanted to dress up in his older sister's clothing. They had sought out the advice of various medical and psychological specialists. The nursery school teachers were concerned. The parents called wanting the analyst to tell them "whether George was a boy pretending to be a girl or a girl in a boy's body." The analyst experienced pressure for answers from not only the parents, but from all the professionals involved.

George had told his parents that he knew he was a boy, but it would be safer to be a girl. Drawing on the parents' strengths and capacities, the analyst was able to quickly establish a setting in which the parents could sit with their anxiety and discomfort, and let their minds associate more widely as to why being a boy might seem dangerous to George. The analyst opened this up for exploration and sat with the parents, helping them to tolerate not having immediate answers and allowing themselves to reflect. Significantly, the analyst contained the urge to supply generic answers, which helped the parents tolerate and express their own sadness, confusion and impotence. After sitting with these feelings for some time, the parents revealed their son's significant medical history. The emotional implications and sequelae of the surgical procedures and medical history had apparently never been considered by the previous specialists whom the parents had consulted. During this session the parents allowed themselves to acknowledge and grasp of the enormity of what they had all been through, and the value of processing what had previously seemed irrelevant to the presenting problem. The parents at this point agreed to meet for weekly parent sessions with the analyst.

Over the course of weeks of sessions with the parents, the analyst learned of the psychodynamics contributing to George's feeling that it would be safer to be a girl. The case vignette offers a detailed description of the many psychic meanings of events and the defenses utilized by both the child and the parents in an effort to manage. There was the experience and meaningfulness of the surgeries, for both George and the parents. The helplessness and frustration, terror and rage. The many confusions and fantasies that ensued reflecting each developmental level. George's belief that the operations were a punishment for being a bad boy. Methods of dealing with helplessness, guilt and punishment by both George and his parents. The sister's self-protective claim that these operations don't happen for girls provided further support to fantasies of advantages for girls. The parents were understandably very frightened and worried about their son's future. There was tremendous sorrow for the father that his son would not be able to engage in contact sports, which had been an important source of pleasure and reward for himself and within his family. The father experienced significant disappointment and loss in not being able to share these pleasures with his son.

Sensitive, nuanced clinical work was done with the parents to expand their understanding of the significance of what they knew and felt. The parents learned how to use their own minds to make sense of their child's communications, both verbal and behavioral. With the analyst's help the parents were able to discover how their own thoughts and feelings provided the clues to the psychic significance of what otherwise seemed mysterious. Although the "problem" at hand did not make logical sense to them, they were making psychological sense of it and discovering connections that they had never before imagined. They worked with the analyst to find language and practiced how to talk with their son about these things.

The analyst very effectively helped the parents sort out their equation of masculinity with contact sports. A more expanded and contemporary vision of masculinity, the hazards of contact sports, and an exploration of how to talk with George about this was especially helpful for this family. Additionally, the broader long-term implications of talking with parents about their feelings of disappointment in regard to their child are worthy of consideration.

While this father was saddened that his son's medical condition required restrictions that curtailed the sharing of a particularly meaningful activity, many parents would have had some type of "disappointment" in regard to their child. It might be a child who is not athletic, a child who doesn't like books or reading, a child who is not artistic, or any number of discrepancies between the wishes of the parent and the strengths of the child. Many parents ward these thoughts off, finding them unacceptable in themselves. They do not allow themselves the chance to acknowledge and process them, or to work them through sufficiently. Instead their feelings are unconsciously communicated to the child. Children know when they are a "disappointment" to their parents, they feel their parents' sad and/or angry gaze. This becomes internalized and shapes the child's self-image, sense of self and self-esteem. The importance of finding a way to explore such feelings with parents cannot be underestimated.

In this case, the clinical work with parents on how minds function when faced with helplessness was also crucial. The analyst provided insight into how George found a sense of control in his belief that he was responsible for his past and future surgeries. As awful as it was for George to feel guilty and responsible, it also allowed him the illusion of control, and facilitated the belief that there were things he could do to control what lay ahead for him. Wanting to be a girl was merely one of his more creative, albeit magical, solutions. The analyst also knew that work was being done in displacement as the parents also needed to find ways to deal with their own sense of helplessness.

The parents made excellent use of the work they did with the analyst. After six months of them working alone with the analyst, George was functioning in an age appropriate way at home and at school, enjoying a full range of activities, and no longer talking about wanting to be a girl. The treatment was terminated with the parents' knowledge that they could return if they found the need. The parents sent a letter after George recovered from his subsequent operation at age nine, indicating that they had used what they had learned from the previous parent work to both their own and their son's benefit.

It is noteworthy that these parents did not feel the need to return to the analyst prior to their son's operation at age nine, as it speaks to what we optimally want parents to take away from our work with them. We introduce them to a way of approaching their child, how to think about and make sense of a child's experience, as well as how to provide holding and containment for both themselves and their child. When parents are able to internalize these capacities and ways of thinking, they feel more competent and effective as parents, and the parent-child relationship is expanded and deepened. They have resources within themselves to make sense of their child, to understand the significance of experience, and to identify the meaningfulness of behavior. Parents typically approach us with a specific problem, yet what we provide equips them for the many types of child and family dilemmas that lie ahead, for a lifetime of parenting.

Commentary 3

This is a lovely vignette for demonstrating crucial aspects of parent guidance that are applicable generally as well as specifically. George's parents entered into the work with all the pain, anxiety and confusion with which most parents enter the work. This is a foreign territory for most parents, so the need to start where they are is essential for the work to progress. Understanding the feelings about consulting with an unknown professional, as well as the feelings of concern about their child, is the *sine qua non* for establishing a respectful working relationship between parents and therapist. And one reason this intervention was so successful was the approach from the start.

From the first contact, the therapist in this case could listen and hear not just the "facts" of the presenting problem, but the enormous fear and confusion the parents were experiencing. The therapist was able to engage the parents as partners from the get-go, conveying he/she needed collaborative help to figure out what this was all about, and that they as parents could be the agent to help George understand and get things straight. The notion of consulting with an expert, as if someone knows more than they about their child, can undermine parents' sense of self; but even more importantly, it can close off the collaboration necessary to getting a complete history and sense of who everyone is. It is not healthy nor helpful to hand over the parental function to one who is not the parent. Given that parents entering into this kind of work can feel inadequate and/or guilty, with injured narcissism because their child has a problem that they could not prevent nor help, it is important to keep the ego task of the work in mind, helping the parents to engage their ego, observational capacities. And it is helpful to keep in mind one's own goal of strengthening parental functioning. This is not an exercise in parents handing over information and our receiving it. We are actually trying to help change the way parents think in a way that helps the child and strengthens parental function.

This initial phase, from the phone contact to first meeting, is the beginning of the work; the therapist was aware and accomplished in both hearing and understanding the parents' anxiety and confusion, but not taking on the externalization of anxiety when the father was pressing for George to come to the first meeting. Being aware both of the father's distress, and the therapist's own internal response to that distress, permitted a helpful and hearable response to the father's request. At times, therapists can respond to pressure in a way that is unhelpful. Sometimes, this stems from an eagerness to establish a relationship of goodwill, sometimes from our own internal anxiety about our ability to help.

As therapists, we are trying to understand the underlying processes that produce the problem, symptom, or dysfunction and we can rush to conclusions not only because we, as experts, need to prove we know what's what, but also to avoid the discomfort of uncertainty. As we use our knowledge and integrating functions to try to understand what's going on, we come up with hypotheses that may or may not be on track. In this case, the therapist was able to tolerate not knowing, sitting with the uncertainty, the ambiguities and the process until what was going on was clear. The therapist also waited until the parents were able to think about the issue from a different perspective and were able to hear, either from the therapist or from George, what was going on. The ability to wait, to be confused and unclear, is essential in any therapeutic work.

The following work progressed at a pace that let the work emerge rather than be forced. The therapist was well aware of his/her emotional responses to this difficult and painful history, a history awful for the parents as well as for George. Being able to tolerate our own responses to distressing histories, yet being able to be empathetic and not closed off, requires self-awareness both generally (who we are, what our own issues are) and specifically (what in a particular case taps our own issues and vulnerabilities).

The emerging history—both of what happened and how what happened felt to the parents—required time for the therapist to get to know the parents and time for the parents to get to know and trust the therapist. Relationships take time to build—they can't be established by demand. Thus, the meetings during which the parents began to tell the painful medical history and traumata (for George and for them) permitted a depth that "just the facts, ma'am" does not allow.

Another piece of the process that enabled movement forward was the sensitive work around the feelings stirred up in the father. Becoming a parent is a huge developmental step and as such challenges the ego's status quo. A parent's early history is tapped and stirred up, but from a time that is repressed and not necessarily available in memory. It comes back in feelings that can be overwhelming, surprising and confusing. This does not mean that parents are necessarily our therapeutic patients, but it does mean that there may be an opportunity to help parents, using their observant ego function, to look at and understand their own pasts from an adult perspective. The father's ability to remember aspects of his own past, and to understand and integrate new ideas as a result, enabled him to help his son in ways that were not available to

29

him before. This work, for both parents, enabled them to understand George in a new way, and provided a boost to reality testing as distortions came to light.

As the work progressed, it became more possible to assist the parents with concepts that helped them understand George. This is a primary goal of parent work—to support and enrich the parenting function by deepening their understanding of child development in general, and their child specifically. Thus, the concept that George's behavior had an origin and a meaning—that it was a communication of something he was feeling and something going on inside himself and that there was a reason for his behavior—allowed the parents to access their own deferred and marginalized feelings about the crucial piece of history that made George's struggle around being a boy begin to make sense. The denial of the pain and terror of the major surgeries had led to an inability to understand and integrate this major traumatic event. Once the difficult reality of these events was acknowledged and confirmed, the parents were then able to look at how their own reactions (fear about rough sports, etc.) led to attitudes that reinforced George's anxiety and confirmed his distortions.

The therapist did not supplant the parental role; rather he/she helped the parents find a way to talk with George that permitted him to express what had been warded off—his frustration, terror and rage as well as his distortion that the surgeries were a punishment for his instinctual wishes and behaviors. In a significant way, they were able to help George with both id and superego concerns. Besides helping George with his terror, this open expression also permitted a strengthening and a repair of the parent/child relationship. And one of the most significant outcomes of successful parent work is the strengthening of the core relationship that is the child's first community and world; providing that support, and helping that evolution, has long term bang for the buck.

George was four when the parents sought help, so the work through the parents was possible and important. Because they sought help for George pre-repression, before true symptom formation, much was available to George when the parents intervened. He was displaying a desperate defensive posture rather than a compromise formation as an outcome of repression. What is so satisfying about the ultimate outcome is that George's development was freed up and he could progress. At the same time, the history wasn't denied, which permitted a healthy approach to reality, allowing George and his parents to accommodate to his physical limitations and to face the upcoming interventions that would reawaken the anxiety, conflict and distortions for all concerned. Thus, the ego work is central to the successful outcome of this intervention. The therapist's ability to help the parents and the child observe not just the external world, but also their internal and affective worlds, gave everyone the ability to handle future development and future events with insight and understanding.

One measure of the success of this intervention is the fact that the parents stayed in touch, communicating how they could access the understanding from their work together to help all of them during the surgery at age nine. That, and the later communication when George was fifteen, reflected the sustained knowledge and understanding they had derived from the earlier work. This is a primary goal of parent work—not just to help the child through the parents, but it is also to help the parents through the work around their child. This was successfully accomplished in this case.

Editorial Reflections

Unlike all the other chapters in this volume, this one describes clinical work where the child was never seen, where the therapeutic efforts took place between analyst and parents, working together on behalf of the preschool child, in a treatment structure formally described first by Erna Furman (1969). We have included this example to demonstrate the wide range of types of parent work. It also turned out to illustrate many themes that emerged in other vignettes and commentaries and sets the stage for some theoretical considerations that arise when we venture into the relatively unknown territory of parent work.

We learn here of the intense pressure of parental anxiety and concern for their child, how it pushes therapists to respond quickly to relieve distress, and how fruitful it can be when we resist that pressure and take the time to more fully map the landscape with parents, tolerate uncertainty together, and collaborate in making sense of the initial picture before rushing to generic explanations or premature treatment plans. This chapter confirms the finding that time is needed to build a relationship of trust within which an alliance can be formed with parents.

More specifically, it illustrates that the pressure comes from parental helplessness and their defensive need to attribute omniscience to "the expert." We also have to acknowledge that to be seen as an expert and to respond accordingly exerts a powerful pull on the therapist. The parents had already seen many experts, and all had responded with answers, including a referral to this therapist as an expert. When we work with the parent-child relationship, what are we tapping into in the parents? In all cases parents come feeling helpless, but here the analyst did not respond with omniscience, but by waiting and building a collaborative relationship with the parents, a partnership in which three adults were working together to figure out why the boy was acting like a girl.

Another consequence of feeling helpless as a parent is the feeling of guilt that is described in the vignette; a feeling that is often deployed as an active self-scolding that strives to diminish the painful passivity of helplessness. When this was revealed, the analyst strove to help the parents to identify "reasonable concerns" that could be met with practical actions. This work had a lasting impact. When the parents corresponded with the analyst at the time of George's nine-year-old surgery, "The mother added a note that she had begun to panic and feel guilty and overwhelmed, but had stopped herself, with the internal reminder 'That won't help! What will?' She then went about giving George (and herself) the realistic reassurance that most likely all would be well."

What impact does change in the parent-child relationship have on the child, and at what level? The work described in this vignette changed the way the parents thought about themselves and their child, and how they understood the meaning of his behavior and feelings. They worked through and came to terms with the differences between the child they had imagined and the child they had, dealing with the kind of disappointment that all parents have to face to some degree. They understood that their helpless panic, among other effects, had interfered with their primary love for the child.

The interpretations offered by the analyst and delivered by the parents addressed id and superego issues in the child, and also engaged with his ego's interactions with reality. They seemed to affect his internal representations in ways that proved long-lasting. As we consider this application of working with parents, it seems that the age of the child may make a big difference in how deep the work goes, whether a child's trauma can truly be addressed solely through work via the parents. With this preschooler, his worries and confusing behaviors seemed to represent a desperate defensive posture, rather than a true compromise formation of symptoms. With an older child, we might consider that individual treatment would be needed to reach unconscious elements. The point is well-made in the third commentary that "treatment via the parent" work is best undertaken when the child has not yet experienced the onset of what Freud (1901) termed "infantile amnesia." Before repression has set in it "makes sense" to the children that their parents know about their early life and can share with them the memories they have of that time, thus "reconstructing" for the child something that may have been forgotten or not clearly remembered because of the early age of its occurrence.

A technical point we can take from this case and generalize is that the analyst should resist the seductive pull to being the omnipotent and omniscient one and instead take the time to develop a working relationship with the parents, affirming their actual expertise in certain areas and validating their capacity to stay in the open system of the reality of their parental power, their knowledge and their love for their child.

CHAPTER THREE

THE IMPACT OF PARENTAL DELUSIONS

School-age

Clinical Vignette

This account of work with the parents of six-year-old Jake refines questions about work with a parent with faulty reality-testing and provides a roadmap to its perils as well as possibilities. I hope to clarify questions to hold in mind as we attempt to help children and families with layers of intergenerational trauma leading to distortions, which in turn can lead to emotional abuse of a child. The most urgent recommendation I can share with peers embarking on work with such complicated families is to set up a safe and coordinated professional network/framework from the beginning; the possibility of doing further harm is great, as this piece of work sadly demonstrates. I will also address the analyst's unconscious resistances to ensuring and safeguarding these working conditions.

As a new graduate, I was happy when Dr. B., a senior psychiatrist, referred Ms. K. to address concerns she had about her three children. I was eager to impress the referrer, though my wish to impress was not conscious enough to turn over in my mind as a cautionary signal. I imagined Dr. B. imbued me with healing qualities as Ms. K. had recently become a more complex patient, and he wanted to see if I was up to the task—a bit of a dare put to a junior colleague, even a dare to fail. In any event, putting aside the unconscious dynamics between colleagues that all too often get overlooked in referrals (which warrants further discussion in our field in general), Ms. K. came to see me five times on her own and once with her husband, Mr. K. She was worried that a recent crisis was impacting her capacity to be present for her children.

Six months earlier, a sighting of her former stepfather at an airport, in which no conversation took place, opened floodgates to traumatic memories from childhood, a time when she had felt isolated from peers because of an injunction to keep secret a sexualized relationship with this same stepfather. Ms. K. said she had been expelled from a group of good friends in third grade when she became paralyzed during a sleepover as each girl was made to tell her deepest secret. Ms. K. could not tell and worried if she made up a secret that God might find out, so she remained silent, refusing to tell. The girls felt betrayed since they had all told their deepest secrets, so they ostracized the eight-year-old Ms. K.

I felt for this mother's story, although it was likely a screen memory, organizing multiple experiences of injury and abandonment. It also showed Ms. K.'s piety, her inability to play in her mind for fear of a judgmental God, which caused me to query trauma and neglect for its potential to embrittle psychic operations. I took Ms. K. to be a faithful reporter of events as the referrer had not mentioned anything regarding a tendency towards distortions. In the one meeting Mr. K. attended in these initial consults, he disagreed with his wife's strong sense that people at their children's school did not fully welcome them. Ms. K. saw herself as being denigrated and excluded in her family, professional and social life.

Three months after these parent meetings, Ms. K. called very worried about Jake who was testing a year below grade level and being bullied by classmates. Initially, the parents had been most concerned about their middle daughter Amalia's daily tantrums whereas now they were most concerned about Jake. Interestingly, a similar story of expulsion from the social group emerged about Jake: he had been very close to a boy in his class until the friend began to tease him for being a "cry baby," which made all the boys steer clear of him. Jake was not keeping up with his fast-paced class, so he had been referred to the resource room for extra help. The school had also flagged inattention and possible ADHD. The eldest son Fred, eleven, was an outstanding student who hid behind books most of the time and was friendless. As a result of our parent meetings in the context of my work with Jake, within a few months, all three children were seen by therapists.

An early observation of Jake was the disjunction between his kindly, handsome face with bright brown eyes and his tentative movement and speech, so short on agency and confidence. Jake began the first session by asking me what I would like to do, carefully exploring my face in case I might not like his preferences. When I answered that this was his time to talk or play with anything he wanted in the room, his eyes darted, and he seemed anxious in the face of so much choice. I wondered what he liked to do in his free time, and he shrugged. He liked the new box of colored pencils and the silly putty, pulling both near but not moving to draw or mold the putty. When he asked if it were all right if he drew, I was relieved as I worried that he felt too anxious to do anything to let himself feel more at ease. He drew a sports car with big wheels, focusing on details such as a flame on the body and silvery hubcaps. He looked for validation with his choice of shapes and colors, asking me if red or orange would be better for fire, gray or black for a tire? I had the sense of a boy who was very careful to live his life "in the lines," so as not to make any waves. In the second session, we took turns hiding a toy in the room that the other had to find. Jake put his figure out in the open for me, ensuring I would easily find it (him), and complained when I hid it a bit more, thinking I was trying to trick him rather than to make it more fun. Precarious loss felt imminent if all was not out in the open. When he made mistakes in speech, he looked frightened as if I might criticize him, as when he called a toy train a "tain." I had the sense of a bright boy whose reasoning and creative risk-taking had been dulled by things not adding up or making sense in his world.

Two months into this once-per-week treatment, Jake and I played a game at his behest to bolster his math skills. I was once again very aware of how quick he could be when he felt more relaxed as he had all the math facts and rules memorized in no time. And yet, despite this, occasionally, even if he had correctly calculated a repeating sum on three occasions, on the fourth, he would look away and not be able to figure it out for several moments. He would then giggle and after some moments of re-finding his focus would provide the correct answer. When I suggested his mind had wandered off somewhere as he had got it right three earlier times but then he went quiet on the fourth try, he looked embarrassed to be noticed, as if he had misbehaved for having had a wandering thought. I said it would be so interesting to know where that thoughtful mind of his had got to so we could help him use his very good brain at school more. He smiled for the first time, excited someone had noticed he could be clever.

During Jake's first year of treatment, the parents frequently missed their bi-monthly parent meetings. I repeatedly raised with them my need of their help to aid in the continuity of the work with their son. Privately, mother would complain that her husband disparaged therapy and this was his reason for not making time for the meetings. It was most common that I met with Ms. K. alone due to father's schedule and ambivalence about parent work. Father came to a quarter of the meetings with mother—and mother was upset that he had not taken up her many-years-long request for marital therapy. When both parents were present, I began to understand why father kept his distance. Ms. K. would accuse him of being disrespectful for playing tic tac toe with the children during a very long religious service. On another occasion, she angrily complained he never permitted her to go to the gym. One grievance led to all the grievances: she had wanted marital therapy for years—why was this the first time he made it into a therapist's office?—she would implore. At these times, father would ask how she preferred he help keep the children from making noise during lengthy services or remind her of his offer to put the children to bed she could go to the gym. Ms. K. felt overwhelmed by the demands of working full time and having to come home to make dinner then put the children to bed, particularly considering the recent sighting of her abuser. She wished Mr. K. could do the bedtime routine without getting the children too wound up, leaving her with the responsibility of calming them down. Father would defend himself saying he thought the children enjoyed rough and tumble play after their long, formal school day. Her retort was that made it impossible for her to put them to bed.

I asked more about how routines had become established in their current family, as well as when each had been a child. Ms. K.

remembered how many nights she had put herself to bed as her ambitious single mother put herself through college then graduate school during her first eight years of life. She remembered being tucked in some nights by her mother after a story but also being alone in her house, one time slipping on a runner and being frightened when her hurt lip produced a lot of blood. She put her age at "over ten," as if ten-year-olds are old enough to take care of themselves after school. In the course of our work together, she would realize she was younger than ten during that injury as she recalled the kitty she was running after had died when she was closer to eight.

Her parents had divorced before she was three; father financially supported his young family though he lived several states away. This detail made me wonder if dad's "rough and tumble" play with the children was stirring for Ms. K. her longing for her father long lost. Mr. K remembered rowdy bedtimes with his younger brother and his parents becoming frustrated with them but at the same time feeling his parents understood it being fun to wrestle. Regarding current routines, he said he offered to put the children to bed most nights, but that Ms. K. insisted it was only she who could calm them.

A year into working with Jake, the parents' irregular attendance grew worse. I contacted them repeatedly to meet, but to no avail. Ms. K. explained to me on the phone that she was having memories of abuse from childhood and needed distance from her husband. I learned she had stopped going to her own psychiatrist after starting the children in treatment as she said she could not take more time off from work, a detail I found worrying. Now she needed time separate from her husband to sort out the traumatic flashbacks and therefore could not spare further time to come to parent meetings. In my weekly meetings with Jake, he reported that his dad was mean to his mom. He said he had not invited her to his office party, an annual event they usually attended together, and his mom was really upset. He said he did not like him, he behaved like a "jerk" and "isn't nice to my mom." I was increasingly concerned and confused yet my invitations to the parents to meet were ignored. When I finally persuaded the parents of the urgency of coming in together, Ms. K. could barely look at dad and felt very rejected by him as she imagined he was sleeping with an office colleague to explain why he did not invite her to the office party. When he explained that he wanted nothing more but to have her accompany him but she herself had insisted he go on his own as they didn't have good babysitters at the time, I felt the same confusion as when early meetings with mom did not add up. mom shouted she knew what he was doing, and she would not interfere with his new love life!

Up until this point in the parent work, there had been so many urgent matters regarding Jake's needs that I had not prioritized talking about Ms. K's faulty reality testing. Also, I had avoided raising this as Ms. K.'s reaction to Mr. K.'s divergent views of events showed me how immovable were her versions, a further detail alerting me to likely serious past trauma. Ms. K.'s disapproval of Dad for overexciting the children in the evening and thereby making it impossible for her to put them to bed remained the top subject. Fury erupted over his complete negligence of her wish to work out after dinner. I had thought it had been resolved in a previous session when he easily agreed to let her get to the gym after dinner any time she wished. To Ms. K.'s mind, however, he had refused since he did not say "Go to the gym tonight and I'll ensure I don't rile up the children" each evening. A confusing dialogue ensued in which Mom insisted that she asked regularly, and Dad insisted that she was free to go any time she wanted. I again suggested they work out a schedule here since our earlier plan had not worked (gliding headlong into the displaced issue). Ms. K. then screamed there was no way to exercise if he riled the children up so she would have to forego fitness until they were grown. Given how important exercise was to her mental health, there was no way she could live with him anymore, she said in a raised voice. I wondered to myself if she had another lover, and whether this was the reason she was so keen to suddenly leave her husband or to look very fit, or why she had insisted he had a lover? Aloud, I wondered if anything else could be beneath the gym issue, and she angrily told me I had no idea what it was like at her home. Mr. K. asserted it would be fine and he could handle putting the children to bed as he had done it many times. This would be one of many childrearing management questions in which the divergence of mom's and dad's reports was so wide that my head spun after our meetings.

A week later, the grandmother called me. I had met her when she brought Jake to sessions during her regular visits. She had been in touch with Ms. K.'s new psychiatrist after an awful event the previous weekend. She reported that Ms. K. had taken Jake out, stopping in at a pawn shop to sell a valuable watch Mr. K. had given her. When they returned home, mother nonchalantly told father she had sold the antique Rolex he had given her. Father cried as this felt out of the blue and cruel, and later left me a voicemail explaining he did not understand what was happening and had no idea what to do. Grandmother left another voicemail explaining that her daughter (Ms. K.) was no longer speaking to her and was asking to be left alone as she was flooded with traumatic flashbacks of having been repeatedly raped as a child. In front of the children, Ms. K. told the grandmother to "F--- Off! I'm traumatized from being raped as a child and I never want to talk to you again!" According to the grandmother, Ms. K. had never communicated with her this way before. She did not know what Ms. K. was talking about and admitted she had left her daughter alone too much as a single mother but never would have knowingly put her in harm's way as her daughter was indicating she did.

Now the entire family was in crisis. Ms. K. decided to check herself into a psychiatric ward but, as it was a voluntary unit, she left after four nights then locked herself into a spare room in the attic of the family home, telling her husband she needed to be alone as she was besieged with thoughts about the past abuse. I spoke on the phone to mother, expressing sympathy for the deluge of flashbacks and urged her to try to see the children as they missed her and were scared about her well-being. We agreed that she would meet Jake at his next appointment as she did not want to come downstairs for fear of seeing Mr. K. or her mother. Jake was relieved to see her at his appointment but was freaked out by her new youthful wardrobe and magenta hair. He drew a picture for her of the family, with a heart above them, which she left behind.

Mother reported she did not agree with the hospital's diagnosis of her as she knew it was PTSD, so she would not take the meds they prescribed. Ms. K.'s ability to function was rapidly deteriorating. Mr. K. begged mom to eat family dinners so the children could see her. I had several phone calls with Ms. K. at this time in which she reported that she was repeatedly sexually abused as a child by several different men—father, stepfather, neighbor, coach—and she insisted her own mother knew of the events and indeed, sanctioned them. She reported it had been a male babysitter who had repeatedly abused her, and the next day reported a neighbor had been let in at her mother's behest, and then during an emergency parent meeting to brainstorm next steps, she accused her husband of sexual assault. He cried, saying he was deeply saddened as he had thought they both had enjoyed their intimate times together. When she responded with sarcasm he was genuinely upset. It was incredibly difficult to bear witness to the maelstrom of feelings and accusations that mother's fixed ideas unleashed on all members of the family. Mr. K. and her own mother had become *personae non grata* and I was next, now that I was trying to help protect Jake from Ms. K.'s *idée fixe* that father was the source of all evil, just as her stepfather and mother, and all the other men had been before him. This was my first experience of a patient whose story regularly changed. Given the disorganized thinking, it was plausible Ms. K. had experienced multiple traumas in childhood, and we knew she had been neglected—her mother admitted as much as she was a young, single mother—but the detail that her own mother knowingly paired her with an abuser was very hard to imagine given grandmother's sincere reporting of events.

Ms. K. next spent the winter holidays doing a full-time outpatient program and locking herself in the attic bedroom upon her return home each evening. She reported she was doing her best to spend quality time with the children, and Jake reflected this in session with great relief. The grandmother moved in to help and Mr. K. took time off from work to spend time with the children. Nonetheless, I still regularly heard from grandmother when she brought Jake to his weekly session about his difficulty sleeping in the night, begging his grandmother or dad to stay until he fell asleep. The children missed their mother terribly, and though she was physically present she struggled to give them the attention they needed. I saw the parents during this time, and we spent a lot of time working out what Mom *could* give to the children despite her preoccupation and very low energy levels. Slowly mom allowed herself out for thirty minutes with each child, and it was moving how much these interactions meant to both the children and Ms. K.

Jake, formerly so bereft of curiosity, now implored me to tell him what happened to his mother: "You must tell me what happened to my mother when she was a little girl." During the height of the crisis, he had overheard multiple overstimulating arguments and conversations. I was relieved to hear his urgent curiosity and simultaneously pained that I could not answer the questions, not only because I did not fully know but also because what his mother had reported would have been developmentally inappropriate for Jake to hear. He had heard enough of his mother's outbursts to know it had to do with a man touching her, and he was daily exposed to his mother's sense that Mr. K. was an unsafe, unkind man, leaving Jake utterly confused regarding who was safe and who was not. Jake's attachment to his mother made it very easy to take on her point of view and agree that dad was an unsafe man.

I began to wonder to myself if dad was an unsafe man. Was Ms. K. correct, that he had repeated the sexual trauma with her, or as a sexually traumatized woman, did she associate being intimate with feeling traumatized? I will never know but I did come to find father's reports consistent while mother's always changed. Grandmother also reported how much all three of the children relied on their father during this time, so emotionally absent was their mother. He consistently expressed heartbreak that the woman he wanted to marry and with whom he had wanted to raise his children now met him with revulsion and fear. He was compassionate that she might be in the midst of a trauma-induced state of mind but he too experienced profound hurt and loss at this time. Additionally, the grandmother, Ms. K.'s mother, and Mr. K. worked as a caretaking team during this time.

When Ms. K.'s outpatient program ended, she had the confidence of a graduate and wanted to immediately separate from Mr. K. She went online to find housing for her and the children, taunting father in front of the children that he could not join them. Knowing that she was in no position to handle such a move or single parenting, I encouraged her to give it some time as the children had just experienced a great deal of instability and loss. She agreed to this initially, but then banned her mother from having contact with the children, whom all three acutely missed after her return home. I became increasingly concerned about protecting the children from the not infrequent hostile, sexualized remarks mom used with Mr. K., whom she now included amongst her abusers. Jake would tell me, conspiratorially, that his father would not be allowed to go to this or that family activity planned for an upcoming weekend: "We're going ice skating and to get hot cocoa, but not *Dad*."

In the now resumed parent sessions, father would ask mother why she sought to exclude him from the outings. Though Father would insist upon joining his family, Ms. K. would complain about his manners or ineptness at keeping the children in line. I tried to persuade Ms. K. to bring her feelings to our sessions or to her own treatment as her negative view of Mr. K. at mealtimes, school events, outings was having the effect of Jake suspecting his own father of not being a trustworthy man. I asked mother if she were able to see how destructive it was for Jake to have the power to taunt his father such as: "Dad, we're getting a new house very soon so we don't have to be near YOU—You've ruined the family."

In one especially difficult session, Ms. K. insisted Mr. K. deserved his son's hostility and accused me of straying from my ethics for not seeing how abusive father was, threatening to call my professional body for singling out her behaviors over father's behaviors. I was impotent in the face of mother's *idée fixe*[2] that her husband was an abuser.

I was shaken by this threat, never before having been accused of such a thing. Frightened, I called my ethics board to obtain advice. When together we read over the criteria for making a report to child protective services as a mandated reporter, the bar was "reasonable suspicion" of physical, sexual or emotional abuse. I was deeply concerned about "parental alienation", when a child for unwarranted reasons shows fear or disrespect towards the other parent. The advisor told me I ought to have made a child protective services (CPS) report as soon as the emotional abuse had become apparent to me, and that, furthermore, this would protect me in case Ms. K. did make a report to my professional body.

I labored long and hard over the decision to call CPS. In the week that followed the difficult and threatening parent meeting, mother canceled Jake's appointment the day of the appointment, and reported she could not attend the parent meeting. I decided I would call CPS to gain advice as to what to do. CPS thought what I described constituted "emotional abuse" and therefore, I was mandated to report it. That both the ethics advisor and the CPS advisor made clear that I was late in making the report, made me feel I was legally mandated to do so.

In their seminal book on parent work, the Novicks write, "We have found that many child workers, including child analysts, may be driven by rescue fantasies, which places the dynamics of the phenomenon within a system of mental functioning that uses a hostile omnipotent

---

2   Pierre Janet used this term in 1894 and his ideas are still cited for their bedrock way of describing how the mind splits off and remains under the influence of trauma when it is left untreated. For an excellent discussion of Janet's contributions to trauma-induced defensive operations see Hart and Horst (1989).

fantasy as a defense against helplessness" (Novick, K.K. and Novick, J. 2005, p.11). This sentence describes our—child analysts'—vulnerability in work with high-risk children. Since the defense of the rescue fantasy and the unconscious wish to get right between a mother and a father (one's own internalized and real parents as well as the parents in one's child practice) to defend against exclusion, want and pain, reports to child protective services represent on an unconscious level a multi-layered omnipotent fantasy. Another sentence from their book sums up the single largest challenge to work with children and parents in one fell swoop, "… we agree with Furman that core identity is formed first with a nongendered mother… It is no wonder, then, that all those who work with children are vulnerable to reacting to and defending against the Ur-Mother. This must be acknowledged, shared, and worked through before effective parent work can be done" (p. 11).

In my own experience, this acknowledging and working through is easier said than done. Though my relationship to the parents had been ongoing, indeed had increased in frequency during this family's crisis, with trust and a working alliance between us, I felt incompetent and helpless in my efforts to help mother modulate her incendiary and sexualized accusations against her mother and husband *in front of the children*. This unfortunate situation was impossible given that mother had changed her own psychiatric provider to a person who did not agree to collaborative casework. Mr. and Ms. K. represented the two caretaking adults upon whom Jake and his siblings depended during mother's exceedingly difficult period of several months' duration. While Ms. K. undoubtedly was re-living real and psychic trauma including fragments of trauma infusing her psychic life to create fixed ideas about current people in her present life, Ms. K. was also traumatizing her family. To Ms. K.'s mind her accusations were reasonable *"because they were true,"* and it was I who was dangerous in

48

attempting to protect the children's attachments and in encouraging a different point of view.

Technically, I walked a tightrope trying to help her feel heard and believed (it was her psychic reality that both her husband and mother were her tormentors—her *idées fixes*), while witnessing Jake lose his capacities to determine cause and effect, reality versus nonreality, safe versus unsafe. Jake loved and depended on his father during his mother's travails but on numerous occasions it was clear he had the impinging worry that receiving the much-needed love from his father increased his abandonment and heartache from his mother. I acknowledged Ms. K.'s strong feelings of injustice over what she said her mother and husband had done to her, and yet—since she was also relying on them to look after the children in her difficult time and therefore to some extent she trusted them—asked her please to bring those feelings to her own individual therapy or parent meetings as it was utterly destabilizing for Jake to hear his mom accuse them of terrible things to do with sex that he did not understand. To her, this was as if I were asking her to not stand up to abusers and my words fell on deaf ears, an experience that ironically left both of us feeling helpless.

I came to feel that this experience of helplessness that prevailed in our work, stemming from mother's earliest helpless feelings in relation to a powerful Ur-mother or similar figure, is a feeling all of us who interface with parents—principals, teachers, social workers, child analysts and others—are vulnerable to feeling and defending against in our work. I continued to witness in my sessions with Jake how identified he was with mom's point of view, at the same time he felt heartbroken and confused to imagine his beloved dad was possibly flawed. Jake's overriding need of his mother meant that he had to query his father's wholeness.

For example, amidst this, Jake implored me to tell him my husband's name, believing he could imagine his hair color and appearance based on his name. I wondered what knowing this information would mean to him, to which he said, "I just know you would pick someone who would be nice—you would know who is a good guy. He's probably nice, not like my jerkface of a dad." I winced, knowing how hungry Jake was for a loving father, while I also felt heartbroken on behalf of his father who felt that his son had so identified with mom's view of him that he had temporarily lost his son's respect. I reminded Jake that he did not know whether I had a good or a bad husband but understood how much he loved and admired his own dad and wished that his parents loved one another so they could love and attend to him more fully. He began to cry and told me how annoying some of the kids in his class were. It turned out that annoying meant he was being teased for making errors at the whiteboard when he volunteered in class. Having worked with him the year before on how much his ability to pay attention in class was linked to all that he was trying to manage in his mind about the family situation, he cried further and said, "It's impossible to pay attention with all the stuff going on at home." I truly felt like hugging him at this moment and nearly came to tears myself.

I chose to let the parents know that I made the report to CPS in the urgent hopes that we could contain the experience together. I explained my concern that my work to help mom modulate her sexualized invectives against the father and grandmother had not been heeded and were causing dire emotional harm to the children. The call to CPS initially made matters worse, as expected. I had weighed the likelihood that the treatment could end with the possibility this intervention might effectively communicate how crucial it was that parental alienation—one parent's attempt to deride another parent or caretaker to the children—cease. In this case, the CPS report achieved both.

Psychoanalysts above all rely on confidentiality for their work, so when a privacy-disrupting act such as contacting CPS occurs, parents, children, grandparents, school and other professionals working with the family have strong reactions to such an intervention. We too are jolted by the legal mandate as it registers a violation in our psyches even as it protects. CPS visited the children at school and later visited the home. The investigation intensified Jake's loyalty conflict. As he had missed his mother so much in the months she had been emotionally unavailable to him, he had tended to agree with mom's derisive invectives against father so important was it to keep his mother close.

In my profound wish to rescue and protect Jake, I linked with an outside agency for validation and support. By the book, it was justified, and professionals were advising it ought to have already been done. After I made the call and Ms. K. became irate and ended the treatment, I deeply questioned whether it had been the right thing to do. For several days, I was in a daze as I worried about the fallout from my actions. The only consolation from my action was that Mr. K. reported it did immediately stop mom from maligning Mr. K. and the grandmother in front of the children.

From the moment of intake child analysts are vulnerable to responding to their unconscious wish to rescue before forming an alliance with the parents. The parents can unilaterally end treatment at any point for any reason and will do so in the event of difficulties in the treatment as this case demonstrates. So, what can be learned? Optimally, the child analyst and parents are united in the goals and the work, and this is acknowledged. At times, we who work with children take directions from the parents or the referring colleague, despite our experience and confidence in our capacities to assess. Evaluating whether parents can engage in the very complex work of helping their child is a significant part of the assessment.

Though I have long made parent work part of child therapy and analysis, referring parents to colleagues when necessary, I had been a little slow to insist on more regular contact with these parents. I sensed from the beginning that some of Ms. K.'s stories did not quite add up, and I was not sure how to respond. I did not know what to do with Ms. K.'s distortions. That I did not insist on regular meetings until it was too late allowed me to avoid thinking about parts of the case that triggered my helplessness and ignorance. Unfortunately, I was not consciously aware of these dynamics. And while earlier, more regular contact with these parents would not have prevented the breakdown of this complicated case, I do wish we could have had a better ending together. I tried very hard to get mother to be seen by a colleague psychiatrist with whom I could work, yet Ms. K. insisted on a psychiatrist who saw no reason to be in contact with the son's clinician. I am probably not the only child analyst who has been deaf to my own signals in the realm of difficult parent work that renders us helpless. I invite us to think more about these vulnerabilities we share despite how uncomfortable it is to be sincere and admit of our shortcomings. Collaboration amongst the mental health team was not possible.

Though I have had the benefit of colleagues' writings and thoughts about the role of parent work in child work, I am surprised by how easily its significance can recede from my mind. When we receive distress calls, be they from colleagues or parents, it can be irresistible to respond to our strong wish to serve and pull a child out of harm's way. Who can resist the fantasy of rescuing from time to time, or of protecting one's own childhood self from injury? Yet, no matter how many times I have the pleasure of working extremely well with parents of child patients or with colleagues in a team approach, I remain vulnerable to the unconscious forces that can thread through clinical work. I may be alone in that vulnerability, but I suspect others share in it.

As I feared and wished, the case did fall apart. Ms. K. was enraged I contacted CPS, and though she never returned to see me, I heard from Mr. K. that she worried it threatened her reputation in her field. Mr. K. also told me that mother's new psychiatrist was aghast at my call. But one good thing did come out of the CPS investigation: Mom stopped attacking father in front of the children. For me, the case ended abruptly which I knew was not in Jake's best interests. I had hoped that the father might continue to bring Jake as the two of us were clearly very close, but he did not want anything to upset his wife any further. He was quite in love with her and hoped she would re-find her attraction to him and hoped by doing her bidding she might.

Long after the case ended, I ran into the grandmother. She reported the parents had divorced, and that Jake had gone on to become a very high-achieving student and mentioned an academic award he had just received. Maybe on balance I performed the Hippocratic oath "do no harm" in that my intervention did get mom to stop deriding father in front of the children, yet abrupt endings are never good for anyone and I really wish that I had been able to say goodbye to Jake with more time to review our time together.

Commentary 1

Well, such a difficult case. And how lovely to have a case presented with such openness and clarity of thinking and willingness to learn from our mistakes if only the lesson we learn is that there might have been nothing more any of us could have done.

We are not presented with detailed sessions, as this is simply a vignette to get us thinking, but, given the important late developments in Jake's capacity to think and to use his intelligence, I am going to speculate that, in spite of the abrupt and premature ending of the boy's treatment, important changes took place internally in him thanks to the therapy. The therapist seemed to have worked hard to embolden him, and to encourage him to believe in his intelligence, and I think this must have helped enormously.

A question which always arises when we work with children who have a parent or parents who is/are more ill than the children are, is how to address this. We have all been taught not to interfere with the relationship between the parent and child, but sometimes there are opportunities to highlight something the child has noticed about a parent, e.g. the weird inconsistencies in the mother's accounts of her own abuse. In the past I might have felt I had to ignore that, whereas nowadays I would be more willing to let the child know I have noticed his observation. Otherwise we are colluding with the parent's delusions, or *idée fixe*, or bullying or manipulativeness. Sometimes the only hope is that the child's sanity and powers of observation will survive until he leaves home in later adolescence. His belief that his therapist probably had married a good man suggests that not only his own sense of his father's goodness and his internalization of his therapist's adherence to the truth via the transference experiences of her, meant that he really had internalized something important about truth and reality that may have saved him.

One thing that worried me a little was the speed with which the therapist identified trauma as the cause of the mother's disturbed accusations. I have little doubt that she is right about trauma as the cause of the *idée fixe* and the condition, but we also need to face the facts about the kind of person—and possible personality disorder we—and the mother's family—may be confronted with. Some years ago I started saying to colleagues that I was unwilling to take on children of psychopathic parents (sometimes one, sometimes both) because, in the end, if I dared to challenge their ruthlessness with their children, even if it was only about cutting down the number of sessions per week (i.e., milder than what was happening in Jake's family), the parents would end treatment. But, of course, I haven't been able to stick to my rule about who I would take on, because I didn't always sense what I was up against when the parents came eagerly and respectfully trying to get help for their child.

What I would say, however, is that after many experiences of treating psychopathic children, I have developed a way of facing up to them without retaliating (it was a hard lesson—we go into this work to help with suffering and we aren't necessarily familiar with the values of the battlefield). I have learned to veil my eyes and not be so open and vulnerable. This has helped with my work with the child, but the issue with parent work is that we are trying to elicit (as the therapist in this case study was doing), concern and responsibility for the child. And for the psychopathic or personality disordered person, this may be a waste of time as their own deep personal needs hidden behind the manipulativeness and demandingness may not be being met. It seems selfish and self-centered, but it may be also very desperate as it was in Jake's mother. Thus, such people need skilled personal analysis for themselves. The best we can do in the parent work is not be too weak, let them know we can see their powerful manipulations, but also be respectful of their deep needs for help and understanding. And further help with this is often the last thing they will consider when their powerful projections indicate otherwise.

Margaret Rustin (1998) wrote a very interesting paper on four levels of work with parents where she suggested that at the first level, with, for example, a very paranoid parent, the most we may manage with him is to manage to listen to his complaints enough to enable the child to continue treatment. The next level concerns giving emotional support. The third level involves support plus insight and the fourth really therapeutic insight.

Let us note, however, that when the emotional abuse is severe as it was with Jake, we do need to call in the CPS and it did help even though the therapy ended. (I was curious who got custody after the divorce.) I have had situations where I did call in the CPS and they took the situation of emotional abuse seriously for awhile but then not. It is the hardest thing to prove in the courts especially if the parent is intelligent and persuasive.

Congratulations to the editors for raising some seriously important issues in this work with children and their families. I suppose, sadly, we have to face our limitations as well as our partial successes.

Commentary 2

Often, it is only in hindsight that we can glean the true depth of a family's pathology, and sometimes, only after a treatment ends prematurely and precipitously. Rarely do we have the opportunity *après coup* to investigate such difficult cases from multiple vantage points of theory and technique. Unlike many publications that document those treatments that result in "good-enough" outcomes, the *Parent Work Casebook* inspires the possibility of advancing our field by giving us access to treatments with unfavorable endings. Fortunately, the therapist of this paper generously offers us reflections of her arduous struggles with a complex family case.

The commencement of a therapeutic journey carries many elements that are pregnant with meaning, but that are often "hiding in plain view." Is it a family member or another professional who sounds the initial siren of distress? What are the precipitating circumstances that propel one or more family members into treatment, and why is therapy sought at that particular moment in time? Who is the "identified patient," and in the case of child analytic work, what traumatic *links* are the children carrying on behalf of other family members? What is the nature of the parental couple: is it a generative, "creative couple," (Morgan 2010) or is it a malignant couple destructive to the healthy development of the children? When a mother or father appears consistently unavailable to participate in parent sessions, what meanings are communicated by such a parent who is *missing in action*? As such questions cannot be answered immediately, the analyst needs to maintain a position of *negative capability* (Bion 1970) so as not to foreclose understanding.

In the case of this therapist, she engaged initially with the mother of "Jake" for several individual sessions prior to meeting the father during a joint parent meeting. The work then continued with Ms. K. for a few months prior to meeting the boy. Rather than regarding this sequence of single and joint parent meetings as a happenstance situation, we can be curious about the latent unconscious significance of this intriguing division of labor. I wonder: what might have been in the way of the therapist investigating this early pattern, or halting it at the outset? In other words, this natural development invites a thoughtful consideration of the family dynamics getting played out, and ways that the therapist seemed to become coopted into a family system in which domination and submission prevailed. The reader comes to discover that Ms. K. succeeded at holding the family and the therapist hostage to her distress and demands. In sum, the therapist seemed beholden to meet the parental couple according to Ms. K.'s terms, foreshadowing ways that the therapist would later feel frightened, helpless, and eventually at the mercy herself or not of Child Protective Services.

"Jake" was characterized as a six-year-old handsome, bright, and anxious boy who suffered with pervasive inhibitions and developmental delays, academically, socially, and emotionally. He seemed to assume the stance of a parentified child, who was paralyzed, or at least, held back by considerable fear that the world was at best, un-containing, and at worst, subject to ongoing neglect and family trauma. Jake's siblings each communicated other symptomatic difficulties for the troubled family, with middle child "Amalia" expressing her anguish in the form of temper tantrums, and the eldest child "Fred" who was "friendless" despite his stellar intellect. Apparently, the parental couple was bereft of a resource within their own relationship to confront their escalating conflicts or to replenish their reserve, let alone to serve as a *container* for their troubled children. Furthermore, they allowed their difficulties to go unchecked, both by resisting couple therapy and opposing joint parent work, despite Jake's therapist's recommendations. Although Ms. K. claimed that her husband was the only one voicing such objections, from the perspective of analytic couple therapy, one member of the couple could be seen to be expressing the desires on behalf of the couple as a unit. It appeared as if the therapist may have been misled in believing that the spokesperson for opposing parent work resided solely in Mr. K., perhaps revealing her bias towards Ms. K. who was the patient initially referred.

We are informed that Jake's mother was prone to terrible emotional collapse, self-described as PTSD. Sometimes she was stricken by paranoia, and major distortions in her thinking that at times she loaded onto her children. Ms. K.'s focused disdain and attack upon her husband later extended also to the referring psychiatrist, and eventually to the therapist herself. The early origins of each parent's difficulties were chronicled by her, more so for Ms. K. than for Mr. K. Importantly, Ms. K. perceived many neglectful and abusive situations, including sexual assault.

In the face of a significantly disabled parent, the necessity for the therapist or analyst to form a secure therapeutic alliance with the apparently healthier parent cannot be overemphasized. In this case, it is possible that there would have been a better outcome if the therapist had succeeded at forming a sturdy working partnership with Mr. K., with Jake's grandmother, or possibly even with both, when Ms. K. was hospitalized, for example.

The referral of Ms. K. to this therapist carried some ambiguity as to whether she was actually in need of both individual therapy and parent work. The particulars of her treatment with the referring psychiatrist were not disclosed, so it can only be surmised that she may have been receiving pharmacotherapy. In the setting of major family trauma, there is a high potential for the parents to eventually experience the analyst as a traumatizing figure in the transference. Alternatively, one or both parents may come to envy the child's treatment which could upend the treatment, sometimes suddenly. If Ms. K. was not receiving individual treatment, it may have supported the child's work for her to receive that from another clinician.

Jake's therapist reflected that it would have been helpful to create a more secure setting for the parent work, exemplified she says by augmenting the frequency of the parent sessions from the bi-monthly occurrence. This analyst concurs. It may have been helpful to establish a clear set of parameters or conditions by which the therapist would agree to treat the child, namely that the parents attend jointly, and at a specified frequency. At a minimum, it seems that this family would have benefited from parent work, occurring at least once-weekly or even twice-weekly, resources permitting. In a similar vein, the once-weekly work with the child was probably insufficient to provide Jake with the scaffolding and opportunity to develop his relationship to his therapist as a developmental and transference object, especially in the face of the formidable counter-forces that he was exposed to within his unstable and damaging home.

The professional network implications are important to consider when encountering a traumatized family such as this one. In particular, forging an alliance with the child's pediatrician at the outset (with informed consent by the parents) can be very useful. As the pediatrician is in the life of the child, often for many years, he/she is poised therefore to share with the analyst a familial, multi-year context that can assist at sizing up the magnitude of risk at an early stage of treatment, and thus strategically position the analyst. If there is a threatened rupture of the treatment, the pediatrician can sometimes reinforce to the parents the necessity of child therapy, or at the very least, can foster the continuity of child work if a transfer of care were to occur.

In the case of Jake, it might be reasoned that an analytic family therapy alternating with couple therapy or parent work could be a potent therapeutic approach. There are multiple family members in need—all three children, the mother and father as individuals and as a couple, and the maternal grandmother. From the perspective of analytic field theory articulated by Enriqué Pichon-Rivière, each member of the family expresses a voice on behalf of the family (group) mind (cited in Scharff et al. 2017). Family therapy could optimize the understanding of each member's communication that resonates with the family voice. An individual therapy for Jake may still have been necessary, but a family therapy intervention may have helped to pool resources together when Ms. K.'s mind was collapsing, or when the couple could not function as a *container*. Even if a family therapy approach were not initially utilized, it could have been a very helpful method to apply at the point of the family crisis, expressed poignantly in the form of parental alienation.

Although it is difficult to say conclusively, it appears that Ms. K. was intent (unconsciously) on poisoning Jake's mind, by preventing him from claiming his own view of his father. This invasive situation could be regarded as a malignant recapitulation of Ms. K.'s own experience of rape that she passed on to her children. Her violent attacks upon herself, her husband, and her family as a whole seemed to continue with an unstoppable force until CPS became involved. Once it appeared that Ms. K. had co-opted Jake's therapist's mind and filled her with all-consuming fear, it is doubtful that the treatment could have continued meaningfully.

Just as this volume ushers in a group mind to consider the complex nuances for such demanding work, perhaps this case illustrates also the value of seeking consultation. Given the strong need for more writings about parent work, perhaps peer consultation may go a long way to advancing our field, and to supporting those on the front line. This therapist is not alone in facing such formidable challenges where it can be impossible to recognize the myriad unconscious forces that threaten to topple the treatment. The work of the Novicks represents a notable precedent, and an exemplar to inspire other similar conversations that we could be having more often with one another.

Editorial Reflections

Virtually every therapist working with children and their parents will, eventually, find themselves in the painful dilemma of having to decide whether a situation within the family is placing the child (or children) in enough danger that the analyst feels compelled to report the matter to Child Protective Services. The reactions of the commentators to this vignette reveal and reflect the sense of helplessness uniformly experienced by therapists placed in such a predicament. Ultimately, this analyst had to make the painful decision.

But the analyst and the commentators direct our attention to earlier points in the process and suggest that things might have been differently handled from the very first contact. This helps us learn from this case and think about others.

1. Referral. The analyst says that we should be alert as to why we accept a referral. There are conscious and unconscious reasons and this analyst discerned the motivation to prove competence to a senior colleague.

2. Referral for what and for whom? Usually the referral is for <u>treatment</u> for the child, not for evaluation, often including a prescription of the frequency and mode of intervention "Do you have time for a once a week play therapy with a six-year-old boy?" is a typical question raised by the professional or parent. This is a potential Achilles heel for all therapists, allowing the parent or referrer to decide who the patient is and what the treatment should be. Why was this child seen once a week and parents bi-monthly? This raises questions about the structure of consultation and treatment, the role of the therapist as designer of the interaction with the family, and, centrally, what we can learn

from the trajectory of treatment about the kind of foundation we need to lay out at the outset to maximize the likelihood of a positive outcome. Several cases described in this volume offer us the opportunity to learn about these matters and to suggest in our final chapter some ways to approach the challenge technically and theoretically.

3. Working arrangements. Safety is fundamental to treatment. What arrangements need to be built into the treatment plan and frame in order to safeguard everyone involved and the treatment itself? One commentator says that he/she would not take on a case if the parents are psychopathic. That commentator adds that it is difficult to tell at the beginning, when parents are desperate and respectful, how they will react later when they are confronted by challenges. The editors suggest that having a period of joint exploration and working with the parents to attempt to effect certain crucial transformations before any treatment plans are made gives a possible testing ground and allows for either further work with parental pathology, getting consultation, and or brief trials of other forms of treatment as suggested by the other commentator, or telling the parents that you cannot work with them, thus saving everyone unnecessary pain, money and wasted time.

Such a long period of exploration and crucial transformations in the parents allows for a recommendation based on everything the parents and analyst have learned (see Novick, J. and Novick, K.K. 2016). The parents then can genuinely accept the recommendation and not impose their own treatment plan, or one they had expected based on interactions with peers or with the professional who referred them to the child therapist.

We might also consider that when parents refer their children for treatment, a part of them, be it at a conscious, pre-conscious, or unconscious level, knows that their own emotional conflicts, typically stemming from unresolved past experiences/traumas, contribute at some level to their child's difficulties. This can occur even if the parents are seeking treatment based on the recommendation of another professional, (presuming the parent is not seriously disturbed, as happened in this case). Once the child is in treatment and the alliance has been further strengthened between the parent(s) and the analyst, then, within the "containing frame" of that alliance, the raw and painful aspects of what has lain dormant (at least relatively so) may press to the foreground. In this vignette we do learn of the mother's experiences in third grade and, as the work progressed, her linking of traumatic experiences to having occurred around eight years of age, with this being proximate to Jake's age at the time of referral and start of treatment.

When it does become clear during work with a child that a report to Child Protective Services is required, it is possible to help the parent(s) self-report. This can occur when the pathology of the parent is less psychotically tinged, when in the context of the alliance the parent can muster sufficient ego strength to do so. A self-report can often occur in the supportive presence of the analyst. The parent may feel enough relief that it is evident not only to him or her but also to the child.

Typically, when this can happen, it is possible for the treatment to continue. Often the parent comes to realize that the emotional issues arising require more intensive personal therapy. It has been our experience that regular concurrent parent work can and probably should continue while the parent starts or continues personal therapy for issues beyond parenting.

Needless to say, however, as this case vignette illustrates, such an outcome is not always possible. When continuing treatment cannot be supported or tolerated by the parent(s), and the parent does not accept the need for personal therapy, the analyst is left to reflect, as does the author of the vignette, on the feelings of frustration, helplessness, and second-guessing that eventuate, an outcome with which the analysts commenting on this case resonate.

Perhaps there is an important alternative "take away" for us all. In spite of what must, at least in part, feel like a failure (especially including regret over not being able to continue the work with the child), as one of the commentators stated (and both implied), "it did help even though the therapy ended." This case is not as much of a failure as the therapist thinks and sharing with others, as in this book, allows one to see the good one has done but also enables everyone to put in place practices which may allow us to do better.

CHAPTER FOUR

PARENT WORK AND DIFFERENTIAL DIAGNOSIS

School-age

Clinical Vignette

In this chapter I will describe work with an eight-year-old boy and his parents. Marco was born abroad and is an only child of his parents who are natives of their home country. The family had emigrated to the U.S. when Marco was six years old. The family's first year-and-a-half in the U.S. had been a confusing time for them as they moved a few times in their effort to find a comfortable neighborhood and home setting where the parents could each work from home. Upon their arrival, Marco had been placed in first grade. His use of English was limited and was thought to be a contributing factor to his apparent academic delays. Unfortunately for Marco, the family's frequent moves had meant that he had to change schools a few times. In each school, in addition to academic delays, he was also noted to be immature, socially anxious, and awkward.

Each school offered speech and language services and encouraged the parents to seek a more thorough evaluation of their son. He was tested near the end of second grade and diagnosed as being on the Autistic Spectrum.

At the time of that evaluation, the parents described Marco's atypical behaviors that included looking at things that went around in circles (e.g., when playing with his beloved small toy cars Marco focused on turning their wheels and watching them rotate).

Distressed by hearing the test results, the parents consulted with an analyst with whom they and Marco had worked for a period of two years before moving to the U.S. She had expressed skepticism and disagreement with the diagnosis and encouraged them to wait until they and Marco had gotten settled in the U.S. where they should seek out an analyst for Marco. With this recommendation in mind they had sought my help.

As we concluded our first meeting, we made plans that I would next meet with them and Marco together. When they arrived for that appointment and as all three entered my office, Marco looked around and decided to take the swivel chair by my desk. By way of introducing me to their son, the parents recalled with him his previous therapist, explaining that, like her, I talk with children about their feelings. Marco remained unresponsive, other than to swivel in my chair and look about the office.

I spoke of the small cars that he had brought with him. In response, he was able to tell me a bit about his cars. His parents described his frequent play with them and he acknowledged this.

The parents had let me know that Marco had an "imaginary friend." When I asked Marco about this and he seemed confused, his father explained to him what I was referring to. When I asked Marco if he could tell me about his friend, he looked at me for a bit and then pointed toward the corner of the room. When I asked him to explain he responded that his friend was standing there; didn't I see him? I thanked him for letting me know and said that actually, I was unable to see him. He smiled slyly and said, "I know, he only lets me see him." As we chatted further, he explained that his friend did not always accompany him, "only sometimes."

At the end of that visit I asked Marco if he would be willing to meet with me a few more times so that we could get to know each other better. After that, along with his parents, we could all decide how we might best proceed. He nodded that he would like to return.

During the three weekly sessions that followed with Marco, he at first spoke haltingly and distractedly in response to questions I asked about his family, school, and neighborhood. Resisting further conversation, he settled into play with the dollhouse. Though it began with slow and cautious exploration, before long he was crashing the family in their car and tossing them about as they seemed confused about where they would live and what they were doing. After a half hour or so of such play and as the time for our visit was drawing to a close, I explained that we would meet again the following week. He could continue to play with the dollhouse or with other toys he had seen in my toy drawer, or he might bring from home something that he might like to show me.

As he talked about toy cars he would bring, he noted out my office window that darkness had fallen. He was mesmerized by the lines of cars and their headlights on the street below. When I asked what he was thinking he paused for several seconds before muttering, "the day is gone." I said, "yes," he had come this week at a later time than when we had met with his parents and so it was already dark by the end of our visit. He stood unmoving and seemed confused. Finally, he repeated, "the day is gone." Not knowing quite what to say I responded, "Yes, but tomorrow will be another day." After another long pause he said, "but I missed today." As he exited the office, I found myself wondering about his apparent surprise, confusion, and comments. I was left to wonder how this could occur in the mind of a boy who had just turned eight.

At the start of the next visit, Marco took from his pocket a couple of small toy cars that he'd brought from home. He rolled them about on the floor. He seemed to have little to say. Gradually, he began to crash the cars about. As they rolled under the furniture, he made comments about how they were lost. Eventually, they would get found only to be lost again. After this play had continued for a while, I recalled with him how it seemed like his play with the dollhouse characters and car the week before. I noted the confusion they seemed to feel about where they would go and what they would do.

As he remained silent, I asked if I could ask him about something. When he paused to look at me, I took this as permission to proceed and wondered with him how it had been to move to the United States from his home country and then to move more times after arriving here. I asked if that, too, must have seemed confusing.

Instead of answering or commenting, he stood and went to look out the window where, like the week before, it was beginning to get dark. As it became darker, he said, much as he had the week before, "the day is going." As I had done the week before, I again commented that, yes, it was turning to evening. After a long pause he asked, "Where does it go?" I tried to explain how the sun had set and how it would come up again the next morning. Though he listened to me he seemed not really to understand and as our time ended and he started toward the waiting room, he commented, "I don't like the day to end."

In our next session, Marco said he wanted to draw and took paper and markers from the drawer. He sat on the floor and drew on a plastic mat I provided. As the picture developed, he drew the two of us sitting on a sofa. In front of the sofa he drew a large television screen.

On it he drew a tree, the sun, which was wearing glasses and had a worried face, and then a boy holding and shooting a gun. Bullets went toward the border of the TV screen. He drew a leg of a person on each side of the screen as though two people were approaching but neither was yet in view. He drew a table that was falling over with several things falling from it. He drew rooms of the house next to the screen and said that he and I would go to the kitchen to make popcorn.

He then switched to another sheet of paper and rapidly redrew the two of us on the sofa in front of a now empty TV screen. He then drew us walking toward the kitchen where we would make the popcorn. At the top of the page he captioned, "1 minute later."

Next, he took another sheet of paper and quickly began to draw the same images of us on the sofa and the blank TV screen. In this picture we had arrived in the kitchen, were making popcorn, and it was popping wildly out of the pan on the stove. This picture he captioned, "2 minutes later."

Lastly, he drew a picture of himself, alone on a couch. It was the end of the day, night was falling. Several pieces of food were on a table or nearby to it. In a final picture, he drew himself with an angry face carrying more bits of food to an already food-covered table.

I told him our time was drawing to a close and said he had time for perhaps one more picture. He got out colored markers and began to draw rapidly. At the bottom he made a tree with rainbow colored leaves. Above was a dark shape that looked like a tornado. At the top he drew dark scribbled clouds but then filled in what looked like eyes causing the final appearance to be like a dark ominous face.

As I thought about the pictures, I thought of what seemed an interesting progression. First, we had watched a confusing scene on the television; then he had us go to make popcorn together, only to have it turn into a wild, out-of- control event. His captions of the progressing time (first one minute later and then two minutes later) seemed an effort to slow time down and mark sequential occurrences, as if to understand things better. At the end, when left alone, he provided himself with food but in a way that seemed to feel overwhelming. His final picture seemed to provide further evidence of his expectation that frightening things could happen to him.

Marco had come with a diagnosis of autism; descriptions of his behavior from teachers and parents seemed to validate the diagnosis as did his initial presentation in my office. But my take-away thought from these first sessions was to think that Marco was a boy who was able and perhaps even eager to have someone with whom to work on sorting out his overwhelmed feelings and experiences.

As our time finished, I said that I would be meeting soon with his parents and we would talk about how we should go forward. I asked if he would like to continue to come and, as if a bit surprised to be asked this question, he looked directly at me and said, "Yes," before exiting the office.

As I began my meeting with Marco's parents, I could see the eager and, at the same time, anxious look on their faces. I assured them how much I had been enjoying getting to know their son. As we talked, I shared that I thought he was letting me know about his worries and explained that I thought I might better understand them if they could provide me with more information about his earliest years. Led by Marco's mother but soon joined by his father, the parents began to pour out to me a painful story.

During Marco's first year he had been with his mother each day while she worked from home. Though she spoke of how she had enjoyed these months with Marco, she described how when he was about eighteen months of age, she had begun to feel "guilty" and thought that he needed to be around other children. She happily described how she had dressed him up in his jacket and hat and taken him in his stroller out into their neighborhood to "look for a school for him." They had found a school nearby that she thought would be a good choice. Dad recalled how they had visited the school and liked both the teachers and the equipment that it contained. Marco was soon enrolled there and began to attend daily.

They recalled that Marco had seemed anxious when they dropped him off but described how they had been reassured by the school's director that he was always fine after they left.

It was then that Marco's mother paused, covered her face, and haltingly began to cry. As she continued, she explained through her tears that during the several months that followed they had gradually become concerned. Marco continued to seem unhappy when they would take him to the school in the morning. To reassure them, the director provided them with photos of Marco at school, showing him sitting on mats with other children, on the playground, or engaged at play with one of the teachers. In each photo, he seemed unhappy and less engaged than were the other children.

Shortly after the first anniversary of Marco having started at the school, when he was approaching two-and-a-half, Marco's mother attended a "Mother's Day" celebration at the school. At the event another mother took her aside and said that she was sorry to have heard from her daughter what had been happening to Marco at the school. The other mother then told of her daughter's description of how the teachers often confined Marco inside the school's darkened bathroom, keeping him there whenever he would not stop crying. She also learned that at other times Marco would be left alone for long periods in a swing in the garden, while everyone else was inside.

Angered and upset by this information, the parents confronted the director who did not deny that these steps had been taken when she had felt frustrated and helpless in the face of her inability to get Marco to stop crying. Though she apologized to them, the parents immediately withdrew Marco from the school.

After a search and careful assessment by the parents, another school was found, and Marco was enrolled there. The parents recalled that Marco had seemed happier and was gradually supported to settle in at that facility. About six months later though, they noticed that he again seemed to be distressed and unhappy. When they investigated, they learned that the director of the previous school had been hired by and had started to work at his new school. Angry that they had not been informed of this, they withdrew Marco from that school as well.

In the weeks that followed they sought and carefully reviewed other school options for Marco. Eventually, they settled on a Montessori School. In that facility Marco had seemed happier. He attended there from the ages of three to five, when the family moved to the United States. During those two years the parents also began to consult with an analyst who worked with Marco and the parents and who encouraged them to find an analyst to continue work with Marco once the family had settled in the U.S.

As they concluded their painful story, both emphasized how awful and guilty they had felt when they learned from the other mother what she had been told by her daughter regarding how Marco had been treated in his first school setting. I sympathized and asked what they thought Marco knew or understood regarding what they had told me. They looked at each other and then acknowledged that they thought he knew nothing about it. They had never known what, if anything, to say and had never known how to go about it.

As the session was ending, I again expressed my sympathy and, recalling what they had said about the photos they had received from the school, I asked if they could bring them to our next meeting so that we could look at them together and think further how best to proceed. They agreed to do so.

Before that next session with the parents I began what we had agreed would be regular weekly sessions with Marco. During the first of these sessions he attempted to play with Lego, something he said he did with his dad. As he sat by the Lego box fingering different pieces, I asked if he thought he might try to follow the directions portrayed in the accompanying booklet, so he could build one of the items portrayed there. He quickly declined, saying he preferred to build his own designs. Several minutes later he had only managed to put together and then take apart several various pieces. As I watched, it became clear that he could not think of how to proceed.

Toward the end of the session, I noted that we were at the last day of the month and asked if he would like to help me change the page of my calendar to the next month. He said he would but when I asked what the next month would be, he could not say. He could not even say what the current month was. As I asked a few additional questions, it was clear that he not only did not know the sequence of the months, he did not even know more than a couple of their names. He was similarly unable to recite the days of the week.

As Marco departed and I tried to make sense of these apparent gaps in his knowledge, I wondered if they provided evidence of someone on the autistic spectrum or was this a defense against retraumatization by a massive withdrawal from and shield against a dangerous external world.

During my next visit with the parents they brought and showed me several pictures they had obtained and saved from Marco's first childcare center experience. What they shared was painful to look at. First came pictures from Marco's first year when he was home with his mother. The pictures were of a happy baby and his happy parents.

When we shifted to looking at the pictures taken at the childcare center, Marco appeared a different child. His face was marked with sadness, worry, confusion and, occasionally, tears. He protested as teachers tried to help him walk on mats. He cried and sat helplessly as another child took a truck from his grasp. He sat in tears on his cot at naptime and as he leaned against a post and then sat alone and forlorn in a swing in the garden. In no picture was there evidence of a boy who felt happy, safe, or secure.

As hard as it was for me to view the pictures, it was equally hard to witness the remorse and grief of the parents as they looked at them with me. It was as if doing so together let them truly see the pain on their child's face; pain they had not before been so able to integrate or take in.

As we talked after viewing the pictures, I shared with the parents how memories of early experiences, though not recalled as actual events can nevertheless remain and be recalled as "feeling memories." (In this way I was providing an explanation of the difference between "implicit" and "explicit" memories.) We discussed how memories from a time before much language was available to a child were often only retained as "feeling memories."

I asked the parents if Marco had ever looked at the pictures with them. They did not recall that he had. They further reflected that until I had asked about the pictures, they had not looked at them for years. The experience had been such a painful one they had just wanted to put it behind them. They had never thought of telling Marco about it. They feared it would only upset him further and upset them all, all over again. I assumed that they too had been traumatized and, like Marco, frightened that they would be retraumatized by painful memories.

I said that I could understand how they would think that way but, after a pause, I said I had an idea to propose. I cautioned that they might find it hard to consider what I was about to propose. I explained that, in spite of what we often think as adults, children can actually find it very helpful to get clarity regarding even very painful events that might have occurred when they were very young, events for which they had no conscious memories. I then suggested that we all meet together and use the time to again go over the pictures, this time with Marco. We could talk about the feelings suggested by the look on Marco's face in the pictures and they could let him know what they had sadly come to learn had been his experience in that first school he had attended. Cautiously, they agreed to give it a try.

When we all met together, I could feel the tension and worry in the parents. After it was clear that they were deferring to me, I explained to Marco how his parents had been telling me about some hard things that had happened when he had been a very little boy. When he had learned how to walk and wanted to be busy with his toys, they had looked for a school in their neighborhood that he could attend.

Mother picked up the story. She told him of taking him out in his stroller and walking through their neighborhood until finding a school that looked like it would be a good one. As she talked, she began to show him the pictures of him at the school. As she did, she acknowledged that she and his dad had come to see that he was not happy there. She then told him of what she had learned from the mother of his playmate about how he was put alone in the bathroom or out in the garden swing. As she spoke, Marco began to crawl onto her lap; he began to hug her about the neck and to lick her face.

His mother began to cry. His father seemed worried and tried to encourage Marco to get down. But Marco stayed on his mother's lap and continued to hug and lick her face.

I spoke and said that I thought that hearing his mother's words and seeing the pictures had brought back a memory for Marco and that as he was having that old memory, he was also remembering how he had wanted to be on his mother's lap and be close to her when he was young and felt that way. Mother held him close and rocked him and wept.

After a bit I spoke again and said that I thought it had been important to share this story and to have these feelings together. I suggested that we continue to meet this way for awhile to talk further. In between sessions they might talk more of this at home, maybe even look at more pictures.

For the next two weeks we continued to meet conjointly, with the parents and Marco together. During the first of those two sessions, they demonstrated how as a family they had loaded all of Marco's baby, toddler and preschool pictures into Mother's computer. In addition to again looking at the pictures from that first school experience, other pictures of birthdays, holidays, outings in parks and gardens, and visits with relatives were all recorded for posterity.

Marco could begin to see how in the pictures from before the first school experience he had been a happy boy. In one picture he was on his father's shoulders, happily scrubbing his father's head. In another, as a small baby, he was lying on a cushion smiling as the family's dog stood beside him. There were happy pictures of playing with Christmas toys with his father; sitting together happily with both his parents and their dog; riding his tricycle in a park near their home.

During the third session, Marco came in carrying the computer. He had determined with his parents ahead of time that he would operate the slide show of pictures that day and that he would be the one to tell me about them.

He began by showing me what he said was his favorite picture. It showed him and his parents posed together over a table. In the center of their group hug was their dog. She had just finished licking her birthday cake off a paper plate at the celebration of her fourteenth birthday. All were smiling broadly, especially Marco who was laughing happily as the dog licked his face.

During the weeks that followed, Marco seemed a different boy in his sessions. He was talkative throughout, played creatively with doll house characters, and regaled me with many pictures that he drew with rapid pen strokes and apparent artistic skill. From his parents I learned that he was doing better in school and was much more cooperative working on his homework at home in the evening. On weekends he was enjoying outings with his parents to the zoo, museums, and movies, and on a couple of occasions had invited and been accompanied by a neighborhood school friend. As well, his parents noted his keen interest in music and had supported him learning to play both the trumpet and the drums.

Toward the end of Marco's third grade year, the parents pursued another evaluation for him to see if he was still identified as showing signs of being on the Autistic Spectrum. This was necessary to determine if he remained eligible for supportive school services. While the report concluded with "diagnostic impressions" of "Autistic Spectrum Disorder without accompanying intellectual impairment, without accompanying language impairment." A review of the testing protocol raised questions but, ultimately, the parents decided to let the report be submitted to the school because it did allow the school to continue to provide Marco with the supplemental services that he benefited from (largely because of the enduring underlying caution and anxiety that distracted him from working persistently and because he continued to struggle a bit with English as his second language).

Throughout the first few months of his fourth-grade year, Marco continued to progress in terms of his academic skills and social development. Our work increased to a twice-weekly frequency with parent sessions occurring bi-weekly, augmented by periodic email communications to provide additional information about both home and school activities.

In his sessions, Marco typically brought several matchbox-sized cars from his collection and used them to enact fantasy stories. Led by a "brother and sister" pair, the group of "friend" cars went on outings together, had overnight stays with one another and generally enjoyed being friends. Of interest was how the themes of this play surpassed the actual life experiences of Marco. Though his play clearly demonstrated his yearnings, he admitted that he still had trouble reaching out to peers to make and maintain friendships. He acknowledged that during most recess periods, he played alone on the playground.

By mid-fall he was showing progress as during most weekends activities with friends were regularly occurring, though encourage-ment from parents and their participation usually were needed for support.

However, in early November of Marco's fourth-grade year, mother learned of a work opportunity in her home country that she felt she could not turn down. It would involve her having to work part-time in her home country, but she would be provided with transportation home at least every other weekend and her son and husband would be funded to travel to see her on the other weekends. She accepted the opportunity.

Things went well for the first few weeks. Marco had daily phone calls with his mother and took pleasure in sharing with her the details of his day. A serious interference occurred however when problems emerged regarding the family's visas. They were aware that they needed to be renewed and had taken beginning steps to accomplish this early in the preceding summer. However, by mid-November they had received no response.

A crisis developed when mother's U.S. visa expired while she was in their home country. She was unable to return to the U.S. until a renewal came through. Similarly, for father and Marco, their U.S. visas also expired with them in this country. As the winter holidays approached, the family faced the reality that they had no control over when or if the documents might be reissued and could not travel without them. As a stop-gap measure, the father's mother came to stay with Marco and his dad. Nevertheless, Marco's affect and demeanor began to regress.

During one poignant session in early December, Marco brought with him a stuffed wolf pup. He created a story of how the pup's mother had died in a fire when she was trying to rescue the pup and his sister from their lair. The motherless pup missed his mother deeply and at night would bay at the moon above the forest calling to her.

During another session as Marco anticipated having to celebrate Christmas without his mother, he struggled to allow himself to feel his feelings. I spoke softly to him, recalling what we knew to have occurred when he was just a small boy missing his mother desperately in a school where he was being misunderstood and mistreated. Marco sobbed bitterly. He said he was hurting so badly he couldn't think. He told me that he had made up five songs about his feelings. He tried to sing them to me, at first only remembering one of them. As we continued to talk about the old feelings though, he managed to remember all five and left feeling a bit hopeful.

The next day, however, he came in again bereft. He had planned to bring his cars with him to use them to make up a story, but had forgotten them, only realizing it when he exited the car to come to my office.

Again, he let me talk about the feelings and their old connections. He began to draw, first making large blue drops that represented his tears. He then filled other circles with jagged lines to show his angry feelings. On another page he drew pictures of the cars he'd left at home, finally breaking down into sobs as he drew a picture of his bed at home with the cars resting upon it in the tin he carried them in.

As the session drew to an end and his crying persisted, he said, "I can't remember any of the songs that I sang for you yesterday! How can I have my feelings back for my mom?!?" We departed the office sadly as I walked him back to his dad. On route he stopped suddenly and said, "I just remembered one of them! Maybe I'll be able to remember the rest." I said I thought that might be the case and we sadly said goodbye.

After the winter holidays I heard from Marco's father who expressed concern that Marco seemed unable to remember what he was learning in school. He wondered if he should have Marco evaluated again to see if there was something that had been missed. In a session, I told Marco what his father had said about his seeming loss of memory. He spoke poignantly, saying, "My mother has blown up my brain! I miss her so much!" I countered by recalling with Marco the work we had done to understand what it had felt like to him when he was so young and was mistreated in his first childcare setting.

I arranged for a Skype meeting with both parents (we had been meeting this way to continue our sessions during mother's enforced absence, but this was an additionally scheduled session). During the meeting I reviewed with them the work we had done before on the effects on Marco of his early experiences. I suggested that mother make two identical scrapbooks of all the pictures that had been used during our conjoint sessions. Father could have one to keep at home where Marco could look at it and the other could be in my office so that Marco and I could use it during our sessions.

Both parents agreed with this idea and by the start of our sessions following the New Year, the two copies of the books were available for use. For Marco, looking at the pictures during his sessions proved most helpful. At first, he could not recall what he was looking at—the locations of where many of the pictures had been taken, the sequence in which things had occurred, and who the other people were who were included in some of the pictures.

I reached back out to mother and she created another version of the book that placed all the pictures in sequence and provided captions of what they represented. She extended the pictures from the time of Marco's birth up to the present, including showing her in her present day setting in their home country. The result was noteworthy as Marco was able to go through the pictures to recalibrate for himself a sense of order in his life. It was clear that he was recovering some of his confidence, hope and good feelings.

In mid-February, still without word about the visa situation, the parents and I agreed that I would write a letter on Marco's behalf, emphasizing his need to have physical access to his mother. They submitted the letter and within two weeks the documents were released.

Throughout the spring there were several trips back and forth. Mother's work project would soon conclude and the family was looking forward to being happily and permanently reunited. In the meantime, Marco and his father travelled to their home country for several extended weekends and for all of spring break. Mother was able to come to her U.S. home on a few occasions. Added to the scrapbook were the pictures they had taken during each of their visits with one another and it was these pictures that Marco enjoyed looking at during our sessions.

At the start of our work, Marco had been described as a child "on the autistic spectrum." Early work with his parents revealed the likelihood of early childhood trauma.

Aided by the parents' making available photos from his first childcare center and then from his life from infancy onward, together we were able to reconstruct—first for the parents and then with their assistance, Marco—an understanding of the painful and traumatic experiences he and his parents had endured.

Marco continued to benefit from the small group support services he received at his school and increasingly attained academic adequacy. More broadly, he remained proficient in both English and his native language and continued to develop both his musical and artistic talents. Gradually, he became more socially comfortable and able to form and maintain lasting peer relationships.

Commentary 1

How does a happy little boy respond to the loss of his mother? How do parents respond when they learn that their child has been traumatized? How can analysts help untangle the resultant difficult diagnostic picture while helping child and parents identify the source of the avoided traumatic memory?

Marco clearly suffered an extended trauma period from eighteen months through two-and-a-half, when the parents placed him in a program so he could have more exposure to other children. Only at two-and-a-half did the parents discover in a serendipitous fashion how destructive the program was for Marco. Subsequently there were a lot of moves for the family. Marco was diagnosed as suffering from Autistic Spectrum Disorder, as his symptoms were very severe. Thus, he received a variety of interventions, without much success.

What did the analyst do that was different? The analyst was an acute observer. The key moment occurred early in the work, when the analyst was trying to understand the nature of unexplainable severe gaps in Marco's cognitive functions. The analyst writes:

> As Marco departed and I tried to make sense of these apparent gaps in his knowledge, I wondered if they provided evidence of someone on the autistic spectrum or was this a defense against retraumatization by a massive withdrawal from and shield against a dangerous external world.
>
> During my next visit with the parents they brought and showed me several pictures they had obtained and saved from Marco's first childcare center experience. What they shared was painful to look at. First came pictures from Marco's first year when he was home with his mother. The pictures were of a happy baby and his happy parents. When we shifted to looking at the pictures taken at the childcare center, Marco appeared a different child. His face was marked with sadness, worry, confusion and, occasionally, tears. He protested as teachers tried to help him walk on mats. He cried and sat helplessly as another child took a truck from his grasp. He sat in tears on

his cot at naptime and as he leaned against a post and then sat alone and forlorn in a swing in the garden. In no picture was there evidence of a boy who felt happy, safe, or secure.

As hard as it was for me to view the pictures, it was equally hard to witness the remorse and grief of the parents as they looked at them with me. It was as if doing so together let them truly see the pain on their child's face; pain they had not before been so able to integrate or take in.

Very early in his career, Freud (1892) was aware of the pathogenic character of hidden/masked memories of traumatic events. Freud noted that "The hysteric suffers, therefore, from memories of psychic traumas which resulted from experiences which could not be fully abreacted, either because the hysteric denies himself one or another means of abreaction, or because the experience took place in a state which was not suitable for abreaction" (p. 37).

This description is a perfect description of Marco's phenomenology. As the subsequent work with the parents and Marco illustrates, a gentle, careful review of that period of time with Marco and his parents resulted in a dramatic progression in Marco's development. The memory of the experience that led to the psychic trauma no longer had to be avoided by either Marco or his parents.

Interestingly enough, when the mother had to go to another country for her work, Marco experienced a temporary regression. But further work, including Skype sessions while the mother was away, enabled Marco to continue with improved social activities and peer relationships.

In the twenty-first century, the mobility of many families is a fact of life. Some of this mobility is the result of increased economic and/or professional opportunity. Unfortunately, too often, many families are forced to migrate because of political reasons, because of poverty, and because of terrible dangers to themselves and their children. Marco's family belonged to the more privileged group. Yet, the work with Marco and his family can provide clues to helping the under-privileged.

There were two central aspects operative in this situation, which made things worse:

1. The parents did not appreciate the impact of the center on Marco for over a year.
2. Marco, in some unknown way must have been vulnerable so that he could not communicate effectively to the parents that a change needed to be made.

In the work, the analyst understood the guilt the parents experienced as a result of their denial and avoidance of appreciating the impact on Marco of their non-action. Furthermore, the analyst proceeded carefully because it was evident that the parents emotionally suffered as they finally appreciated the impact on Marco. It was only after many years that the parents *saw for the first time* the difference between the lively happy Marco of one year and the sad, withdrawn Marco of his later toddler years. Why did they not *see* this earlier? One can only surmise that the parents needed to defensively avoid appreciating the negative reality of the center situation for the year between one-and-a-half and two-and-a-half. Only the concern by another child's mother awakened them to the problem. And only then, when they connected to the analyst when Marco was eight, was the family able to confront the unbearable affects associated with the traumatic memory and move forward from it.

Richard Lane (2018), a neuroscientist, has been able to evaluate Freud's hypothesis about the therapeutic impact of addressing old memories from a current neuroscience perspective. Lane et al. (2015) describe the process which must occur in psychotherapy, whether it be cognitive behavioral, emotion-focused, or psychodynamic therapy. There must be "(1) reactivating old memories, whether through explicit recall or reminders, as well as activating the "old," usually painful affect associated with those old memories; (2) engaging in new emotional experiences during treatment that are incorporated into those reactivated memories via the process of reconsolidation; and (3) reinforcing the updated memory by practicing a new way of behaving and experiencing the world in a variety of contexts" (Lane 2018, p. 509).

The case of Marco illustrates that for this process to work effectively the parents and the children have to be involved. How to use these insights to help more desperate families with children who suffer unspeakable traumas is an incredible challenge.

Commentary 2

It was most astonishing to me how Marco's non-verbal perceptions—containing potential communication—slowly became transformed metaphorically while reaching out to his therapist with whom he was co-constructing meaningful verbal symbols, gestures and the analytic process based on seeing and being seen as well as on his experiences with his former analyst. The spirit of this new analytic couple carried over to the child-parent-therapist system (Novick, K.K. and Novick, J. 2005) and such to concurrent parent work. I will focus only on the development of the mainly optical metaphorical inner and outer realities and the wonderful work of translation of emotional memories of the past in the here and now which took place within a most sensitive and creative child-parent-therapist system.

His parents had moved to the U.S. and thereby imposed on their six-year-old son—who had no say in whether he wanted to leave his home country or not—painful feelings of losing his familiar holding surround with its sounds, smells, food, language, relatives and so forth (Bründl and Kogan 2005). In terms of Nachträglichkeit (Freud 1895), his migration to the U.S. reactivated unforgotten-but-not-to-be remembered traumatic feelings of abandonment, contempt, and segregation during his vulnerable transition from his inter-subjective self to his incoming verbal self (Stern 1985) back home in kindergarten after his mother had taken good care of him all the time before. The consequences of his traumatizing pre-oedipal experiences made his parents look for analytic help by an analyst in their home country for approximately two years prior to their move to the U.S. There Marco had already learned to put feelings and phantasies into words, translating emotional memories into meaningful metaphors within his mother tongue.

From the very beginning the outstanding case report evokes strong visual images and metaphors: not only are we informed about Marco being fascinated by rotating things, in his first session he is looking around in the room while he is being seen swivelling in the therapist's chair without uttering any word; and Marco makes it clear, that his imaginary friend can be seen from time to time only by himself. In his third week of once-per-week evaluation—as a boy of eight in the U.S.—his therapist remarked that Marco " was mesmerized by the lines of cars and their headlights on the street below" as he was looking out of the window of the office while darkness was falling. He could tell his therapist "the day is gone," repeating it in a confused way not being able to accept his (American speaking?) therapist's concept of another new day to come in the future, and finally mentioned "but I miss today." Was Marco bringing forward metaphorically pre-traumatic early mentation and time sense where the object had not been personalized yet in her/ his own right in a new way within the actual presence (Rizzolo 2019)?

It seems to me that Marco had hope toward and a deep feeling for his therapist's openness to the ongoing unpredictable process and his therapist's negative capability (Bion 1970; Green 1973) when Marco communicated their being together and how the traumatic process (Fischer and Riederesser 1998) would be marked in their therapeutic work by means of a powerful sequence of drawings: a "confusing scene" [for the two] on the television, then he had us go to make popcorn: only to have it turn to " a wild, out of control world," and by slowing down time for better understanding by means of the two following drawings pointing to his being alone and the day disappearing. In his inner world (in his body?) obviously his traumatic past had been laid down, a feeling his parents had to defend against, because it had been too painful for them, too; they therefore had never talked to him about it or shared their memory with him, reinforcing Marco's repression of memories once conscious.

The following parent work was structured by the parents now presenting photos, pictures so to speak, to the therapist and also to the analytic couple, photos of unhappy, desperate, abandoned Marco in the kindergarten. The therapist's empathic openness to and the containment of the turmoil of feelings within parents and within the child triggered an up-to-now unheard narrative for Marco, while the parents were commenting on traumatic and lovely pre-traumatic photos. This led to a deepening, widening and loving transformation of the resourceful parent-child relationship (Novick, K.K. and Novick,

J. 2005). In a later session, "Marco came in carrying the computer. He had determined with his parents... that he would operate the slide show of pictures that day and that he would be the one to tell me about them," giving his own re-found new narrative, his own translation in his own metaphors. Marco seemed to become a "different boy in his sessions," He was talkative [!], played creatively... and regaled me with many pictures that he drew with rapid pen strokes and apparent artistic skill."

When Marco was about ten his mother, for professional reasons, had to return to her home country, leaving Marco and her husband behind in the U.S. A new serious crisis developed because unexpectedly his mother could not return to the U.S. due to her expired visa. Again, Nachträglichkeit brought split off affects of his kindergarten time and of his migration to the U.S. with full power into the present. Because of progression and ongoing consolidating of his self along the different developmental lines (A.Freud 1965) in the secure transitional therapy space (Winnicott 1971) his symptomatology seemed more complex and mature, finding expression still in powerful drawings, sorrow and complaints about losing his playfulness and verbal-musical creativity.

Concurrent parent work continued by Skype conferences. The most convincing outcome was two identical copies of a scrapbook of all the pictures that had been used in therapy—one copy for Marco at home with his father, the other book for Marco in his therapy sessions. In the final version mother "placed all the pictures in sequence and provided captions of what they represented... pictures from the time of Marco's birth up to the present, including showing her in her present setting in their home country... Marco was able to go through the pictures to calibrate for himself a sense of self in his life."

An unusual intervention of the therapist as a child expert outside the analytic setting, the writing an urgent letter to the immigration services, helped all the members of the family within a short time to receive their proper visas. And they could cross borders in ways convenient for them. I assume this was of more importance for Marco than it seems on first sight. He was old and mature enough now to mentalize his own capability to switch between and bridge the two nations and cultures on his own while in his past he was placed by his parents without him having any initiative in the placement. I am convinced that this new developmental step in the inner and outer world helped Marco in the second meaning of Nachträglichkeit to redo and heal many of the wounds his traumatic migration as a child at the edge of latency had left on him. In other words, the experience in late latency had a strong impact on unresolved issues which had been carried on in his inner hidden world since his migration to the U.S. at the age of six.

Having to struggle with two languages and two cultures, Marco's artistic gifts helped him to reach out to his therapist in a most sophisticated way, not having to rely on verbal language in his new country which he had not securely made his own. The sequence of his own drawings and those of photos from his birth up to the present told their own story, no matter what kind of language the person would speak who looks at the picture narrative, supporting the internal symbolizing systems. Of course, in child analysis kids often reach out and develop by paintings and drawings. And we therapists are more inclined to use poetic and metaphorical interventions with children patients. But in my experience patients who had immigrated legally or "illegally" in first or second generation, children, adolescents and adults alike, can develop more trust in the therapist who does not belong to their ethnic group, when the search for shared metaphors, images, and poetic language becomes the precondition for co-constructing the analytic space and process. Marco, the child immigrant, in his way helped his experienced therapist to learn "Marco's own language in translation."

Editorial Reflections

This chapter underscores the necessity and impact of concurrent parent work. The analyst and the commentators are pointing to concurrent parent work as not only crucial for differential diagnosis, but also allowing for reconstruction of trauma eventuating in mastery and a changed diagnosis, which indicates a different outcome for the child. In a case such as this, when parents and child have all experienced a trauma, we see that the analyst was flexible in moving from concurrent work with parents and individual sessions with the child, to conjoint sessions for a time, and then back to concurrent work and individual sessions.

Starting as an experimental attempt to decrease the high proportion of premature endings of child and adolescent cases, concurrent parent work has been increasingly used by psychoanalysts in a range of circumstances with encouraging results. This case brings us an eight-year-old child diagnosed as on the autistic spectrum who presented with a number of confirming symptoms and evidenced several puzzling cognitive deficits which further underscored the likelihood of neurological dysfunction.

Rather than simply accepting the diagnosis, the analyst kept an open mind. This included the crucial dimension of keeping the parents in mind and the analyst soon included them in the initial exploration. By working with child and parents, reconstruction of repeated traumatic experiences began to make sense to all family members and the child began to change. The work then shifted to what one commentator referred to as the "child-parent-therapist" system. Each party to this system had experienced the trauma and a creative variant of concurrent parent work allowed the feelings to emerge, be shared, contained, transformed and experienced again but in a non-traumatic form.

The repeated impact of Nachträglichkeit (deferred action) could be elucidated and a reparative process of reconstituting a shared family narrative began. This integration of traumatic memories appears to be one of the major outcomes of concurrent parent work, that is, that disparate and disconnected experiences of events become available for sharing and generating a family history narrative that all parties can own. This is central to strengthening the parent-child relationship. In this case, the parents could bring their own memories to help the child; it sometimes happens, too, that a child in treatment may bring a memory that the parents may not have access to, that can aid the parent work. In successful work, the unconscious of each member of the "team" is activated.

The chapter also poignantly demonstrates the need to recognize and address the extremely distressing feelings of guilt that most parents bring with them when they seek help on a child's behalf. Helping transform these into "useable concern" (Novick, K.K. and Novick, J. 2005) becomes the basis for moving the treatment forward.

CHAPTER FIVE

SECRETS AND LIES

School-age

Clinical Vignette

Aria was eight years old when I met her parents. Extremely attractive and successful, Aria's middle-aged parents were very concerned about their birth daughter's extreme level of anxiety and penchant for using her body to express her overwhelming feelings rather than her words. For the last year Aria had been openly masturbating in the classroom by rubbing her legs together with such intensity her desk would travel across the room. In the developmental history form parents described their only child as a beautiful, academically successful and intelligent girl who has manifested symptoms of anxiety throughout her young life. Before the onset of public masturbation, Aria bit her nails and was intolerant of spending time alone, frequently clinging to Mother when anxious. Angry outbursts and difficulty calming Aria were common in their household, especially in response to parents correcting her misbehavior. Both parents and school had exhausted all known possibilities in attempting to calm and re-channel Aria's sexually explicit behavior.

Subsequent to the four parent and three individual evaluation meetings with Aria, her parents began to accept, with my guidance, that their daughter was developmentally behind in the area of affect regulation, causing heightened anxiety and depression. They agreed that Aria's angry outbursts and open masturbation were signaling her difficulty calming herself when overexcited and uplifting herself when depressed. A four-times-a-week analysis made sense to them to help Aria consistently find words, and ultimately thought and reason, to navigate her way through her feelings rather than her body. Aria expressed enthusiasm and the desire to meet with me as much as possible when analysis was recommended to her. This enthusiasm was consistent throughout Aria's eighteen-month psychoanalysis. The parents, desperate for more knowledge and help in parenting their suffering daughter, accepted the recommendation for once-a-week parent sessions to help them be the best parents possible.

During this beginning phase I was aware of feeling enthusiastic about working with this invested family. I was particularly curious about Aria's choice of symptom and drawn to her welcoming attitude about the therapy. Yet I was also concerned about the intensity of her pain as well as its origin.

The appearance of parental working together melted rapidly when we began the analysis. Father disappeared from the parent meetings, refusing to answer my emails while mother and Aria remained invested in their meetings. Mother expressed disappointment when father refused to attend and confronted father in response to my recommendation, telling him his daughter was more important than going to the gym during sessions and that I would agree to FaceTime with him when he was traveling. Father ignored mother's messages and continued to avoid the meetings. Feeling confident in my connection with mother, I encouraged her to speak of anything providing clues to father's behavior. Mother wept. Six months before, mother had found evidence through phone and email that Father was sexually involved with many other women.

Mother was in her own therapy exploring her feelings and how to resolve this challenging situation. Father refused to attend marital therapy sessions before seeking consultation with me. Both mother and I wondered how Aria's behavior in school was connected consciously or unconsciously to father's acting out. Throughout the analysis I periodically emailed father, stressing his importance in Aria's life and encouraged him to attend. Occasionally he would attend parent sessions, yet he would never acknowledge my emails or any of my interventions directly.

Aria entered her analysis with gusto, expressing herself primarily with action and action words. In an early hour Aria and I played a rubber band game initiated by her. While entangling the bands around our fingers, Aria leaned her body warmly and affectionately against mine. Perfectionism quickly followed when she could not master the task of flicking the rubber bands to the ceiling. When she failed, she violently hurled objects around my consulting room, practically breaking a lamp. I spoke of how hard it seemed for her to feel she must master a task before it is taught to her. I also said her loving feelings are having a hard time calming her big, angry ones and how, like flicking the rubber band, we were going to practice her use of these feelings to calm anger. Aria calmed down and re-entered intimate play. This vacillation between loving excitement transforming into wild aggression was repeated several times in the first three months of her analysis.

During the next session with mother, she expressed concern and anguish when Aria mirrored mother's perfectionism similar to what I witnessed with Aria in my consulting room. I suggested mother help Aria remain calm when Aria learns a task by encouraging her to use words for her feelings and then think through the steps to accomplish the tasks before performing them. I explained that Aria's perfectionism was an attempt to erase her feelings of aggression and concomitant guilt from what Aria perceived as her bad behavior. mother agreed. Mother also believed that Aria's anxious perfectionism originated from father's pressure for Aria to excel beyond her ability in academics and sports.

Through acting out her inner conflict with beanie babies while using me as her object of transference, and through games of hide and seek, Aria continued to reveal anger and sadness from loss through separation, which she allowed me to interpret. Through games of hide-and-seek I provided words for Aria's concern she and mother were lost from each other's minds when mother went on business trips. Through beanie babies fighting, then hugging, she allowed me to give voice to fears that her anger from the loss was damaging her loved ones and her need to repair it. From her beating me with balloons and pinching me, she revealed her desire and terror of damaging her loving but inconsistent objects. Finally, she transformed my words into her own and took them out of the consulting room.

When the family returned from their spring break trip, Aria burst into painful sobs telling mother how horrible it was for her when mother returned to work. When Mother worked, she came home too tired to play with Aria, and this hurt her. Mother, while speaking with me through sobs, realized that she had been neglecting her child. She concluded that she needed to work less and spend more quality time with her daughter. At the end of three months, parents were delighted that Aria was masturbating less and excelling in school. Yet, Aria's use of her nail biting to substitute for the masturbation and her continued meltdowns suggested to parents that she needed ongoing therapy.

Aria's diminished masturbation indicated she was no longer carrying her father's issues, but it was followed by escalation in parental discord over the next three months. Father acted out by arguing with mother in front of Aria, spanking Aria, attempting to reduce Aria's time in her analysis, and constantly insisting on perfect behavior from Aria. Given father's continued absence from the parent sessions, I attempted to modify father's behavior through mother. I told mother that, through spanking Aria and the push for perfectionism, he was acting in opposition to treatment goals. Mother confronted him by passing on this message. He responded by using his words to reason with Aria instead of spanking, but he could not let go of the need for perfect performance. Rather than Aria calmly reasoning with him when working on schoolwork, she became agitated and refused to work. I also suggested mother leave the room when father attempted to argue with her in front of Aria. Mother agreed.

Mother also confronted father's lying and told him under no circumstances would Aria's time in her analysis be compromised. When father resurfaced in the meetings, he refused to talk about anything but Aria perfecting her schoolwork and sports. He refused to engage in conversations about parental interventions or accept responsibility for his actions.

Aria's agitation escalated at home and in sessions, yet she contained her behavior at school. She was rubbing her vagina raw in private and attempted to provoke parents and me to correct her acting out. In sessions, hide-and-seek games while father was on business trips were interpreted as signaling Oedipal strivings as well as family secrets and deception. Was she afraid of what father was doing on his trips? I asked. Was she afraid he was spending time with others and not her and mother? Aria, like father, refused to answer with words, and responded by hurling scissors and other objects in my consulting room. Through displacement Aria sobbed with mother about how Aria felt she was such a horrible mother when her puppy ripped her beloved beanie boos. Mother asked Aria if they should give up the puppy. During a phone call I suggested to mother that Aria would interpret this as parents giving Aria away if she misbehaved. Mother agreed and helped Aria protect her belongings. In session I spoke with Aria about how she was feeling helpless and responsible for parental discord, as well as her pain in response to it. In response to the resulting guilt, she was attempting to punish herself by blaming herself and provoking me to punish her. Aria responded by throwing her arms around me in tears saying, "Thank you, Doctor. No one has ever told me that before." Her provocations subsided in and out of her sessions.

In the next parent session, though father had never acknowledged the effects of the parent work, he was able to empathize with Aria's feelings of loss. He replaced a lost necklace mother had given her as revealed in a session he attended. I acknowledged his accomplishment and deepened connection with Aria and attempted to empathize with his feeling of loss from his childhood. Mother responded with anger, hoping I would be more confrontational with father yet knew I was trying to re-engage him. I told her I was concerned about alienating him further. I gently said I felt she wanted me to confront him to save her the pain and aggravation of doing so. She calmed. I then suggested that she tell him if he wanted the marriage to continue, he needed to attend marital therapy and parent sessions. She agreed.

Highly tumultuous sessions ensued for the next four months in both Aria's and the parent work, revealing their urge to revert to past defenses. As mother became more aware of her desire for divorce subsequent to discovering additional evidence of father's serial infidelities, father continued to embrace denial while concomitantly acting out more frequently. Possibly in response, Aria returned to her old defense of masturbating in school and revealing her desire for sadomasochistic bondage in sessions. Simultaneous decisions of mother's to file for divorce and plan to move to another state where they had friends also occurred at this time. I struggled with knowing the roots of Aria's regression, i.e. her preconscious knowledge of her parent's impending divorce and her father's unspoken infidelities, but it was not my place to inform her. Though Aria's behavior temporarily regressed in school, the behavior just as quickly subsided when her growing ego strength allowed her to accept the traditional and appropriate limits at school and as recommended by me.

Was Aria feeling in bondage with me, her parents, herself or all three of us? While she was tying me up with every prop she could find, I declared that I could have my own body and mind as could she; she responded by squealing with delight, calmed, and then became embroiled in superego conflict. She tested every limit in my office including destroying a lamp when I attempted to suggest her open masturbation with me was in response to mother's absence. She then contritely expressed regret, calmed, and through play with a male character in a game chastised father for his illegal and dangerous conduct. In the midst of this father acted out by abruptly telling Aria that he and mother were getting a divorce. Aria responded by screaming, sobbing and running down her neighborhood street. In her next session she sang the Sound of Music in my consulting room. I spoke of a family first unhappy from horrible loss only to heal and find happiness again. Aria then asked if she would be unloved if her parents divorced. I said she would not. If they divorced it was with each other and never her. Though parents separate and cannot live with one another they can still love

101

each other and their love for her will only grow. She threw her arms around me and said, "I love YOU."

Subsequent to Aria's declaration, father's acting out infiltrated and interfered with Aria's progress and life again. Following her voluntary relinquishment of control in sessions for the first time through freely flying paper airplanes, at the beginning of her next hour father entered her session and in front of Aria said her sessions had to be cut to once a week for financial reasons. Aria responded by attempting to injure herself in session and provoking me to chastise her. I spoke of how she used her out-of-control behavior to prevent feelings of helplessness. She calmed in response.

To the parents I revealed Aria's intense signals of distress in response to the threat. Mother had no knowledge of father's threat because she was out of town when it occurred. I insisted on continuing Aria's analysis as scheduled and parents agreed. In a later session, mother revealed the family's extreme wealth. Father continued to deny Aria's struggles and the impending separation. Mother continued to plan for the divorce while Aria was told they were moving to another state. Aria expressed her feelings about loss of me by masturbating openly in my consulting room. I spoke directly to her about how using her body to soothe loss was not working. In a following session I said I was not trying to take away her use of masturbation, I was simply trying to help her find other choices. Aria calmed.

Aria directly expressed with words in session and at home her sadness and concern about the big goodbye. I followed by speaking of the move as a good goodbye and a happy opportunity to return to friends and to a new home or possibly two homes with new pleasure and opportunity with two parents. Aria made me a crown titled the Queen of Love in response. Mother discovered STD drugs in her husband's drawer. She felt overwhelmed and hurried her visit to their new state to consult with her lawyer to plan an efficient exit plan from the marriage during the move to that state. Father then told mother a woman was attempting to black mail him by revealing the woman's affair with him to mother. Mother suspected a pregnancy and found further evidence that father was being blackmailed by the woman. Aria's behavior escalated in session yet not in her outside world. She vacillated from calm to rage followed by provocation. In session when she attempted to provoke through openly masturbating, I spoke of how she was blending pleasure with anger to calm the anger. I said her big feelings are signals of something wrong but do not have to be destructive. An outpouring of feelings about the divorce followed. Nightmares of twin girls being murdered were reported by Aria directly to me. She expressed great relief when I said divorce is not the same as death and neither she nor her parents were going to die from the divorce.

Aria visited the new therapist I found for her in her new state and liked her, but was saddened knowing this meant leaving me. Fears of loss were expressed by running into my office sobbing, throwing her arms around me, and saying people on the stairs called her an orphan. I held her and told her they were mistaken; she would never be an orphan with two such strong parents. Through email father lied, saying he and mother wanted to cut back Aria's time in her analysis. I reminded him of the agreement that they must provide a thirty-day notice before changing Aria's schedule. He was furious but backed off.

Aria's terrors of death and abandonment through divorce were realized in my consulting room by Aria and mother. Mother was out-of-town and unable to take care of Aria while father was attempting to cut Aria's analysis. Father responded by unnecessarily going to work and leaving Aria to her own devices. Aria enacted this through a game; we played two sisters whose parents died and the left sisters on their own. While I spoke of her fear of being left an orphan, Aria sobbed. In a parent session Mother revealed father's abandonment of Aria and mother's parallel fear of father abandoning Aria. I spoke to Aria about how mother would have plans in the divorce agreement to make sure Aria was adequately taken care of if anything were to happen to mother. Aria calmed. Before their last trip Aria shared her feelings for the first time to father. He was touched and shared this with me. I validated Aria's message of him being a loving father and he bolted from the parent work forever. In the last two weeks, Aria openly said she would miss me; I said I would miss her very much but would use the knowledge she was going to such a wonderful home to ease my feelings of loss. Aria calmed and built us a house of love.

In the last two sessions Aria and I played all of the games we played throughout the analysis, including hide and seek to cope with feelings of loss and catching her in a sling made of a scarf to symbolize our presence inside of her to guide her. She sang the song, "The day that I met you I knew you will always be a part of my heart." I confirmed these lyrics as a part of our relationship. When she attempted to deny this, I showed her a sculpture her mother gave me as a goodbye gift. It was two chain links made of stone. I asked her to try to break them apart. She could not. She smiled in response and again sang, "The day that I met you, I knew you will always be a part of my heart."

At the end of her analysis Aria had completely ceased her public masturbation, she preferred using her words to express herself at home and in public almost exclusively over the use of her body. She was successful in school and was the lead in the school musical. Parents and Aria reported her more frequent calm, her success in school, her ability to happily play alone, and her enjoyment of steady relationships with friends and family.

Commentary 1

Here are a few thoughts and comments that came to me while reading Aria's most touching material regarding her parents and her feelings, and her behavioral "reflections" of them and their difficulty. One wonders if the parents' referral of her and identifying her problems was an "undercover," unconscious way of approaching the underlying ones in their marriage. The child's treatment becomes something of an "unspeakable" revelation of feeling about their issues together and as individuals. As it was, it seems Aria in her own right was able to gain new and important thoughts and feelings around the troubling pressures. Did her mother? She appreciated perfectionism in herself. Significantly she was able to go ahead with the divorce and begin a new life. Father unhappily was not.

The problems of perfectionism that are found in Aria's parents seem to me to be one of the most trying here, with the idea of "limited goals" coming to haunt particularly in regard to her father. Perfectionism, as it is linked to omnipotent fantasy, with its deep wishes of gratification mounted against the primitive anxieties, creates formidable defenses. It seems the whole personality itself is felt to be threatened in the parent when we seek to explore it in the child and, of course, when we touch it in the parenthood. When the insistence on perfection in its many guises is projected onto the child by the parent, we know the child is subject in herself to all the anxiety and depressed feelings of failure, inadequacy and helplessness, with losses of love and value that the parents feel. Their feelings of being incapable of resolving them and finally being overwhelmed by them would also be hers. Aria's acting with her body did seem to illustrate these feelings in her. At times when the family/parents were especially strained, Aria exacerbated her masturbation as a soother; however, she masturbates but there is no feeling of pleasure in it. As such, it appears to be a failed attempt to ward off depressive feelings around her unsatisfied, longed for wishes for love and narcissistic supplies. Slow, gradual linking a child's expression of feeling with that of the parent's own feeling as it becomes evident can sometimes move a parent into more empathic connections with themselves and child. Finding alternatives, or new ways of attempting mastery of these old anxieties, is often a long process against ideas held tightly by generations of internalizations. (A kind of "bondage"? Indeed, often fraught with punishments when perfection is not met.)

As the elaboration of unconscious fantasies is so fulsomely enchanting in the mind, and as they also include difficult-to-master, highly conflicted destructive ones, they are deeply resisted. I thought the therapist wonderfully was able to touch Aria's most anxious feeling regarding this and help her toward her loving/being loved feelings, in the face of her destructive ones. This could, and seems to have, helped her mother.

Aria's father had not the ability to tolerate the threat of psychological exploration of Aria's troubles. Fears of her anxieties so linked to his own attitudes and behavior likely promoted his adamant withdrawal (flight?) from the parent work and his pressure to end Aria's analysis. He seems to have looked for ways to ease the anxiety by defensively seeking the reassurance of extramarital affairs. An old tried and true behavior for him that gratifies him narcissistically but likely as empty as Aria's masturbation? I wonder what his early relational life was and conjecture that he faced inadequate resolutions of his own early issues having to do with wounding kinds of frustration. That difficulty would have left him with a lack of maturity with a poor ability to support his daughter's progressive development through her own trials of need. His defensive actions appeared to take center stage when Aria lessened hers.

I loved Aria's "Sound of Music" material and the therapist's use of it. It did make me think of the other song, "A girl like Maria" (what do we do with…) but then, think of the difficulties the Trapp family had to endure when the war came. Divorce has its own vicissitudes with the increase in feelings of imperfection, loss of control and failure. Old pressures as we know, continue to be acted out in the divorce relationship (lawyers and courts offer a fine stage to enhance and excite). Aria's enactments of sadomasochistic excitements, reflecting her preconscious awareness of her parents' interactions in the impending divorce, were, it seems, harbingers of serious concerns for her in the future; particularly in adolescence with its loosening of infantile ties to the parent and a time of finding new methods of securing trusting connectedness and love in conflicting sexual and aggressive feeling states. I was happy to know she would have another therapist but sorry this therapist could not continue with her and her mother. In an ideal world, continuity would be maintained in this truly therapeutic relationship, fraught as the case is with contentious feelings and divorce. The parting gift of interlocking unbreakable stone links seems to offer strong bonds that hold and chains that bind. Aria's loving feelings I hope will go on to hold sway over her "big angry ones."

Commentary 2

Every child and adolescent analyst knows that without an ongoing, positive relationship with the parents, the treatment with the child will be in jeopardy. The analyst must be able to help the parents become an "integral part of the treatment process while at the same time respecting their child's right to privacy and need for an entirely separate, independent relationship with the therapist" (Altman et al. 2002, p. 301).

From the onset of treatment, the parents and therapist need to find a productive method of working together so that the child is not placed in a position of betraying loyalty to either the parents or the therapist. Both child and parents must understand that the therapist respects that "the child has her/his own mind and thoughts, feelings, and fantasies" (Schmukler et al. 2012, p. 58), that are uncovered and expressed in the treatment room and are private. However, when family secrets get divulged, the analyst is often put in a very precarious, yet adventitious position. The analyst's excellent analytic work with eight-year old Aria and her parents is a superb example of why working intensively with parents is imperative in understanding the child's symptoms and analytic material that develops in the play, as well as guiding the parents as they come to better understand their child's difficulties and pain. Furthermore, the case of Aria and her parents reveals how injurious family secrets become the child's unbearable burden.

Right from the beginning the analyst states interest and curiosity in Aria's presenting symptom. In the parent meetings Aria's father immediately abdicates his responsibilities, and in addition begins to sabotage the treatment. The analyst perseveres and attempts to connect with the father through the mother, however, father's behavior is extremely telling. Mother breaks down in sobs and confides the family secret, whereupon Aria's symptom can begin to be understood. The analyst worked brilliantly with her young patient, offering her words to explain her feelings so that she no longer needed to use her body to tell her story of worry over separation and loss. Another important part of Aria's analysis was to help her with her struggle with perfectionism. As the analyst worked closely with the mother, (and the father through work with the mother), she was able to assess the defenses and conflicts that the parents brought into the treatment. In this way she was able to get through to the father that his demands of perfectionism were detrimental to his daughter and he was able to hear that and make necessary changes in his interactions with Aria. The analyst was also able to help the mother with her own difficulties in this same area, and only then was Aria able to be helped with this issue that was deterring her development.

Child analysts and psychotherapists have come a long way since the days when the problem of privacy and confidentiality was solved by not including the parents in their child's treatment. Kerry Kelly Novick and Jack Novick, in their book *Working With Parents Makes Therapy Work* (2005), demonstrate "diverse techniques that protect the child's privacy, that help parents tolerate the frustration of not knowing everything, that foster greater communication and sharing between parents and child, and that redefine separateness and autonomy between them" (p. 53). They state: "Confidentiality should be maintained in support of privacy and not as a reflexive collusion with secrecy. The goal is to make any secrecy a legitimate object of analytic scrutiny and understanding so that the patient and his parents can find their way to fruitful sharing and communication of whatever is important to each and all of them. The analyst's task is to support these goals by respecting the privacy of thoughts and feelings" (p. 124).

If the analyst had not met with the parents in a therapeutic manner, I would speculate that Aria's analysis could have headed in an entirely different direction, perhaps a journey down the wrong path that would not have been as helpful. Aria's successful treatment was actually very short, only eighteen months in duration. I feel the analyst was able to help the patient in such a short time because of the intensive work with the parents. The analyst was able to work intensively with this family keeping in mind what each individual was capable of, what would be tolerable, and most important, what helped the child. The analyst preserved the privacy of the child's inner world (thoughts, fantasies, and feelings), while simultaneously uncovering a harmful family secret.

In closing, this short vignette demonstrates the need to teach young child and adolescent psychotherapists and analytic candidates new techniques in working with parents that integrate the family and support parent/child development as well as child development. Anna Freud stated that a child's treatment is ready to end when the child is back on track developmentally. I think we should add to her important declaration that parent/child relationships also are on a developmental track and need our help when they become derailed.

Editorial Reflections

What is a child to do with the "confusion of tongues" (Ferenczi 1949) and the enigmatic messages received from adults regarding sexuality (Laplanche 1997)? These shape a child's developing personality under any circumstances, but how does a child deal with a consciously kept sexual family secret? As one commentator observes, "Family secrets become the child's unbearable burden." In this chapter we also see how secrets and lies become the analyst's hard-to-bear burden as well. One of the many challenges Aria's analyst faced in the work with her parents was the common enough situation of learning something from the parents and having to hold that knowledge in mind without sharing it with the patient.

Through trying to understand the father's ongoing resistance to joining in the parent work, the analyst learns of his serial infidelities and the mother's increasing inability to tolerate them. The analytic work that Aria valued so deeply had helped her feel understood enough to contain her compulsive masturbation for a time, until the marital relationship deteriorates beyond repair. When the symptom returned, her analyst "struggled with knowing the roots of [her] regression: her preconscious knowledge of her parents' impending divorce and her father's unspoken infidelities, but it was not my place to tell her." The analyst was able to intervene in a way that supported Aria's latency desire for helpful limits on the sexual impingements of which she sought to rid herself and for which her superego tormented her.

Despite the burden imposed on the analyst by the escalating tension between the parents and its visible impact on Aria, it also seems clear that Aria's gains would not have been achieved at all, much less sustained and consolidated, without the regular and frequent concurrent parent work. Even when the father did not attend and tried to sabotage the analyst's efforts, the fact that the analyst kept both parents in mind and was mindful of their presence in Aria's mind and feelings seems to have been crucial in the effort to restore not only the child to a path of progressive development, but the parent-child relationship to as realistic a foundation as possible.

When parents confide such a secret—or any other—in parent work, the analyst can share their burden by becoming its custodian (R. Furman 1995), holding on to a reality no longer denied, helping the parents understand the connection with the child's symptom, and relieving the patient of the need to "reveal the unspeakable," as the second commentator notes. The analyst strives to contain and use the received knowledge to inform both the analysis and the parent work, recognizing the impact of the secret but not becoming so distracted by it as to become unable to work on other essentials in the emerging material. Ideally, over time, the analyst may help the parents find age-appropriate answers to what and when to tell their child, mitigating the pernicious effects of secrecy, while keeping private those details that would be unable to be integrated by a young child.

In regard to secrets, the distinction between privacy and secrecy has been extremely useful in work with adolescents and their parents. The suggestion that privacy was to be protected but secrecy was to be engaged with, and ways found to share the secret, gave analysts the freedom to help parents and children share or keep private when appropriate.

This case adds a further distinction which may prove useful in helping parents share aspects of a secret with the child. It illustrates that the *content* of secrets can be usefully separated from the *effects* of the secret. In this case the content of the secret was father's sexual affairs, but the effect was mother's rage, tension between parents and mother's decision to divorce father. The analyst seemed to make this distinction, guided as she was by the child. The material seemed to revolve around issues of separation and loss and at one point the analyst assured the child that the parents would take care of her even if they separated.

This vignette also makes us reconsider another aspect of parent work—the absence of the father. Previous experience has led us to stress the importance of having fathers be part of parent work. This case may also raise our consciousness about the reactions of some fathers to advice or help from a female analyst. We should consider that, in some cultures, this would be seen as shameful.

We might have expected this case to fail since the father actively opposed the analysis, had his own agenda, and seldom participated in the parent work. The fact that the analyst kept the father in mind, used mother as a conduit to give him the benefit of the analyst's advice such as to stop spanking and use different forms of discipline, and that the analyst was able to convey that both mother and father had problems of perfectionism which the girl had identified with— these gave father the feeling that he was included and aided him in accepting help without being shamed and humiliated. This vignette also alerts us to one of the many potential obstacles to growth posed by parental character aspects, in this instance, the different versions of perfectionism carried by each parent. The parent work allowed for addressing and mitigating some of their effects.

CHAPTER SIX

NEVER-ENDING TOXIC DIVORCE

Older School-age

Clinical Vignette

In this vignette I will describe my work with Chris, who was nine years old when I first began seeing him, and my parallel and ongoing work with his parents. I saw him in a four-times-a-week analysis for two-and-a-half years and then in a twice-a-week psychotherapy for another two years. I will provide a brief description of the family members and family dynamics, the difficulties encountered in establishing a therapeutic relationship with the parents and the reciprocal relationship between the work with the parents and the work with the patient in the analysis, how the parent work facilitated progressive movement in the analysis and how this in turn fostered the development of a better relationship with both parents.

When Chris entered treatment he was encopretic, regularly wet his bed and was prone to angry outbursts. He also had serious learning difficulties, was dyslexic and had difficulty focusing and attending to tasks. Most developmental milestones were normal except that he spoke very little during nursery school and kindergarten, a trait that was evident in the early stages of the analysis as he tended to be quiet and express himself through play rather than words. Chris's parents separated when he was four and he did not see his father on a regular basis for at least two years. Shortly after the parents separated Chris's mother's boyfriend-partner moved into the apartment and initially and throughout most of the analysis there was considerable conflict and tension between Chris and mother's partner.

Chris's mothers' parents divorced at an early age and her mother shortly remarried. At the beginning of the analysis she was estranged from her biological father. She had a difficult relationship with her mother who had a volatile temper and treated her like a child, often criticizing her mothering of Chris. Mother could become quite angry, and her tendency to binge drink often led to frightening episodes of loss of control.

Chris's father lived alone at the beginning of the analysis and regularly spent time with Chris and his brother. It was clear that he cared deeply about Chris but had very little insight or understanding of Chris's feelings. There was a history of serious mental health problems in his family as his father was recently hospitalized with a diagnosis of manic depression. Father's mother was described as somewhat eccentric and disorganized, but also critical.

Chris had one sibling, a brother two years younger, described by the parents as the opposite of Chris. He did well in school, was popular with peers, comfortable and talkative with adults and did not wet his bed or have angry outbursts. Chris was envious of his brother's school success, ease of social interaction, and parental approval and chronically felt unfairly blamed for altercations with his brother.

I initially met with mother and father together for several sessions. Mother accused father of abandoning Chris for over two years after they separated and not paying his fair share of child support.

Father countered by claiming that mother systematically blocked his attempts to see Chris, suggesting that she and not he was at fault. It soon became clear that the level of hostility between them made it difficult for a constructive dialogue to take place. I decided it would be more beneficial to meet with each parent individually. In these early sessions, however, a core issue emerged that was repeated in different contexts throughout the analysis. This was mother's need to block Chris's access to father, and father's feeling of helplessness and impotence in addressing mother's control. This also emerged in mother's transference to me when she became resistant to continuing the analysis at a frequency of four times a week.

In my initial meetings with father, I explored his feelings about Chris beginning treatment with me. He said he felt therapy was another of his wife's decisions over which he had no control. He didn't trust me and saw me as another of his ex-wife's agents. He also was pessimistic about the effectiveness of treatment and feared it would confirm mother's perception of Chris as frail or weak. His willingness to tell me about these concerns in our early meetings surprised me. In this respect I think it helped that I was a man. He could see me as someone who empathized with his pain and rage at his ex-wife for devaluing and excluding him from important decisions about Chris's life. In doing so, however, I had to be careful not to over identify and join him in his hatred of his ex-wife as this could compromise my ability to develop a therapeutic alliance with her and maintain an analytic perspective on the individual and dyadic dynamics in play. At this early point in our relationship, I was reluctant to point out that seeing himself as a victim of his ex-wife's attempts to exclude him protected against seeing his tendency to provoke her to retaliate and made her seem like she was maliciously keeping him from seeing Chris.

In contrast, particularly in these early sessions and throughout our work I was careful to stress the constructive aspects of his parenting, consistently reminding him of his importance to Chris and the extent and value of his knowledge and understanding of Chris. As he began to trust me and see me as helpful and supportive, his resistance diminished and he began to engage with me on a regular basis. He consistently attended sessions and would call me after his weekends with Chris to give me an "update" when something occurred with Chris that distressed him.

Establishing a therapeutic alliance with mother was more difficult than with father. Her attendance was inconsistent. She sometimes "forgot" appointments, and tended to favor phone sessions rather than coming in person. In our initial sessions mother was able to describe Chris's difficulties in detail and at times became empathic and sensitive to Chris's problems, but all too often she became furious and enraged at Chris when he, initially passively and then later actively, didn't accommodate her demands. I often found myself identifying with Chris's helplessness and impotent rage and struggled to inhibit my impulse to sadistically counterattack and control mother. This experience heightened my awareness of the sadomasochistic elements in their relationship that emerged with clarity in the work with Chris and with mother. At these moments I found that I could avoid being drawn into an enactment if I patiently listened to mother's complaints, allowed her anger to dissipate and found places where I could validate her point of view and convey some understanding of her anxiety. Once her anger subsided she was able to recover loving feelings for Chris, develop some insight into her behavior and begin to see him as a separate person.

Mother also tried to get me to take sides in disputes with father over vacation time and visitation. In these situations, as in others,

I restrained my temptation to offer advice and suggestions and instead focused on helping her elaborate the nature of her fears and conflicts, enabling her to reduce her anxiety and arrive at a reasonable solution.

When I first began seeing Chris in analysis he often had "accidents" and tantrums at his father's house and complained that father didn't take care of him or have the right food. He filled the early sessions with repetitive sadistic play and returned to it later whenever he felt narcissistically humiliated, crushed and powerless by people or events over which he had little control. I wondered as to the meaning of the play. He was consciously voicing his anger at father, and the play revealed an attempt to omnipotently master fears of bodily harm, perhaps stimulated by fears of retaliation triggered by the absence of father at age four, and by father's criticism of him, but it also coincided with mother's reports of incidents in which she became furious and enraged, yelling at Chris for not listening to her and accommodating her demands. His complaints also seemed directed more toward maternal rather than paternal functions. I thought his sadistic play, which was consciously associated with complaints about father, was also related to less conscious feelings stimulated by these experiences with mother. He would later provide validation for my hypothesis.

As the analysis progressed he began to focus on his envy and jealousy of his brother. As he was telling me this he would engage in sadistic play, destroying and repairing damage to a figure in the womb of a clay figure. Eventually, he began to voice some of these complaints directly to father, particularly his resentment of father's criticism of him, his unfair favoritism and idealization of his brother and the amount of time father and brother spent together. Chris's emerging ability to put his feelings into words provided an opportunity for me to deepen my work with father as he took these complaints seriously and became concerned that he was favoring the younger brother.

In our sessions father began to become aware of the devastating toll Chris's learning disabilities had on his self-esteem and the degree to which it stimulated intense envy of his brother's academic and social skills. Father connected his tendency to criticize and punish Chris to father's identification with his parents, and their angry punitive attitude towards him as a child. He remembered how angry and unfairly mistreated he felt. As a result, he became more empathic with Chris's conflicts and able to intervene less punitively and more effectively in the out-of-control angry conflicts that often occurred between Chris and his brother.

This was in marked contrast to mother who tended to "yell" at Chris and blame him for the fights with his brother. Mother was also very fearful and tended to allow her fears to inhibit his strivings for independence. Chris's relationship with his father significantly improved as a result of our work together triggering a shift in the analysis and in his relationship to me. Whereas before he would exclude me, relegating me to the role of outside observer of his sadistic play, we could now play interactive games together that expressed his wish to be known by me, and his protective need to control my access to his feelings. In addition, as he became more secure in his relationships with father and with me he became less fearful of his anger at mother giving voice to it in the sessions and at home.

As this occurred, Chris filled the sessions with a litany of complaints about his relationship with mother. She didn't listen to him, made decisions without consulting him, and didn't tell him the truth about important people and events in his life. A theme ran through these events, a painful feeling of helplessness and powerlessness to effect change. As he told me incident after incident where he felt powerless and ignored, he often returned to his characteristic omnipotent sadistic play, cutting up the clay figures and putting them back together or staging exciting bloody fights between soldiers and dinosaurs. At home he was becoming more openly defiant, more verbal and overt in his opposition. At these times mother became furious, impatient, demanding, punitive, and even physical. She felt he was getting worse and thought about reducing his sessions.

After these incidents she would often call me to vent her anger, relieve her guilt for losing control and obtain my support for her behavior. I listened carefully, waiting for her rage to diminish and, as I described earlier, I tried to find places where I could empathize with her point of view and address her anxiety and concerns. I found that providing her with a safe space to express her feelings and acknowledge her behavior without fear of criticism seemed to improve her relationship with Chris. She began to realize that her impatience, anger, and demands on him may not have been helpful or appropriate and that they were connected to his "accidents" that she now could see as his way of expressing his feelings about her behavior. She also could see that her behavior mirrored that of her mother who had a volatile temper, was prone to angry outbursts and vindictively punished others. Chris and mother could now enter into a meaningful dialogue about the issues and avoid turning conflicts between them into power struggles over dominance and control.

The changes in Chris's relationship with mother were also reflected in the sessions. Chris became much more verbal telling me about events of the day and his conflicts with mother, her partner, his brother and friends. He rarely returned to his sadistic play, and when he did the connection with events outside the sessions was more easily recognizable. Chris also became able to see his role in provoking mother and mother's partner, with whom he often repeated the control struggles that were so familiar in his relationship with mother.

It was particularly difficult for mother to tolerate Chris's improving relationship with father and this created a crisis in the family that was triggered in part by details of mother's relationship with her father, of which I was unaware. Shortly after Chris's return from our summer break mother became resistant to continuing the analysis at four times a week. Soon thereafter mother refused to let Chris and his brother see father and told them that she wasn't allowing them to see their father because he didn't pay his child support. Chris was again faced with a situation in which he felt enraged and helpless to alter an important decision. During the time mother refused to let Chris see his father, Chris compensated for the loss by speaking to father every day, often by cell phone while hiding in the bathroom. Their regular communication and the shared sense of anger at mother seemed to bring them closer.

At this point my work with the parents focused on the conflict between mother and father and mother's reluctance to let Chris see his father. father said, "Every time Chris sees me his mother tries to undermine me." He then offered an association to her biological father and her estrangement from him. "Maybe she has something against all fathers." I said that was possible but by not paying the child support he was confirming her perception and protecting her from seeing her contribution to the problem.

I spoke to mother a few days later. She defended her decision not to let Chris see his father. I asked her about her biological father whom she had described as distant, incompetent, and abandoning. She surprised me by revealing that he was in fact a well-educated successful professional with whom she had been quite close throughout her childhood and early adulthood. All of this changed when he was unable to meet a financial obligation. She, and particularly her mother, became enraged at father and they did not speak to him for over ten years. mother repressed her hurt and longing for him and in identification with her mother turned passive to active and acted upon her retaliatory rage. In the process, however, she suffered the painful loss of her close relationship to father.

It was now clear to both of us that her rage at Chris's father for not meeting his financial obligations had roots in her relationship with her father. She had difficulty however, seeing her need to have Chris and me suffer the same painful fate she did, for this required recognition of her own sense of loss and the self-destructive consequences of her actions. Yet in our sessions there was a dawning recognition of this. She then reconciled with her biological father and started to become aware of loving feelings for him and of his importance in her life. These feelings helped her moderate her rage at Chris's father as a transference figure, eventually enabling her to become more supportive and appreciative of his relationship with Chris. She also became less resistant to the analysis and to our work together.

In the course of our work mother, father and Chris changed, as did the relationships among them. Chris developed the capacity for more constructive modes of self-assertion, directly expressing his wishes and desires and finding compromise solutions to get them at least partially met. He became more able to access loving feelings for his mother, enabling him to tolerate her limits on his behavior and her periodic emotional outbursts and loss of control. He also developed a closer, less conflicted relationship with father. He came to view father as a positive supportive figure who could help extract him from destructive aspects of his relationship with mother and provide strength, and sublimations for his aggression.

Changes in the parents facilitated this process as father's more active and assertive presence and mother's increasing ability to relinquish her needs for control made the inevitable frustration and disappointment associated with the unrealistic nature of Chris's demands and the problematic nature of his parent's behavior less dangerous, more easily symbolized, and less prone to be concretized in bodily functions, or expressed through sadomasochistic interaction.

Many theoretical and technical issues arise when parents are concurrently involved in child psychotherapy and child analytic treatment. Chief among them is the possibility of compromising effective analytic work by impeding or restricting transference fantasies, shifting the focus away from intra-psychic conflict to interpersonal conflict and by introducing supportive interventions such as advice, education, suggestion, permission and prohibition. Although the parent work presented challenges for managing transference and countertransference and for maintaining an analytic attitude, I do not believe these difficulties were sufficiently problematic to foreclose the value and potential of the parent work.

Commentary 1

I find it remarkable that many child therapists and analysts treat children, even intensively, while maintaining minimal contact with parents. I currently treat a man in intensive psychotherapy whose young daughter is in analysis. He and his wife feel perplexed by the girl's behaviors and desperately need help, but the analyst apparently views such an intervention as tangential because he meets with the parents only intermittently. I am working on another case in which a therapist is seeing a four-year-old girl who allegedly was sexually abused by her father. The therapist has almost no contact with either parent because of "confidentiality concerns."

Such situations lead me ponder how therapists lose track of the reality that, no matter how important they are, parents are in the trenches influencing the child day in and day out and, of course, are infinitely more important to the child in the long run than any therapist can be. In reflecting back on my own work, I must acknowledge with some distress that I, too, have been guilty at times of this type of shortsightedness in my work with adolescents. I see a few obvious explanations. One is that we get so caught up in our relationship with child patients that we lose track of their environment outside our offices. Second, we therapists, often unconsciously, need to see ourselves as better parents to the child than the actual parents are. (This has many possible roots, including therapists' unresolved conflicts with their own parents.) Third, parent work is hard. Many therapists/analysts feel ill-equipped to deal with its many challenges, especially parents' strong negative reactions to therapists, driven in part by the acute narcissistic vulnerability inherent in needing help with one's children.

This third point leads me to a discussion of the case at hand. Chris's analyst takes parent work very seriously and wanders deep into the trenches with the parents. He recognizes that he elicits strong transference reactions in the parents—stimulated in part by his important role in Chris's life—and works persistently with these reactions, appreciating that the parent work will not proceed constructively without such arduous work. The analyst's steadfast, determined investment in the parents and the resultant positive alliances he forms helps to explain his success and why so much parent work does *not* go especially well: When therapists treat parent work as peripheral, parents feel marginalized, which exacerbates their narcissistic vulnerability; additionally, therapists lack the time and space to understand, and constructively deal with, parents' strong feelings. In this particular case the parents come to trust the analyst because he takes them seriously and gets to know them well, including their histories.

The analyst uses parent work beautifully to help Chris in different ways. He utilizes his *in vivo* experience of Chris's suffering to help the parents empathize more with Chris's emotional distress. His father, for instance, becomes much less punitive and critical through increased insight into Chris's learning difficulties. Conversely, the analyst, by dealing directly with the parents' negative transferences (instead of dodging them, as most therapists do), gains hard-won understanding of the parents that he applies to the individual work. For instance, by persisting in understanding and managing the mother's controlling, angry mode of interacting, the analyst can help Chris deal better with her. The analyst's work with Chris informs the parent work and vice versa. I cannot imagine Chris making the progress he did without the intensive parent work. Parent work in post-divorce households creates particular challenges and opportunities for therapists. Chris's analyst is immediately confronted with this reality when he realizes he cannot meet with the parents together because of their mutual antagonism. I agree that it's optimal to meet with divorced parents together but necessary to accept when doing so is counterproductive.

I would like to address a few tasks I see as critical in helping parents help children through difficult divorces. I would guess that the analyst did some of this work in parent sessions, though he does not articulate it explicitly. In her book *Between Two Worlds*, Elizabeth Marquardt (2005) describes how children, especially in tense post-divorce households, often feel as if they are living two separate lives with no way to knit them together. Parents rarely ask about life in the other household, and, if they do, it is done critically or dismissively. Therapists can help parents assist children with this troubling experience by encouraging them to speak openly, and encouragingly, about life in the other household.

Bitter parents, such as Chris's, find doing so difficult. They complain to their children about the other parent or angrily contradict his or her account—"No, he is lying; he was the one who wanted the divorce." Such comments, very common, exacerbate children's tension states and their painful sense of helplessness at their inability to reconcile their parents' divergent visions of the family circumstances. Through what I believe is a critical intervention, therapists can model responses that empathically address these binds and do not push children further to feel they must take sides: "Well, I know your dad says I wanted the divorce. I see the situation quite differently. I know that puts you in a tough spot. It's hard when two people you love see things so differently." My experience is that many parents are eager to address these matters thoughtfully with their children but simply don't know how. I think the analyst set the groundwork for such interventions by increasing each parent's appreciation of the other's parenting role, especially the mother's appreciation of the father.

Chris's analyst observes that Chris struggles with a "painful feeling of helplessness and powerlessness to effect any change," which he attributes to ongoing frustrations with his mother. In addition to difficulties with his mother, I wonder about the impact on Chris of the actual separation and divorce. Because Chris was four when his parents separated, he spent formative years with them together. Parental separation, even when it relieves bitter parental feuding, confronts young children with their lack of influence over critical people and events and contributes to their investment in omnipotent fantasies of control as a defense against helplessness. Parent work can be crucially important in this context when therapists help parents help their children bear the losses that inhere in divorce and engage a constructive mourning process. The positive working alliances this analyst developed with Chris's parents provide the necessary foundation for this sort of work to take place.

Commentary 2

This case can serve as a "poster child" for the assumption that "working with parents makes therapy work." We have the patient, a nine-year-old severely disturbed boy, who came with serious learning difficulties, enuresis, encopresis, uncontrolled rages and difficult behavior, failure at a normal school, no age-appropriate friends, estrangement from father, battles with mother, stepfather and younger brother, a boy who in general seemed like a very poor prospect for outpatient intensive treatment. In his early therapy work he seldom talked, played compulsive repetitive sadistic games, and seemed unable to relate to the therapist.

His parents were divorced and unable to be in the same room together or maintain any joint parental responsibility for their child. The mother lied to Chris and the therapist, replayed childhood traumas, and treated Chris as she had been treated by her controlling mother. She also seemed to feel as if both son and ex-husband were her hated father. She apparently had no insight into the possible impact of her behavior.

The father acted helpless to deal with his ex-wife, who effectively excluded him from any relationship with his son. He was highly suspicious of the therapist, seeing him as an agent of the mother. He too had no insight into the impact of his behavior on his child or on his reliving of his childhood with a very disturbed father. The stepfather also had a battling, sadomasochistic relationship with the patient, so the boy was isolated, alone, blamed, humiliated, with no resources or support.

I note several specific aspects of the analyst's technique that created turning points, as well as saving this treatment in crises:

1. By making concurrent parent work an integral part of the treatment, the parents were seen separately on a regular basis. This case highlights the importance of including fathers in concurrent parent work and adds to the accumulating evidence that including fathers is essential to successful child/adolescent therapy.

2. From the start, the analyst focused on establishing a therapeutic alliance with the parents. He helped them gain a beginning sense of competence and understanding. Forming a therapeutic alliance with the parents is probably the most difficult technique to teach but is the *sine qua non* of successful concurrent parent work. In his brief summary the analyst could not convey the words he used, the tone of the words, or how, despite the obvious pathology of the three parents, the analyst could respect them, find areas of functioning he could admire and support and help them access the "primary parental love," which had been totally submerged in their sadomasochistic rage.

3. Once he had gained their respect and created an atmosphere of safety from judgment, blame or humiliation he could begin to suggest certain changes.

4. A major turning point was when the mother could use the parent work to begin to see the value to the boy and to herself of a positive relationship with father. Similarly, the analyst helped

father recognize his importance to the child and not allow his anger to interfere with his primary goal of access to the child and being the best father he could be.

5. This had a profound impact on the alliance with the boy as he now felt that he had a competent ally in his therapist and eventually in his father.

6. As the parents felt more trust, they could explore together with the analyst their own traumatic histories and begin to see that certain parts of the trauma were being repeated with the child. This was another turning point, bringing important changes in parental behavior (e.g. mother's reconciliation with her father, father seeing his own father with less denial). This led to a significant diminution in attacks on the child and an increased capacity to see him as a separate person with his own strengths and vulnerabilities. The work with both parents became much deeper and extensive. The analyst used all the techniques one would use with an adult patient (defense analysis, reconstruction and linkage of current behavior with childhood traumas, transference and so forth). The one difference is that the technique used could be termed "focal analysis," analysis focused on one area of personality. In this case it was the parental functioning of both.

7. Increasingly, they were enjoying their child and finding moments of "primary parental love," a major step in the movement through the phase of parenthood.

This case makes it clear that we should move beyond the question of whether or not concurrent parent work is useful and focus on the techniques that are needed, the stances that make a difference, and the personal "emotional muscles" we need for such work.

Commentary 3

As Chris begins his analysis, his parents have been separated or divorced for some five years. However, they remain wedded to conflict and hostility that evidently characterized their relationship both during and after their marriage. Some divorced couples can function reasonably well as parental partners even when they are no longer a marital pair; others cannot give up waging war with one another no matter the cost to their children's emotional well-being. Over time I have come to feel that a recommendation for analysis for a child may be untimely or even contraindicated when parents are actively in the process of divorcing, though adolescents can sometimes more easily separate their own troubles from those of their parents. When the dust and dustups settle, the likelihood of parents working together on behalf of their children is greater.

It probably goes without saying that it is advisable from the outset to be clear what the analyst's role will and will not be vis-à-vis parental discord. Following the dual treatment goals outlined by the Novicks (Novick, K.K. and Novick, J. 2005), the explicit aim of the work remains the restoration of the child and each parent to the path of progressive development. When the parents' relationship is as acrimonious as it was for Chris's mother and father after five years of being apart, it would be understandable if the analyst wanted to avoid the expectable strife and obstacles. Yet Chris's analyst did an admirable job steering a steady course through the stormy waters. I have some ideas about some factors that contributed to the significant and beneficial changes that were made possible as the analytic work and the parent work unfolded.

One of the hallmarks of a child's successful resolution of oedipal conflicts is the growing capacity to be in threesomes during latency and beyond, based on a recognition that to actually get rid of the rival parent would also mean the loss of a loved and valued object. Identifications with both parents enrich the self and compensate for the disappointment of having to wait for one's own romantic partner and offer hope for a future love. The more the loving side wins out and tames the aggressive side, the kinder and more accepting the superego will be. The fact that Chris's parents separated when he was four posed a developmental interference for him, as he did not have to grapple with two loved parents whose grown-up love for one another excluded him. Chris's mother's decision to bring another partner into her home soon after separating from his father complicated matters even more. But we also learn from the analyst that neither parent seems to have come to parenthood having achieved the level of oedipal development that shows in mutuality and reciprocity in relationships with others. Instead, their passions center around ambivalence, criticism, and who's-the-boss conflicts. We hear that their parents had similar difficulties. This is not to assign blame, but to be realistic about the analyst's task. How fortunate that this analyst *was* able to put his own capacity to function in threesomes into the service of the work.

The early attempt to actually meet as a threesome with Chris's mother and father soon proved counterproductive but even after deciding to meet with each of them separately, the analyst was able to avoid leaving one or the other out or siding with one against the other. The guiding threesome in the parent work appeared to be mother-father-analyst on behalf of Chris, even if it was only in the analyst's mind at first. The analytic work required two threesomes: Chris-mother-analyst and Chris-father-analyst, rather than Chris-parents-analyst as in some happier families. All of these triads required the analyst to recognize and respond to strengths and potentials, while at the same time knowing painful realities full well.

The ability to be empathic with each of the individuals in the work was an indispensable feature this analyst brought to his role as a new object for identification. Equally important was the fact that he could work with, rather than join, the repetition of excluder-excluded ways of relating.[3]

While this case highlights how difficult parent work can be when parents are at odds, in other ways it is representative of work under any circumstances. The analyst identifies several pitfalls. One is of overidentifying with one parent, in this instance with the father's rage in feeling controlled and made impotent by Chris's mother and her attempts to intrude on his relationship with Chris. The analyst is aware of his countertransference and the risk of identifying with Chris's sadomasochistic attitudes in relation to the parents. And he is aware of how all three externalize an extremely harsh superego, provocatively inviting him to become a critical parent. These dangers are not specific to work with divorcing parents.

Similarly, the therapeutic tasks are the same as in any other. In order to develop a therapeutic alliance with the father, the analyst encourages him to talk about his feelings about being left out of the decision to start analysis, his view of the analyst as an agent of the mother, and his pessimism about the outcome. In order to establish a basis for working together, the analyst stresses the constructive aspects of his fathering, emphasizes his importance to his son and his unique understanding and value, and addresses Chris's loyalty conflicts and the father's own expectation that the analyst will be critical or

---

3   Not all exclusions signify oedipal ones, of course, and we get hints from Chris's bitter feelings about his younger brother that he had not been helped to "be three" with a parent and his sibling either. We do not know enough to speculate on why this younger boy seemed to function so much better. However, the parent work and Chris's analytic gains did attune the father to his contribution to Chris's upset and led to more effective parental handling of conflicts between the boys.

try to come between him and his son. It was harder to engage with Chris's mother as a partner in the work and both the transference and countertransference were more heated in the relationship with her as the treatment evolved. The analyst discovered that he could sidestep enactments (most anyway?) if he recognized and conveyed his understanding of her pervasive anxiety. The analyst learned that validating her point of view and allowing her to express her rage and guilt helped keep the work going and ultimately led to improvement in her relationship to Chris. The challenges and techniques to deal with them are useful examples for us all.

So often at the beginning of difficult cases we observe that a downward spiral has been set in motion, with parents' and children's worsening problems negatively impacting each other. In Chris's case we witness an upward spiral—as the parents see how they have repeated their own experiences of being parented, they become more able to see Chris as a separate person whose behavior and toileting symptoms reflect inner conflict and pain. As he feels more understood by his analyst and at home, Chris gets better at communicating more directly. This, in turn, helps the parents feel like better parents and they bring even more of themselves to the parent work with less fear of criticism. Every reduction in the level of hostility between the parents allows Chris and his analyst greater freedom to explore Chris's inner world.

The analyst eloquently described how important it was to function as a "third" whose presence allowed Chris and his parents to move along in their development:

"In the course of our work together mother, father and Chris changed, as did the relationships among them... He became more able to access loving feelings for his mother, enabling him to tolerate her limits on his behavior and her periodic emotional outbursts... He came to view father as a positive supportive figure who could help extract him from destructive aspects of his relationship with mother and provide strength, and sublimations for his aggression."

Despite profound early interferences and the distortions to his oedipal development due to his parents' animosity, these words offer the hope that Chris may yet become a loving husband and father himself.

Editorial Reflections

This chapter gives us a window into the common situation of working with parents who are "divorced, but wedded to conflict and hostility." The basic challenge to the analyst was how to form and sustain a therapeutic alliance with the parents, in the face of obstacles from within them and potentially within the analyst. The analyst and commentators suggest to us that constant awareness of the state of the alliance and flexibility in engaging with loss, mourning, loyalty conflicts, and negative transferences, while acknowledging and building on strengths and promoting love, were critical to a good outcome for all.

The techniques that made that possible were regular meetings with parents, the courage to use the whole repertoire of interventions (such as interpretation of defenses and transferences), and insistence on father's involvement. Above all, we see the importance of what the analyst brings to the situation, that is, the qualities of patience, empathy, and respect, as well as the capacity to hold in mind, even when the parents faltered, the necessary "threesomes" that all needed to grow into. The impact of the analyst's conviction of the central role of the parents in addressing and ameliorating Chris's troubles is a powerful argument for the utility and necessity of including such work in the structure of any treatment. Only then could the patient and each parent truly and realistically come to recognize and respect each other as separate individuals.

CHAPTER SEVEN

PARENTAL GHOSTS FOR TWO MOTHERS

Older School-age

Clinical Vignette

Robert was a ten-year-old when we first met. He was referred by his school's social worker. I worked with him for two years in four-times-per-week psychoanalysis followed by once-weekly psychotherapy. Robert is an only child, adopted by two middle-aged lesbian women. He is of dark complexion and striking features; he wears his hair in a Mohawk style. He is funny and quite witty at times. He has always been easy to relate to, as he is playful and eager to connect with someone who is predictable and curious about him. Recently, he has begun to speak about the consulting room as "the island of calm and laughter."

The school decided to refer Robert after a meeting with his mothers who expressed concern about his overall socio-emotional development. The meeting was prompted by a fight in the playground between Robert and a boy in his class, where he spit and kicked and called obscene names. This was the first time that Robert had behaved like this at school; however, his mothers said this often happened at home. At the time of referral, they reported difficulties in self-care, affect regulation (persistent tantrums and physical attacks towards both mothers and physical property) and consistent oppositional behavior at home.

Robert was adopted at six months of age by a white American same-sex female couple from an orphanage in another country. At the time of adoption, the couple had been together for eight years. Both mothers had a history of emotional and physical abuse as children at the hands of their fathers, so when they were presented with Robert's history, they felt they were in a special position to understand his early experience of neglect and abuse and help him grow and develop in spite of it.

His biological mother took Robert to the local orphanage when he was two months of age. The information given to his mothers at the time of adoption was quite limited but the document indicated that he was the third child of a very young mother who had suffered at the hands of an abusive partner. Not much was known of Robert's father except that he was incarcerated for murder at the time of Robert's birth. Robert was extremely malnourished and had signs of having been burned on both his legs and arms at the time of adoption. According to records shared by his mothers, at six months, Robert had the weight and development of a three-month-old.

The situation at the orphanage was quite precarious; he inhabited a dirty crib, which he shared with another infant. His mothers, Lisa and Wendy, remember vividly when they first met Robert. They described how difficult it was to hold him. They spoke of his little body, tense and frozen.

Following their arrival in the U.S., Lisa found herself unable to bond with Robert as she felt his physical attacks (biting and scratching) awakened her old feelings of rage towards her abusive father. Wendy took over most of Robert's physical care during the first year but actively resented Lisa's rejection of the child. Eventually, Lisa became better able to care for Robert but her relationship with him remained fueled by ambivalence (Lisa is often quite unpredictable in her reactions and comments, for instance, she openly calls Robert an "asshole" just after a tender exchange).

As Robert grew older, he continued to exhibit uncontrollable tantrums accompanied by violent physical behaviors towards both his mothers. By the time he was referred to me for treatment at the age of ten he had been evaluated by several local specialists and diagnosed with ADHD, Oppositional Defiant Disorder and Reactive Attachment Disorder and had been medicated since the age of four with both anti-psychotic and stimulant medication.

After a one-month diagnostic period, I began seeing Robert four times per week. Agreeing with the parents on a clear contract was an essential element that included their understanding of my way of working (psychoanalytic framework). I emphasized the importance of establishing a commitment to parent work and to bringing Robert regularly to sessions.

When I first met Robert, he was attending a special school for children with emotional disturbances. His teachers described him as a "puzzling child." At home, he often had long periods of rage in which he would curse and ransack his room, which by now had been reduced to a mattress on the floor and a few items. His mothers spoke of his continuous need for physical care and described frequent episodes of encopresis and enuresis at home. At the time of referral at ten, he would still stand in the middle of the bathroom with feces running down his legs waiting to be cleaned, mostly by Wendy. As I heard their initial description of Robert, I felt a sudden mix of dread and compassion. For instance, they described his physical features in what I felt was a rather demeaning way. In response, I felt a sudden rush of indignation.

Most importantly, however, was the obvious lack of narcissistic investment these mothers displayed regarding their son. There seemed to be a focus on how damaged he was and a fear of the kind of man he would turn out to be. Would he be like his biological father or their own fathers?

Robert had a good relationship with his cousin, a girl two years older. He also had a strong relationship with Wendy's family, especially her uncle, a positive role model for him who would often show up and calm Robert down by taking him out for an ice cream. I was encouraged by Robert's internal representation of himself as someone who can love and be loved. I found this extremely hopeful and shared this with his mothers, who at first responded by saying sarcastically, "Well, he sure has a way of showing us how much he loves us!"

At the first session Robert was waiting sitting on his mother's lap while reading a magazine. The waiting room was full, but there was one free chair. I greeted "Mommy Lisa" and proceeded to speak about her not being alone here today. Mommy Lisa introduced me to Robert who ran to the corner of the room towards the small chairs and table. Robert sat there with a book looking at the wall. I felt myself being observed by everyone in the waiting room while Mommy Lisa loudly exclaimed, "This is the shit I have to deal with all the time!"

I said I thought it seemed difficult for Robert to come to the room with me, a total stranger, and added that it would be ok for him to come in with his mom. I said I would be waiting in my room and I was hoping we could get to know each other with mom's help. I signaled to mom that I would be waiting and smiled at her; she seemed a bit embarrassed and angry at the same time (in my mind I thought she was saying: Sure! Run away you coward!). I could hear mom telling Robert to get off the chair and come with her.

Five minutes or so after, Robert and Mommy Lisa showed up at my door. I stood up and greeted them. mom sat on the sofa and Robert sat next to her with his head nestled in her chest at first, then moving to placing his head on her shoulder. (I kept reminding myself that this is a ten-year-old boy). He is quite short for his age and moves like a much younger child. He speaks in a very high-pitched voice most of the time. I introduced myself and asked Robert if he had any thoughts as to why he was here today. I said it looked like he was not so sure about being here and I referred to what I thought he was trying to show me in the waiting room. He looked at me from under his mom's arm and smiled; I smiled back. I made a curious face that made Mmm laugh, she added: "I think she is a bit puzzled with you, my son. Welcome to the club, Doctor!"

I replied: "What do you think Robert, should I be invited to your club?" He smiled and stood up, began to explore the room, he looked at the box sitting on top of the playing table in my room and pointed to it and made a noise as to get his mother's attention. She replied: "Use your words." I invited Mommy Lisa to try to imagine what Robert might be thinking and feeling and said: "He can only show us today; I think the nervous feelings are making the words difficult." As Mommy Lisa was going to begin speaking, a different Robert emerged:

Robert: "I have words you stupid; I am just being a jerk."

Lisa: (laughing) "I think she is not used to that kind of language."

Analyst: "I think Robert is telling me that he could talk if he wanted to but he is choosing not to. What do you think Robert, is that what you meant with being a jerk?"

Robert: "You know what a jerk is?"

Analyst: "You mean behaving like a jerk?"

Robert: "Yeah!" (he continues to walk around).

141

Analyst: "Well, it means not being nice, making people feel bad, being rude. Did I get it right? I can also see by how much you are moving that maybe you behave like a jerk when you are nervous."

Robert: "Yeah, you did, you get it, aren't you clever?"

Analyst: "I think we are all getting to know each other and that makes people behave like jerks sometimes."

Robert looked at his mom and told her it was ok to leave now and started to push her body. I said now he was using his body and his words! He laughed and the two of us laughed a bit too. I wondered if before Mommy went outside and waited for Robert we could talk a bit about what we were doing here, it seemed to me that Robert might need some help from Mommy? Mommy Lisa said they had talked about it at home, she thought Robert was just nervous as he always is when he meets a new doc.

I turned to Robert and asked: "You have met many doctors?" *He nodded in agreement and added:* "And they are all jerks!!" *and laughed loudly. Lisa told him to tone it down.* "Hmm," *I added,* "Can you tell me a bit about that?

Robert: "Not Dr. T., he is nice, I like him and he gives me medicine that calms me down so I am nice at school. He told me you are his friend, are you his friend?"

Analyst: "What do you think?"

Robert: "I think you are and you like each other, you probably kiss in the mouth." *(Laughed loudly and his mother with him).*

Analyst: "It seems like Robert is feeling comfortable here now (I refer to Mom) but he is also worried about losing Dr. T. He is also thinking about what kind of friends Dr. T. and I are, he is curious about the different kinds of friendships like many kids his age are."

Lisa: "I'll say. Can I go out and take a break, buddy?"

Robert held to his mom tightly in a hug and added: "Go, I want to look at the animals in the box." *Lisa left the room. I introduce Robert to the idea of the therapy box and explained the rules.*

Analyst: "Why do you think your moms want you to come and speak to yet another doc?"

Robert: "Dr. T. wanted me to, so I am here, I never do what my moms want that, they are both dicks!"

Analyst: "Not Dr. T.?"

Robert: "No, he is cool! He gets me, he is a real nice guy. He said I need to learn to think about feelings but I don't like to, it sucks. Can we just play and you tell my moms I am thinking about feelings?"

Analyst: "Well, I am not so sure I can stick to that deal. I am a feelings doctor after all."

Robert: "You suck then!" (His affect shifted quite rapidly.)

Robert lay on the couch and put the pillow on his face. I waited. I said our time was nearly over and wondered if we could continue this conversation tomorrow. We can start by just playing and we see where we go from there. Kids, I said, can say a lot of things with their play, sometimes just playing is ok and it can feel like work too. Robert looked from under the pillow, then he added: "Tell me when I can go."

We sat in silence, I walked with him to the waiting room where his mom was waiting, talking to another mom. I said goodbye to both; Robert ignored me and sat on his mom's lap.

During the early stages of the analysis, Robert struggled to leave his caregivers in the waiting room, hiding under the table or crawling into a fetal position in the corner of the room. Often, he would crawl into my office and sit under the play table for a few minutes before starting to create a forty-minute story with the small cars in which they went back and forth repeatedly in a compulsive and numbing fashion. These sessions often ended with Robert hiding under a pretend tent (made out of the throw in my office), asking for darkness in the room. We named these times: "needing to go into the cave"

143

moments and we understood them as times when my words and my mere presence felt too much for real Robert. During these times, Robert and I were able to get in touch with the primitive fears that I believed lived in Robert as unspoken memories and were actualized in our relationship whenever a sense of closeness appeared between us as a result of me naming something going on between us or in the play. For example, if I wondered why the little red car was chasing with such anger the big blue daddy truck and tried to guess, Robert would reply by changing his tone of voice to a baby tone and said: "that is not something I can talk about, maybe another day." This would usually be followed by a request for the cave.

Concurrent with my work with Robert, I met with his mothers every week and was able to experience in the countertransference many of the feelings of excitement, guilt and fear that informed Robert's internalized objects. Robert's early experience of neglect lived on in his body and had laid the foundation for his lack of internal integration. However, what represented a real trauma for him was the ongoing and cumulative experience of not being recognized and loved by his two mothers, whom he longed for so much. I came to understand that Robert had grown up with the experience of not being loved for himself but for what I thought he represented to his mothers—the chance for a new partner with whom to re-visit their own conflicts with their own parental figures, a way of replicating their own early familiar dysfunctional relationships. The ghosts in his mothers' nurseries constantly haunted Robert's relationship with his mothers. I often felt haunted myself and frozen when in the presence of a ten-year-old who behaved like a lost and scared infant.

During the early part of our work, I experienced what I understood as Robert's pervasive lack of safety in relationships and a profound absence of agency and integration. However, as our work progressed we were able to experience more "moments of meeting" where he was more accessible to the influence of a new "developmental object." In this way, he had become more able to allow himself the experience of being recognized by me with both his good and bad parts. In turn, I felt increasingly recognized by him as a real person and not just as the container of his projections. During my sessions with both mothers I was able to reflect on my experience of Robert and invite them to explore their own feelings towards their child. In this way, together, we constructed a safe space where to explore both the love and the hate they felt towards their child.

As he entered pre-adolescence, Robert began to introduce age-appropriate interests that he brought to our sessions. The analytic setting became a place to "play" with new ways of being, a place where Robert began to imagine what I was thinking and feeling and allowed me to do the same regarding him without succumbing to states of fear and disorganization so often.

During my sessions with his mothers I would introduce my developmental understanding of Robert. I did this in order to invite both moms to develop a more balanced view of their child by emphasizing both strengths and weaknesses. I found moving away from pathologizing his behavior was a real challenge as both parents still clung to the idea of a clear diagnostic label which would lead to a "cure" of his difficulties.

In the meantime, during sessions where Robert felt flooded, he would attempt to explore symbolically his feelings in displacement through the use of the teddy bears in the room without succumbing to states of dissociation and extreme regression. These states were partly prompted by Robert's wish to explore his fantasies around his biological parents.

Parallel to this process, my work with his mothers as parents and as a couple informed their understanding regarding the impact of their own childhood traumata in their parenting. They, too, began to recognize Robert away from their own "ghosts." Their reflective functioning capacity had improved as evidenced by their capacity for flexibility and use of appropriate humor when attempting to manage Robert's challenging behaviors. We managed to "normalize" his behavior and integrate the developmental lens into our work through the use of the concept of developmental lines (A. Freud 1965). Both Lisa and Wendy had become increasingly able to think more effectively when challenged by Robert.

During the end of our second year of analysis, our work was interrupted for nearly a month as both mothers experienced serious medical conditions. In response to this stressor, Robert became very regressed again in the consulting room and at home. In spite of this, both parents and teachers continued to report improvement in his learning and his capacity to manage his anxiety. His psychiatrist had reduced his medications and he was currently only on medication for ADHD. However, as a result of financial and logistic reasons, our analysis never resumed after this and we continued working once per week. In response to this loss, the theme of the cave returned. I would often be asked to sit and witness his storytelling through the use of the teddy bears in the room. However, it did not have the same primitive feeling it had during our early sessions.

Perhaps Robert's behavior (hiding under a cover, turning all the lights out, crawling, hiding in a fetal position, speaking like a baby) in the consulting room had been the response to the analytic holding relationship in which he had been able to relinquish some of his defenses and allow regression to a place of psychological rebirth. By surviving the frequent experience of exclusion from his mind in the consulting room and ever so gently inviting myself into his conversations with the stuffed animals, it was my impression that Robert and I were reconstructing the pivotal developmental experience of finding each other's minds in the context of a predictable and secure relational environment after an unexpected rupture.

The following is a session with Robert's mothers during our third year of working together, in which they continued to explore their frustrations in the context of a renewed therapeutic alliance. Robert's attendance had been quite erratic during the previous month or so. However, his moms continued to attend their sessions regularly.

Lisa: "Well! We want to talk to you about Robert's recent behavior, he is being really challenging. I don't know, maybe we need to think about his diagnosis again, he is becoming older and it is a bit messed up the way he behaves."

Analyst: "I can tell that you are both very concerned about his growing up, he is definitively showing signs of becoming a teenager, it is a scary time for parents and kids; with Robert it's a bit confusing sometimes, I imagine, as his young needs come in unexpectedly."

Wendy: "Yes! True! People don't get it! It is exhausting to be explaining all the time, like when we are in the supermarket and he starts whining like a baby and trying to get close, too close, and people are staring."

Lisa: "I have told you! Who gives a shit!"

Analyst: "Well, hold on! I think we all give a shit; that is why we are here."

Lisa: (laughs loudly). "Yes, yes, I get your point, but at this moment, truly, with the stress at home—to be honest, I can care less about what the cashier at Stop and Shop thinks!"

Analyst: "I see you are suddenly quiet Wendy."

Wendy: "Well, once Lisa starts, I just give up."

Lisa: "Oh come on! I am always the bad one."

147

Analyst: "You know, this tends to happen to us in here, suddenly Robert is lost somehow, left out of the room. I can see how it is so tough to not want to do that, he sure makes it hard to want to think about him sometimes when he is challenging."

Lisa: "Well, he is getting bigger and sometimes his aggression and his shit get really scary."

Analyst: "Well, I wonder if we can stay with that for a minute. Aggression seems to come in all sorts of packages in your family, like for most families. It is scary and people seem to want to go to battle right away instead of being scared."

Wendy: "Well, you know, that is a theme for us definitely that came out in previous family sessions in the past. I think we have been in such a hurry to fix Robert that we have been running a lot and trying to see whose fault is it."

Analyst: "And I think I am hearing loud and clear that you are at a bit of a loss about what I am doing with Robert and time is precious as he is growing fast."

Lisa: "You said it! It is frustrating."

Analyst: "I am aware of the sacrifice financially and timewise you both make and I think instead of running like Wendy says and trying to fix it, maybe we can spend some time today thinking about the fear you all feel."

Lisa: "You think we are overreacting?"

Analyst: "No, I don't actually, I think you are genuinely concerned about Robert's future and about the impact his behaviors are having on you and his cousin, but I guess, together we go into problem-solving mode and we don't seem to spend a lot of time trying to figure out how to manage his behaviors while understanding them. I know (responding to Lisa's non-verbal behavior) it is a tall order, feels unrealistic maybe?"

Lisa: "Fuck yeah! The other day, I found him standing completely naked in the hallway. His cousin was over and she was calling for one of us to get him to cover himself, she was calling him a pervert and shit. I think this is our fault because we have a very open policy about the body and sexuality in our home."

Wendy: "Well, don't put it like that, we have boundaries. It is just that maybe they need to be revised."

Analyst: "Well, rules and boundaries need to be explicitly rewritten as kids get older; of course this has a very complex meaning when it comes to Robert, maybe?"

Lisa: "Yes, it is confusing—how many twelve-year-olds do you know that speak to stuffed animals under the sheets in the middle of the night? It is kind of freaky really!"

Analyst: "What image comes to mind when you tell me about this, Lisa?"

Lisa: "Well, to be honest, of a pervert that lures kids with stuffed animals."

Wendy: "That is so wrong!!!" (laughs nervously.)

Analyst: "Well, it sounds to me like—Lisa is speaking about a fear?"

Wendy: "She always goes there though. It's a thing of her family."

Analyst: "You see how we get into the blaming game very quickly" (laughter in the room).

Analyst: "I was wondering, Lisa, if you could tell me a bit about what happened that time when his cousin was calling Robert a pervert."

Wendy: "I came up and told her that is not a way of talking to him, and she said: 'But Lisa does!'"

Lisa: "Ok, ok, I see what you mean—we can't help ourselves!"

Analyst: "Well, I think we have spoken about the words many times before. But I wonder about what fear was making you react like that, why it was so difficult to think at that moment. And I know there are many moments like this so..."

Lisa: "Then I came up and I screamed at everybody and Robert was running and crying like a freaking baby and his cousin was angry."

Analyst: "Everybody seemed to have been angry and also scared?"

Wendy: "I think we do need to revisit the boundaries with the kids; it is getting out of hand again."

Analyst: "I think we need to do that here too, it seems it has become hard to make it here these days and I want to make sure that both of you know I have noticed, can we talk about it? I think, Lisa, you were trying to say something about this at the beginning of our time today?"

Lisa: "I think we, I am worried about our boy, what is going to happen to him, he is growing up and he is such a freak sometimes."

Analyst: "Someone that has to come to therapy four times per week!"

Lisa: "Yes, that. Even though I get it, like you say it's not that he is sick, it's that he has a lot of catching up to do, but what kind of a grownup person is he going to be?"

Analyst: "What kind of a man?"

Wendy: "Yes, sometimes it feels like he is never going to grow up inside, but his body is sure growing up."

Lisa: "We know he is a mismatch kind of guy, but we think maybe it is time for him to see a male therapist."

Analyst: "Someone that can be more of a male role model?"

Lisa: "Yes." (hesitantly).

Analyst: "It sounds to me like we are talking about several things here; they seem a bit muddled."

Wendy: "I think we need to revisit the treatment plan, the goals, I think we feel lost."

Analyst: "Also, left out from the process, like you are only the chauffeur sometimes, like you mentioned last session, Lisa." (some laughter).

Wendy: "Listen! We are not going to sort it all today, but we wanted to ask you, do you think Robert is going to make it? Do you think maybe we should be thinking of sending him somewhere?"

Lisa: "And repeat his freaking trauma!!!"

Analyst: "This is a difficult conversation letting Robert go, me go. You know it is perfectly normal for parents of adolescents to want to let them go, but this is also different, wanting him close and wanting to let him go is something that you have both experienced with Robert frequently throughout his life."

Lisa: "Tell me about it! But we are committed to this kid! We are!"

Analyst: "I know you are, we all are."

As evidenced by this session, my work with Robert's mothers, challenging as it has been, has proven extremely important in terms of developing a common language to think about what lies behind his behaviors and most importantly to present him with interpersonal responses which challenge his internal representations of himself as the dirty, damaged little baby who needs to hide under the cover with all the other ugly and damaged babies (teddies). Unlike other times in Robert's life, the adults in his life are working hard at making sense of his behavior empathically and understanding his internal experience in a way that provides him with the experience of safety from which to grow and develop.

My work with Robert continues, as well as my now monthly meetings with his mothers. It is my impression that having a developmental perspective as the main frame in the work with this family has been of the upmost importance. What do I mean? Well, firstly, my clinical formulation has been informed from the very beginning of our work not only by the child's developmental history but also that of his mothers.

Also, instead of adhering to a categorical diagnostic understanding of Robert's difficulties, a dimensional approach to his functioning facilitated the development of a common language between the parents, other providers and myself. This language included ways in which to address his issues of affect regulation from a mentalizing stance, that is, from a curious and genuinely inquisitive attitude towards what lies behind Robert's behaviors but also paying attention to how it impacts the adults' own thoughts, feelings and behaviors in response.

By developing a strong therapeutic alliance with these parents, one based on a clear social contract, we have managed to weather multiple storms. Robert's mothers still struggle with the legacy of their own childhood traumas, however, they seem increasingly able to differentiate their own difficulties from those of their child.

The fact that our work began when Robert was ten years old was extremely helpful to these mothers' capacity to contain and manage Robert's affective storms during what has turned out to be a challenging adolescence. Despite his emotional challenges, Robert continues to successfully attend a mainstream high school where he receives special education support. He has friends and is thinking of engaging in technical training as a car mechanic after high school. His mothers have become more collaborative in their approach to school, encouraging his perception of school and the surrounding community as his own and, most importantly, a safe place to grow and develop as a young man.

Commentary 1

Children do not grow up in isolation. They grow up in an environment, a context. We hope that the family system provides the good-enough environment that Winnicott (1971) so eloquently describes—so that the child can thrive. This "good-enough"-ness is interfered with if the caregivers' own development is compromised in ways that keep them from adequately responding to the developmental needs of their child.

Such is the case with Robert and his parents, Wendy and Lisa. In my experience, it is most often the case with children and adolescents who come into treatment. It borders on impossible for a child to progress in psychotherapy or psychoanalysis without the involvement of parents. We know that nature and nurture are inextricably intertwined, that the brain changes in response to what stimulates it from the environment, and that the environment is then perceived by that brain that was changed. If the child begins to change in the context of psychotherapeutic treatment and is placed back into the same environment in which the presented difficulties were formed, those changes from psychotherapeutic treatment will be extraordinarily hard to sustain.

When the family system changes in concert with the child, the opposite can occur. There is a synergism—the child changes, the parents change, their relationships change. This is what is demonstrated in this excellent case vignette. As each member of the family triad changes, so does their interaction.

The analyst is a clinician who shows enormous talent, sensitivity, forthrightness, and developmental knowledge. She also writes about Robert, Wendy, and Lisa in a way that draws us in immediately.

153

Her openness in presenting both what she said and how she felt was extremely helpful in bringing us right into the room with Robert and his mothers. I felt that Robert's description of the consulting room as an "island of calm and laughter" was a direct reflection of who the analyst is: she came across as calm in the face of intense conflict and confusion, as someone with a warm sense of humor. That humor aided in diminishing some of the intensity of poor Robert's self-hate *and* in relating to two quite different mothers with their own demons (Levy-Warren 2005). The way she was and the consulting room formed a new emotional context for Robert and his mothers, an entirely new culture for all of them, and an opportunity for a rebirth for Robert and a re-beginning for his parents.

The analyst exemplified the very best of participant-observation, a concept that was most developed in anthropology (e.g. Malinowski 1929; Evans-Pritchard 1940; Mead 1928). She was in the room with Robert, joined him in his imaginative play, but was able to observe both herself and the interaction with Robert in a clear and productive way. It was a pleasure to join her in her work. The quality of her writing drew the reader in so well that we, too, felt like participant-observers in the work.

She came across as very present and warm with Robert's mothers, which allowed each of them to feel safe and connected to her and the analytic work she was doing with Robert. It provided a critical cushion for the treatment.

The analyst used herself as a developmental instrument, some-one able to join Robert wherever he was, from a developmental standpoint. She joined him and was then able to articulate what it felt like to be there. That allowed him to translate his bodily and emotional experience into an experience describable in words. All of this served to move Robert into more of a representational world, a world in which experience could be translated and communicated. This happened because the analyst was able to imagine herself in the places, even as far back as early infancy, that Robert revisited in his use of the consulting room, play, and interpersonal exchange.

She understood his encopresis and enuresis, his need to re-create the dirty crib of his childhood (e.g. mattress on the floor), his insistence on continuous care, and his "cave" in the context of the "rebirth" he needed. This was both because of his very early experience with his biological parents and the orphanage, and his experience upon arriving in Wendy and Lisa's home, with two caregivers who had trouble connecting to his essence (because of their own traumatic histories) and focused more on his behavior.

With her understanding and connection to Robert, the analyst was able to gather important information about his state of mind. She communicated this to his mothers, which gave them a more expansive and compassionate way of seeing their son. She served as a translator of Robert's experience, both to him and to his parents.

Robert arrived in treatment with development that was, at its most mature, in latency. His mothers seemed caught up with that same period in their own lives: they were focused on good and bad, right and wrong, black and white. They needed (and need) to be moved along themselves, developmentally, so that they can allow Robert to progress into adolescence, a time in which things are seen with far greater complexity and ambiguity.

This is proof positive of how parenting has its own developmental trajectory. Adequately parenting a young child is a different experience from adequately parenting an adolescent. When the analyst mentions the need to revisit ideas about physicality in the home, she is alerting Robert's parents to this reality.

The analyst brings us a case in which the necessity of thinking developmentally with children and adolescents AND their parents is aptly and amply demonstrated (Levy-Warren 2018). She mentions the necessity for finding each other's minds in treatment—with which I totally agree—but she also shows us the equal importance of finding each other's hearts and spirits. Thanks to this analyst, and the authors/ editors of this collection for giving us the opportunity to think about these critical issues in our psychoanalytic work.

Commentary 2

This is the case of a latency age youngster who was adopted by two women at the age of six months, who presented numerous clinical challenges for the analyst who functioned as a new developmental object and a safe holding relationship for his mothers.

Unfortunately, it was Robert who was seen as the symptom carrier and was seen as *problem child* rather than both his mothers' past dysfunctional family dynamic which contributed immensely to Robert's dysregulation.

The establishment of secure relationships with consistently available and supportive caregivers during early childhood is the basis for healthy psychological development across the lifespan. As we know there are advantages to having secure attachments to primary caregivers, which include the capacity to regulate emotion and the abilities to establish basic trust, peer acceptance, social skills, confidence, and a positive self-identity.

In Robert's case, I do not think that these two mothers were able to establish early on a secure attachment with Robert. They brought along the ghost of their own childhood trauma to their parenting interactive sphere with Robert. He had a problematic attachment to his adopting mothers. He longed for their love and care, which made him more anxious whenever they exhibited unpredictable bouts of anger and lack of capacity for affect regulation.

Robert was seen by a number of mental health professionals who offered various diagnoses, such as oppositional disorder, ADHD and Reactive Attachment Disorder, which contributed to the overall confusion among professionals.

Robert, a very vulnerable infant, was extremely malnourished and had signs of having been burned on both of his legs and arms at the time of adoption. He was malnourished, traumatized, unwanted, and was an abandoned infant. His mothers went through the challenging process of international adoption. As we know, mothers who adopt children internationally are likely to encounter a host of challenges and greater complexity in establishing affectional bonds to their adopted children (Ainsworth 1985; Bowlby 1969). Robert also brought to the new adopting parent-child relationship his own pre-adoption attachment histories of having been abandoned and abused.

These two mothers have also had a difficult history of preadoption family dysfunctionality; they were advanced in their ages and missed being pregnant. Then they were offered a six-month-old child. The caregiving system which comes from the mothers' own internal working models of attachment is guided by a set of mental representations about themselves as caregivers of their child.

The analyst patiently included the mothers in concurrent parent work to establish a gradual therapeutic alliance with a successful outcome. Her clinical formulation informed her to keep in mind the child's and his mothers' developmental histories as her guide in her clinical intervention. She was aware of Robert's problem with object constancy, affect, and narcissistic regulation right from the very beginning of her work.

She worked with Robert in child analysis, with the parents in concurrent parent work, and with other care providers to develop a consistent and unified shared language to help the mentalization process. She helped Robert to develop a higher order of mental functioning. He learned to realize that there could be hope in slowly grasping the idea that he is not defective. Her work with Robert helped him to communicate in a verbal-symbolic way in a safe place in order to develop a sense of agency and self-representation.

One of the poignant analytic encounters described was when Robert was hiding under a cover, turning all the lights out, crawling, hiding in a fetal position, spoke like a baby in the analyst's office as his response to the analytic holding relationship. The analyst is invited to have conversation with a stuffed animal which shows a progressive movement to relinquish some of his primitive defenses and primitive regressive pull. Including the analyst in his conversation with the stuffed animals demonstrates reworking and reconstructing his past developmental deficit.

This is an example of an adoptive child with history of early trauma who had inadequate integration of inner representations. This child experienced his own intensified aggressive feelings toward his adoptive mothers, which in turn can interfere with the integration of good and bad object representations as well as their self-representation.

The analyst continued her parent work concurrent with the analytical work with Robert. This intervention was crucial to the maintenance of the holding function for the mothers.

Commentary 3

This vignette presents a case with many challenges for the analyst in both working with the child and with the parents. Robert, who was ten years old at the start of treatment, and his two mothers each had experienced significant trauma, including deprivation and abuse. His analyst felt that "what represented a real trauma for him was the ongoing and cumulative experience of not being recognized and loved by his two mothers, whom he longed for so much." The analyst concluded that "Robert had grown up with the experience of not being loved for himself but for what ... he represented to his mothers, the chance for a new partner with whom to re-visit their own conflicts with their own parental figures, a way of replicating their own early familiar dysfunctional relationships."

A developmental perspective informed the analyst's parent work which focused on helping Robert's mothers reflect on their emotional reactions to and understanding of Robert, especially as it related to their own histories of abuse and how their pasts interfered with their responding empathically, thoughtfully, and flexibly to Robert. The analyst's goal was to help Robert's mothers to "present him with interpersonal responses which challenge his negative internal representations of himself, to provide him with an experience of safety, and to address his "issues of affective regulation from a mentalizing stance."

The analyst has definitely been helpful, and her work with Robert's parents has made a crucial contribution to Robert's positive developments in treatment. Robert's behavioral difficulties at home and school have lessened, his school performance has improved significantly, and the family has been able to "weather multiple storms." Robert's mothers are said to be better able to "differentiate their own difficulties from those of their child."

At a time when Robert and his parents were all responding quite positively to his four times/week analytic treatment and the parents' once weekly sessions, there was an unanticipated major disruption. A monumental shift occurred when, after two years of treatment, "both mothers experienced serious medical conditions" which interrupted treatment for almost a month. Thereafter, because of "financial and logistic reasons," treatment with Robert was decreased to once weekly and parent work to once a month. Robert initially regressed and became disruptive at home. His mothers became more worried about Robert's future and discussed both his possible need for a new therapist and for residential treatment. However, treatment has continued on this quite limited basis for a few years (Robert is now in high school), but we have little information about this time period.

As I mentioned earlier, this is a challenging analytic case. With the goal of thinking about various ways one might work with parents, I have chosen to present how I understand and would approach the treatment of Robert and his mothers. My model of understanding and working with the effects of trauma would lead to a different emphasis in parent work. This alternative approach, similar to and informed by the Novicks' (Novick, J. and Novick, K.K. 2016) work on two systems of self-regulation, focuses on the experience of trauma leading to the development of a protective, but maladaptive, internal structure or habitual way of dealing with the pains of life. This defensive structure blocks the taking in, metabolizing, and internalization of the parents', as well as the analyst's, loving and helpful responses. Much like computers, humans can be equipped with and shift between two different operating systems. The open system leads to progressive individual development and loving connections. The closed system becomes the preferred operating system due to the experience of too much danger and emotional pain. This closed system blocks individual growth and connectedness. As one young boy who was in analytic treatment and had experienced significant trauma said, "You should call yourself a 'Love Dr.' Our work is about how loving feelings get changed into hating feelings and how hating feelings get changed back into loving feelings."

In applying this model, Robert's mothers and Robert all shared an unhelpful closed system belief in magical solutions. Here the magical conviction is that traumatized children only need to be given enough love and understanding to overcome the past. At the time of the adoption, Robert's mothers expected that because of their own experiences of abuse they would be equipped to be understanding, caring and fill Robert with love. He would then grow and develop despite his early history of neglect and abuse. In turn, their fruitful nurturing of Robert would repair their own past hurts. This line of thinking led to much parental disappointment and resentment as his mothers quickly experienced Robert's "physical attacks (biting and scratching)" and paradoxical rejection of their attempts to bond with him.

Their interactions with Robert were complicated by their own difficulties with accepting Robert's expressions of love for them (mother Lisa "openly called Robert an 'asshole' just after a tender exchange"). Parent work concerning mother Lisa's rejection of Robert's tenderness could have facilitated a more sympathetic and forgiving approach toward Robert's rejection of their love. Each shared a fear of love and vulnerability and felt a need for hostile, omnipotent protections. Difficulties with loving and being loved are the result of maladaptive ways of coping with the experience of too much pain and fear. However, these protections lead to more pain because they block precisely what is most wanted and needed, feeling loved and loving.

Analytic treatment can help people shift from a predominance of closed system functioning to a preferred reliance on open system mechanisms. However, building feelings muscles, like developing physical muscles, requires more frequent work. Intensive treatment would offer both Robert and his mothers the opportunity to strengthen their open system functioning. Each could become better able to give and receive realistic help and love. In turn, each could develop the emotional muscle to tolerate sadness related to past hurts, current disappointments and vulnerability, as well as concerns about the future loss of loved ones through absence, through growth and individuation, or through death. Rather than unrealistic hope in magical solutions, the analyst can offer real optimism that the hard work of helping their children grow can help parents face difficult feelings and grow in ways that parents would not otherwise do.

In the first session with Robert and Mother Lisa, Robert explains his silence by saying, "I have words you stupid; I am just being a jerk." With this recognition, Robert offers an opportunity for the analyst to demonstrate to his parents how they can support the development of important open system strengths. Both analyst and parents can reinforce Robert's awareness that he has choices and add that his choices have both helpful and unhelpful consequences. Moreover, he can decide to be caring or hurtful. In the above statement, Robert is saying clearly that he recognizes that he is choosing to mistreat a person who is trying to help him. Robert's analyst, or at home his mothers, could support this recognition and emphasize that he could do better if he tried and that he would feel better if he chose to be a "good trier." This approach would follow the general principle of encouraging and supporting open system functioning. Sincere efforts would include taking chances and having the courage and strength to be open and caring. With open system functioning, one can risk loving connections and loss rather than resorting to the closed system use of fake power, angry outbursts or withdrawal in response to closeness, feeling understood, or helped.

This perspective offers an alternative way of conceptualizing and responding to the sudden disruption of treatment. In addition to any real concerns regarding finances and logistics, the extreme reduction in frequency, which occurred after significant growth in both Robert and his mothers, could represent a return to the use of closed system functioning. The underlying threats at this point in the therapeutic process would involve the deepening connections among the analyst, Robert, and his mothers, as well as their eventual separation from and loss of the analyst. An additional source of pain would be the sadness evoked as Robert and his mothers become more connected as well as more separate as individuals. Not only is Robert growing older, but he is also developing emotionally.

The drastic curtailment of treatment could be seen as an expression of Robert's and his mothers' central conflict regarding enjoying and benefitting from what they most want and need, loving and helpful relationships. His mothers' concerns about Robert's increasing difficulties and the possible need for a change in treatment could be addressed as reflecting their recognition that Robert, as noted from the beginning, urgently needs intensive treatment. This understanding could help both parents and analyst become more committed to finding a realistic way to increase treatment to at least twice weekly for Robert and twice monthly with the parents. Even this minimal increase in frequency could potentially have major benefits.

Editorial Reflections

Early in the contact with the parents the analyst responded to their description of the ten-year-old boy with a "… sudden rush of indignation." One of the major challenges of concurrent parent work is that we are faced with a set of people who do not define themselves as patients but who are often more disturbed than the individual adult patients who come to us for help. Adult patients come because they recognize that they have problems, that they are suffering, and they are asking for help for themselves. Many parents, and this case is a prime example, come with complaints about their child and resist any attempt to explore their role in their child's problems. In this case the parents were demeaning, hostile, and seemingly unable to imagine what the child feels. They seemed unwilling to explore the meaning of his behavior. The initial contact with parents who have made the child the carrier of the family's dysfunction turns many child analysts against the parent, leading them to identify with the child and wish to rescue the child. These cases often end in premature withdrawal unless we stay aware of the danger and address the obstacles throughout.

Regular parent work allows the analyst the time and space to develop an alliance with the parents, to respect them and acknowledge their positive wish to help the child. It may take time to get past their disappointment, rage, and helplessness and find their primary love for their child. Until the analyst helps the parents uncover some elements of primary love, embarking on therapy is a risk, as the parent might respond to help with shame, humiliation and rage, feeling that the treatment proves that they have failed as parents.

In this case, the analyst could help the parents begin to see that they were using the child to deal with their own traumatic history and begin to understand that he too was dealing with trauma in the best way he could.

The fact that the analyst could stay engaged but equidistant between the parents and child and between the two moms allowed the case to change so significantly. The commentators point to the sensitive technique employed by the analyst to serve as a container, a developmental object, "someone able to join Robert wherever he was from a developmental standpoint." They comment on the analyst creating a safe place for the warring moms and child to grow. They are equally appreciative of the work done separately with the two warring moms. After two years of analysis and regular parent work there was significant positive change as acknowledged by the child and the parents. The boy's move into pre-adolescence created a new crisis, testing the analyst's ability to understand the new pressures and try to help the mothers move along to become parents of a pre-pubertal male child.

At this point the process changed significantly, but we don't have enough information to fully understand what happened. Externally the mothers each had a serious, month-long medical situation. We should add that the boy was now into puberty, showing the external signs of masculine development.

As noted, these helpless experiences followed significant growth in open-system functioning, in realistic competence, joy, and love. The boy reverted to his out-of-control anger and behavior. The mothers reacted by wanting to change therapists and/or have Robert institutionalized. The mothers insisted that for logistical and financial reasons they would have to reduce the boy's therapy to once per week and the parent work to once per month.

One of the commentators found the model of "two systems of self-regulation" (Novick, J. and Novick, K.K. 2016) useful for

165

understanding this sudden shift and the fact that this highly effective therapist was unable to find some open-system solution to the parents' and boy's closed-system attacks.

This chapter brings us close to the limitations of parent work (and its role in a child's treatment) imposed by parental pathology. One commentator considers alternative techniques that might engage with the defensive resistances that can arise when there is distinct treatment progress and/or life circumstances intervene to render the adults helpless and therefore vulnerable to recourse to old closed-system defenses. We are also struck with the challenges faced by analysts in staying emotionally available even while under attack.

CHAPTER EIGHT

PARENTAL DENIAL IN ASSESSMENT OF DANGER

Young adolescent

Clinical Vignette

Anna and Thomas came to see me about their fourteen-year-old son Paul. After a recent chaotic day, Paul had confided to his father, "I wish I could just kill someone." To Thomas's ear, his son was overwhelmed with frustration with his impulsive, demanding younger brother. It had been building for years.

Paul's older brother, Mike, had an autism spectrum disorder and was happiest when alone. Nick, the younger brother, brought chaos to things around him. Paul, in the middle, had always been quiet and accommodating. For years, he had put up with being dragged to therapy visits for the other boys. Paul did seem to lack a guiding interest or passion. He disliked school. He played sports only because his parents required it. He never had friends over.

I met with the parents twice about their concerns but found I could not draw a good picture of Paul as a person. A wise supervisor of mine might have said, "the object doesn't ring through." In part for this reason, I went ahead and asked to meet with Paul at an early point in my consultation with the parents.

Paul was tall and athletic... and still-faced, expressionless. He spoke so quietly that I frequently had to ask him to repeat himself. He told me a very different story about the day his father had described to me. He hadn't been irritated with his little brother that day and wasn't talking about frustration. He was talking about killing. He wanted to kill someone and learn what killing would feel like. Only then did a little animation come into his face. He imagined killing would be "interesting."

But, the legal consequences for murder gave Paul pause, so he had no plans to kill. Nor had he hurt anyone, destroyed property or set fires, though all those things interested him and featured in his daydreams.

What most interested Paul was the enormity of what he could take from someone. So, killing a young person would probably be most satisfying and killing someone older, who had fewer years left, would be less "interesting." It didn't feel right to Paul that the thing he most wanted to do would be something he could never do. He hoped a psychologist could help him. He did not know what kind of help he needed. "You led your father to believe that you were angry at Nick," I said, "but that was incorrect." "Yes," he agreed. "How come," I asked? "Why upset him? Better he not know," said Paul. "I don't want him to treat me any differently."

Paul said he felt neither anger nor resentment... nor friendship or love. He did not love his parents, grandparents or friends. He had never had a teacher, coach or camp counselor he had liked. He had never loved a pet. There was no one he'd miss if he never saw them again. He described his world as "bleak."

Paul was preoccupied with thoughts of death and killing. He spent his time daydreaming about car accidents, scaffolding collapses, fires, and other scenes of people being hurt "in the worst possible ways." He said that the daydreams brought him no pleasure, but they did help him relax, and he noticed he would think about these scenes at night before sleep.

Paul was adamant that I keep his secrets. He was wary that I planned to continue meeting with his parents. Though mindful of Paul's privacy, I sought ways to raise concerns with his parents. "Paul lives as if he is alone and without close relationships," I said. "He suppresses his feelings and doesn't think of himself as an angry or frightened person. But he spends a lot of time thinking about things that seem driven by intense anger and fear."

The father said he hadn't known, but that none of this seemed a surprise, given the overt antagonism he himself had grown up with. He described a history of conflict over wealth and power waged in his family over several generations. His mother, whom his father had divorced decades before, suffered from a major mental illness, likely schizophrenia. For years, she had lived on the street, cut off from the family's resources. Now, she lived under Thomas's guardianship at a sanitarium.

Thomas and his children had been written out of his father's will, after his father disapproved of Thomas's choice of Anna as a spouse. Thomas had always been open with Paul about the conflicts within his family, perhaps too much so. "You can't trust anyone, I've told them. You've got to watch out. Bad things can happen between people who once loved each other."

Anna told me her mother and sister had autism spectrum conditions. She and Thomas had met through family friends when she was visiting from a different city and he was on leave from college. After marriage Father worked at a family business and Mother was devoting herself full time to the children.

"I was very close to Paul until Nick was born," Anna told me. "Nick took me over and now I'm very close to Nick, physically and emotionally. And it hurts me to say so, but that contact, that closeness with Paul was lost. I don't seem to remember how he reacted. A nanny came to take care of the older two boys. They didn't like her at first, then came to, but she only stayed six months." ("And then?") Shrugs. "Sorry, I don't remember. We just made do." Anna said she was "depressed" for several years after Nick's birth. Couple therapy and individual therapy had helped. I asked what it was like to hear how angry Paul seems to be and how concerned I was. It was concerning, Anna agreed. "It hurts me so. We are lucky we can do whatever is necessary to help him."

I made several recommendations to the parents—that we meet steadily to address their concerns as Paul's parents; that we extend the evaluation period and arrange for psychological testing for Paul; and that I see Paul more frequently. On the one hand, it seemed premature to draw Paul into more frequent contact, given the very early state of my alliance with his parents. On the other, Paul's preoccupations were worrisome and required assessment and monitoring.

In the end, the point was moot, as the parents agreed to more frequent sessions for Paul, but Paul himself declined. Paul's parents also asked me, "What can we do?" I asked them to tell me about the texture of their time with him. "We rarely have time just with him," the parents explained. "We think of him as a shy, awkward person and respect his silence. He seems easygoing and adaptable and so we have little reason to express concern."

"Show gentle interest in him," I suggested. "Ask about himself, his thoughts and feelings. Perhaps at a quiet moment, tell him what you've told me about losing him. And, let him know you see he's distant. Let him know you wonder why."

Paul was agreeable to continuing to meet weekly. I also continued meeting every other week with his parents. They told me Paul's spirits were improving and that he was speaking more openly and freely with them. They were hopeful that the therapy was beginning to help and that Paul was engaging with them more comfortably.

But to me, Paul was saying that things were "the same," as bleak as ever. Paul did, though, begin to complain more of injustices, like bad officiating at soccer games and teachers at school with left-wing agendas. He fantasized about revenge.

Paul's parents and I puzzled over the differences between what they observed about Paul and what Paul told me. They approached the discontinuity by insisting about what was true and what was false. Paul's report, they thought, needed to be corrected. Paul said he had no friends, but the parents disputed that and wanted the record corrected. Paul said things are unchanged; no, Paul is more open and even initiating a little and things are better. It seemed there was no room for Paul to have experiences separate from his parents'.

I explored this space with the parents. Paul sometimes saw things differently than they did. Sometimes that might be because he might misunderstand something or didn't see a wider context. But sometimes that might be because he valued different things than they did. Could it be true, from Paul's point of view, that he did have no friends?

I occasionally asked Paul if he had anything for me to take up with his parents on his behalf. A chance to communicate more openly arose when Paul asked for my help in convincing his parents to let him purchase a knife. The knife he had in mind wasn't a scout knife or even a folding knife. It was a knife he knew from video games, an enormous assassin's knife, designed for cutting throats from behind.

I spoke to Paul's parents about Paul's wish to buy the knife from Amazon. They asked for an update about Paul's anger at his younger brother and had no difficulty coming together to say "no" to the knife. "I've seen the damage family members can do to each other even without weapons," Thomas said. "Nothing good comes of having weapons in a home." "What are you thinking about?" I asked. "My father used to beat me," he said. "He'd give me a choice, a belt or a thin stick. He was brutal. Paul knows, I've told him."

When a suitable moment arose, I asked Paul what he knew about his father being beaten by his own father. "He's told me about it," Paul acknowledged. "What was it like to hear that?" "Interesting," Paul said, shrugging with a hint of enjoyment. "Interesting in a way that you liked, your grandfather beating your father." "Yeah, giving him a choice and then… making him choose is like… interesting."

Paul had met with a neuropsychologist for testing and, soon, preliminary feedback was available. The neuropsychologist told me Paul looked quite "normal." He saw no evidence of thought disorder, prodromal psychosis, or autism. This was problematic news. The diagnosis left standing to explain if Paul's ominous preoccupations was psychopathic personality. The tester had already arranged for consultation from a forensic neuropsychologist experienced in assessing psychopathy in adolescents. I did not share the preliminary findings with the parents.

In our meetings, I continued to encourage Paul to speak more openly about what was on his mind. I drew his attention to the very few feelings he let himself experience. One day, another patient who also attended Paul's school arrived very early for an appointment and crossed paths with Paul as Paul left. About Paul, the other patient said, "I recognize him from school. We both play football during recess. That kid has only two moods, neutral and angry."

Paul's parents and I discussed Paul's emotional remoteness. Each parent saw Paul as acting in their own image: Thomas thought of Paul as trying to navigate a high intensity family by screening things out and withdrawing emotionally, a strategy he himself had relied on, even in his marriage. Anna saw Paul resisting being drawn into things he disapproved of, not lowering himself to the level of his younger brother and his loud and defiant ways.

As the school year ended, I learned that Paul's mother would soon depart for a wedding in her home city. She would take Nick, her youngest, along and leave him with his grandparents for the summer. The entire family would visit the grandparents later in the summer and reunite with Nick. I didn't anticipate that the mother's departure would have an impact on Paul. But, as her departure approached, Paul reported that "curiosity" no longer adequately described his interest in killing. He said he now felt "a hunger" to experience killing.

The next week, Paul revealed detailed planning to kill Nick. Paul explained he knew which floorboards he could step on as he walked through the family home and into the brother's room without awakening his parents. And, he laid out a rationale for killing the rest of the family afterwards—"Logic dictates," he shrugged, "no witnesses."

Although Paul still said he felt deterred from acting on murderous wishes by fear of consequences, his shift from "curiosity" to "hunger" suggested an intensification of his aggression. At the same time, his rationale to kill his entire family raised my concern about incipient disordered thinking and compromised judgement. The day after Paul's mother left, I found myself on the phone with Paul's father arranging to see Paul again before our next scheduled appointment. I alerted the father that I would be assessing Paul for risk and potential hospitalization when we met.

Over the course of that next meeting, I concluded that Paul could not safely be contained on an outpatient basis. I secured Thomas's agreement to take Paul to a local Emergency Room for evaluation. From the ER, Paul was admitted to an adolescent inpatient psychiatric unit.

During our first meeting on the inpatient unit, Paul was stony and guarded. He argued that my decision to send him for evaluation was groundless. I explained that I had promised to do all I could to keep him safe, including safe from doing harm, but he felt like I had violated his trust. A mental health worker knocked on the door to tell Paul that his mother was on the phone long distance. She wouldn't be able to call again until the next day. I indicated he could take the call, but Paul waved the worker off. I wondered why he hadn't chosen to speak to his mother. I also wondered why she was calling from afar and not already on a plane coming back.

By the end of the week, Anna had returned and the neuro-psychologist who had tested Paul was ready to present his findings. Up to that point, Paul had not released me to speak about our meetings and I had divulged a minimum of information. But the neuropsychologist had explained that the test findings would be shared with Paul's parents before he interviewed Paul. So, for the first time, Paul's parents heard a full account of Paul's interest in killing and lack of felt connection to others. They listened quietly.

The tester described Paul's superior intellectual abilities, absence of psychosis and absence of a developmental history indicative of an autism spectrum disorder. At fourteen, Paul was not old enough to receive a DSM-V personality disorder diagnosis. And, because the

174

only criteria Paul met for "Conduct Disorder" were ideational and not behavioral, Paul would not receive that diagnosis either.

Paul's scores on the specialized instruments for psychopathy were high and well above the cutoff, but the tests were only normed for people sixteen years old and older, so Paul's scores were not "valid." His diagnosis was "inconclusive."

Conversation turned toward how Paul had come to be this way. Paul's mother began to reflect on Paul's ways, his distance, caution, withdrawal. His difficulty tolerating affect. She compared Paul's difficulties with those of his older brother, Mike, diagnosed with Asperger's. The points she made about Paul's emotional sensitivity, interiority and awkwardness in relationships raised another diagnostic possibility: a sub-clinical autism spectrum condition. Given the discouraging options on the table, this one seemed, perhaps, more hopeful. The tester thought about it and signaled his openness. Perhaps Paul was related but injured; distant but within human reach; not cold and psychopathic. I experienced a release of tension and a flash of hope.

I met with the parents a few days later. Anna was eager to talk about the shortcomings of the testing. She seemed to be drawing too much reassurance from the absence of a conclusive diagnosis. The parents appeared less concerned by the reports of Paul's unloving relationships and interest in killing than I expected. At first, they were more troubled by the delay the tester had taken in reporting the findings and in contesting the validity of instruments. But, over the course of the meeting, they acknowledged deep concerns about Paul and confusion about what to do.

I spoke of how you learn to bear feelings in relationships. Paul has held himself remote from relationships. A relationship-based psychotherapy makes sense. And, at fourteen, time was of the essence. Anna acknowledged that there had been years she had been emotionally unavailable to Paul. If we opened up space for Paul to see himself as injured by his mother's remoteness, could he open himself again to human caring? We discussed treatment options: outpatient options, residential options. The parents and I agreed that, if it were possible to keep Paul safely at home, it left open the best possibility of renewing family connections. I proposed a six-month trial of intensive treatment at four times a week and the parents accepted.

Paul's behavior on the unit had been without incident but there was concern that Paul might act violently upon release. The doctors had not identified a target for medication and had not prescribed any for him. Paul was terse and superficial in his self-assessments but not overtly defiant. What might indicate it was safe to discharge him?

The inpatient doctors, Paul's parents, Paul and I worked on a plan for intensive outpatient treatment to commence with Paul's discharge, go on hold when Paul and his family departed for their family trip to mother's relatives, and resume in late August when both Paul and I would be back. The trip was deeply important to Paul and his parents and they made assurances they would keep Paul under close adult supervision and away from his younger brother.

Paul was discharged after three weeks in the hospital, a long stay by today's standards. As they packed for the family trip, Paul and I began to meet again on an outpatient basis.

Paul wanted to contest my decision to send him to the hospital. Paul said that he was not the only one in his family to know which floorboards made noise and which ones didn't. How could I have made the judgements I'd made, knowing him so little!? I had no choice, I explained. I used all I knew. Perhaps going forward he would let me know him better?

Paul insisted he deserved an apology. He also believed I was far too stubborn and arrogant to make one. He and his parents had discussed it. They had never seen any inclination in me toward apology. I wondered whether there were others in the family whom I was reminding him of, who were this way too, harsh and unapologizing? Paul was unable to answer.

Eventually, I felt I could say, "Given how I knew you, I could not have made a different decision. Had I known you more and understood more, I might have." Paul seemed appeased. We made plans to resume meeting after his trip and mine. I wondered how the five-week interruption would be for him. Paul was silent.

Caution about our plans for the fall seemed reasonable. Paul had opposed more frequent appointments with me in the months before hospitalization. It seemed worth wondering whether he would follow through on the plan and whether his parents would hold to it if Paul became reluctant.

In our first session back after our August hiatus, Paul opened by saying that he had something to talk about: Everything he had told me and the neuropsychologist had been a lie. Perhaps there was one day he'd been angry at his little brother, but he'd never thought of killing anyone. He had no idea why he'd said any of that. But, unless I was willing to forget everything he'd said before, he would switch to a new therapist with whom he could start afresh.

I struggled for composure. "Really! Lying? That's so interesting," I said. "I see nothing interesting about that," Paul said. "I wonder why you would have lied?" "No idea." "It would take a lot of energy to lie and keep the lies going. It must have been important to you." "I'm not interested in that," Paul said.

"And, if I were to put aside everything you've told me?" I asked. "We would start fresh." "And, then what would you say?" I wondered.

177

"Everything's fine and I have no reason to be here." I explained to Paul that I wouldn't be able to forget what he'd told me or to pretend that I had forgotten. What would be the benefit of that, I wondered? Have people done that to you, acted like they hoped you would forget things?

I told Paul we wouldn't be able to continue if he held to that condition. We could stop now or, if Paul were willing, we might delay the decision. Could we take some time to see if, despite his anger, we could take up his feelings and rebuild trust? We had been through a good deal together. Perhaps it would be worth it to him. Paul cautiously agreed. A few days later, he added another condition—that I give up my power to hospitalize him. He imagined some legally binding statement I would sign. What if I came to think that he was a danger to himself or to someone else, I wondered aloud. Then, you would have to talk about it with my parents and they'd have to agree before you sent me, Paul said. I noticed that Paul's parents mattered to him in a way he had not acknowledged before. Imagining his parents protecting him from someone seemed new.

I asked if I could discuss his conditions with his parents and Paul said yes. "Paul," I told them, "is tempted to put conditions on the therapy that would make it impossible to continue," I explained. Thomas looked surprised and embarrassed, but Anna said, "Paul is still very angry with you. Wouldn't anyone be? You asked him to tell you more about what he was thinking and, when he did, you put him in the hospital!" "That's so, but the things he told me were very concerning for his safety... and yours," I said.

"Perhaps," Anna said, "but the testing came back inconclusive on the question of whether he's a danger or not. And, we still don't have a written test report! If we did, if the testing had come back weeks or months ago, all this could have been avoided. Or, if you'd gone ahead and seen him more frequently back in the spring, when you first asked." "I did want to see him more," I reminded her, "but Paul refused. And none of us saw a reason then to press the issue. And he would have hated that." "And, why was it okay for Paul to come with us on a long trip and not see you for five weeks, but then now he has to come here almost every day," Anna challenged.

"You are also angry with me." I said. "There are things I've done you've disagreed with and other things I've failed to do that you are also upset about."

Anna responded, "What I am saying is that I can understand very well why Paul is still angry with you. My feelings toward you are unimportant."

"Not so," I answered. "Your feelings toward me are important, too. Paul is facing big decisions here that are much too big for him on his own. He is going to depend on you two to guide him and help him. And I see him turning to you now and relying on you in a way that's different than before."

Thomas said, "I see that. But when someone says they don't trust a person, I don't know how much of an impression someone else's opinion is going to make."

I countered, "You know things that Paul doesn't yet know about being with other people, acknowledging and addressing problems between people. Sometimes things feel so difficult it's tempting to end the relationship. In this case, I think that, if it's possible for Paul to stay and work things out with me, it would be very good for him. The distrust and anger he's feeling is connected to the problems that have brought us all together. Paul gets angry and distrustful and then remote and cold."

Thomas spoke about his experience of repairing relationships—his family of origin is rife with conflicts. His relationship with his sister

179

had been worse, was now better, more collaborative in caring for their schizophrenic mother, involuntarily confined at a psychiatric nursing home after years of living on the street.

Anna described the relationships in her family as intact but formal and superficial. Most challenging for her has been working on her marriage with Thomas. Staying in the marriage was a challenge for a time but she has been more positive about it in the last year or two. (While writing this, I had a dream of Anna high up on a gondola, balanced on a mountain peak.)

Thomas said, "I see Paul as torn between liking you and feeling like he could depend on you versus feeling like you betrayed his trust. Well, I think that a person gets to choose his own therapist."

"Yes," I said, "but what about the situation where Paul has chosen me, but is then having problems with me?"

"I think it's important then that we support him," Thomas said.

"Can we also think about what aspect of Paul is most important to support. There's a part of Paul that is against relationships and doesn't trust and is closed to people. And, there's a more delicate and sensitive part of Paul that is able to trust and that is open to relationships. The second part is the part I think needs your support. Paul can stay remote and cold with me. He can get another therapist, but not one he's been through difficult times with like he and I have."

Thomas responded, "I can tell him to work it out with you if he can, but I can't speak for Anna. I do think working through difficulties is an important life skill."

Anna was unsure. "I don't know if I can do that. It feels like I'd be not with him and not on his side. I would be telling him I don't trust him."

"I know that you feel a great sadness about having lost the closeness you once had with Paul," I said. "You could attempt to address that by supporting whatever decision he makes here. Or you could see if you and he could work together on a big decision like this."

"I see that point, but I think the choice of a therapist is a very personal one," she said.

I agreed but said, "Remember that Paul did choose me. And, even though he may disagree strongly with decisions I've made, I've been trustworthy."

In a number of the sessions that followed, Paul was able to discuss productively his feelings of anger and distrust. He confided about shifting tensions with his parents and explored what led to his hospitalization a little bit. But these achievements were undone by subsequent upticks in Paul's anger and suspiciousness. Within the month, Paul had become more derisive in our meetings and more suspicious of my motives. A therapist friend of his mother's had told Anna that the fact that I continued to meet with Paul during his hospitalization was highly unusual. "No one does that," she said. The friend's words fed into the mother's suspicions, and then Paul's.

"It's like you were trying to trap me into therapy with you," Paul said.

"What would be my point in that?" I asked.

"It's not my business or of any interest to me. We've decided we're done. My parents are finding me a new therapist. But there is one thing I don't understand: If I have to come here four days a week, why was I well enough to travel with my family and why did you go on vacation yourself?!"

"If I were really concerned about you, I would have kept you here and stayed here with you," I responded. "At least that would have been consistent. Maybe what a really concerned person would have done."

181

Paul retorted, "I see what you're doing and you're twisting my words. What I'm pointing out is that you've been inconsistent in your argument that I need to come here almost every day."

"You're annoyed with my inconsistency," I responded. "Either I want you here or I don't, the back and forth is hard."

A couple days later, Paul's parents informed me that they would seek other care for Paul and discussed his termination with me. I recommended Paul continue with me until new therapy arrangements were in place and transfer could take place without a gap in treatment, but his parents did not accept my recommendation.

Thomas and Anna surprised me by joining Paul and me at our final meeting. Thomas said to me, "This isn't about you. The money just isn't there to continue this, especially with the other kids growing up and having their own pressing needs."

Commentary 1

We are presented from the outset with a toxic brew—the combination of the lack of a coherent picture of the young man after two sessions with the parents combined with Paul's all-too-easy revelation in the first meeting of his preoccupation with killing and the experiences that he would have as a murderer, actualized through his fantasies. From the perspective of the work with the parents, the abiding question for me would now be: Why doesn't the object ring through? The possibilities are of course protean.

Given the lack of understanding of how Paul is experienced currently and historically by the parents, of the current parent-child relationship, and of Paul's internal world, ego structure, and typicality or atypicality, I think that guidance of the sort that the analyst offered to the parents (ask about himself, his thoughts and feelings … tell him what you have told me about losing him … let him know you see he's distant) is a bit scattershot and without the information to know if this is helpful at this point in the process. But, alarming situations stir efforts to do something active.

We do begin to learn some important clues. First, we learn that the paternal grandmother has a chronic schizophrenic illness, that the father has been disowned by the paternal grandfather (because of his spousal choice), and that Paul has two maternal aunts with ASD in addition to his affected older brother. In addition to the evident questions that this raises about possible incipient psychosis or neuroatypicality in Paul, I begin to wonder about the unconscious meaning of Paul for one or both parents. In working with them, one could at this point try to explore their experiences with their impaired relatives, particularly in the sectors of emotional remoteness and violence.

The analyst sensitively picks up on both parents' difficulties with tolerating Paul's subjectivity—"no room for Paul to have experiences separate from parents." They want to hold him to factual content; you do have friends. Is there difficulty in this sector related to their painful experience with psychotic and autistic subjectivities? Are they afraid that Paul could become some version of insane, whether psychotic or autistic? And, if so, does the most worrisome rendering of this dynamic include the possibility that one or both parents are defending against their unconscious effort to promote insanity in Paul? Is this part of the answer about why the object does not ring through?

I don't know what to say about the terrible dilemma with regard to whether to hospitalize or not. It was hard for me to imagine any good outcome from the hospitalization, including any realistic possibility that Paul's level of dangerousness would diminish other than possibly in the short run. However, best practice and perhaps the analyst's own legal exposure were clearly on the side of hospitalization.

I was a bit surprised that the analyst did not "anticipate that the mother's departure would have an impact on Paul." Surprised from the standpoint of someone not involved, but then again, not surprised when one takes into account the countertransference defenses that expectably develop with someone whose inner world is as disordered and terrifying as Paul's is likely to be.

From this point on, there are two overriding themes—trust and the lack thereof, and separations and abandonments, with accusations flying around. We see for the first time that there is a deeper, pathological tie between parents and child. Suddenly, the house of mirrors is not just with Paul, but with the parents. We see, in mother's construction of events that she, in her heart, is not coming to grips with the seriousness of Paul's dangerousness. We can only speculate about why, but once again the question of an unholy alliance between them cannot be dismissed. Paul's father is overtly less allied with his dangerousness, less allied with his suspiciousness, seems to have an orientation of repair rather than repetition. Conceivably, he was a force behind the scenes supporting the therapeutic effort. But the need for avoidance won out.

The yeoman efforts of the analyst to reason with the parents were of no avail, and one could have expected that on the basis of the paranoid position that the mother had settled into. We now see a worrisome area in which she cannot see her child's separateness at some core emotional level, adding another dimension to why the object did not shine through at first. The object still doesn't, as Paul is constructed rather than seen. Meanwhile, the analyst had become the abandoning bad object, the accusation that the mother had had against herself. I wonder; has badness been purged from a merged mother-Paul, and for the moment, rather than Paul carrying this projection, the analyst was the current beneficiary. Realistically, all was lost.

Most tragically, in the end, Thomas capitulates. He settles into the lack of honesty that seemed to be an option in this family: "This isn't about you. The money just isn't there." Ever the protector and attempted healer, whether for his mother, sister, or troubled spouse and family.

There are some children who cannot join in a treatment alliance and are not treatable. Painfully, in my view, this is one of those children. There are some parents who are not able to join in a parental alliance around a particular child and are therefore not able to truly support a treatment. Equally painfully, in my view, these are such parents. The toxic brew that appeared on this analyst's doorstep turned out to be even more of a toxic brew than it first appeared.

One footnote. Neuropsychological testing can provide some interesting information including phenomenological diagnoses, but we learn little about the inner life of a child. Projective testing would have been extremely interesting and helpful. But alas, it is not something that is easy to come by these days.

Commentary 2

We are challenged reading this report of fourteen-year-old Paul, who presents having confided in his father "I wish I could just kill someone," with what are the next best steps to help this family. Following the initial two interviews with the parents, the therapist notes he could not draw a good picture of Paul as a person and chooses to meet him and by implication perhaps earlier than he would have normally met another child being evaluated for therapy. But then this was an unusual circumstance; this just turned teenager was voicing homicidal ideation which the father took to mean more specifically fratricidal ideation.

What is going on?

And, how as a therapist, do we establish adequate parameters in our therapy to help a child and family safely explore the nature and source of such extreme ideation?

During the interview with the therapist, right away Paul lays out a non-specific wish to kill someone and learn what killing would feel like, imagining it would be "interesting."

The therapist reports Paul hoped a psychologist could help him but didn't know how. Paul unfolds a "bleak" internal landscape daydreaming about car accidents, scaffolding collapses, fires, and other scenes of people being hurt "in the worst possible ways." These daydreams he reported brought him no pleasure but did help him relax and help him at night before sleep.

Early questions arise about how safe Paul is with his ideation, is he psychotic, under the influence of an unknown source (internet, substances, individuals), enraged, and/or are these ruminations of an obsessional nature? If these preoccupations are of an obsessional nature, are they primarily defensive—against what—aggressive and/or libidinal impulses and feelings? At fourteen, has he entered puberty? Has he had masturbatory ideation that has been disruptive to his internal mental state? Against loneliness? All questions which would take some time to explore in a trusting therapeutic relationship.

Paul asks that his verbalizations/secrets remain between therapist and patient. Why secret? Is Paul aware of reasons why such "killing ideation" might be problematic to some? Has there been a discussion of the difference between a secret and privacy/confidentiality? A therapist duty to warn of imminent harm? How was the individual therapy and parent consultation work outlined in the initial interviews?

Might this have been a stage in this early phase of work to delineate the need for safety and perhaps how some verbalizations such as "killing ideation" might cause some people to worry more than others? Perhaps referencing the initial call for a consultation—mom's and dad's worry about his (Paul's) words expressing a wish to kill.

Dad had zeroed in on a wish to kill his younger brother, Nick, when Paul had reassured the therapist that he hadn't had that specific wish. Had there been frustrations, anger, or maybe just some exciting rough and tumble between brothers that had gotten out of hand? How did the family express their feelings, particularly anger but also their love/affection for one another?

In parent consultation there was much data on early difficulties, the marriage was disapproved by paternal grandfather, paternal grandmother is reported as suffering from a schizophrenic type illness (now under the care of father). Maternal grandmother and mother's sister are reported to have had autism spectrum conditions. Paul's mother suffered from depression, there had been marital tension and years of therapy. Father had been whipped by his father and asked to choose the instrument—belt or thin stick, and then written out of the will. Father had shared this information "perhaps too much" with Paul. Had father indicated or implied his own feelings—perhaps his own wish to kill?

Mother reports "I was very close to Paul until Nick was born." We aren't told at what age but mother reports that she doesn't remember how Paul experienced loss of his mother. Paul was initially angry at the nanny but then got along only to lose her six months later.

The therapist usefully recommends considering this early phase of contact between therapist, patient, and parents as an extended evaluation, a neuropsychological consultation be arranged and meeting more frequently with Paul. The therapist has some internal reservations about beginning to meet with Paul more frequently and at the same time is aware that there is this underlying "killing ideation" that needed monitoring. Interestingly, parents agreed to the increased frequency of sessions but Paul declined.

Steadily meeting with Paul's parents, more information regarding the early history emerged. Parents reported "rarely having time with him" and "respecting his silence." They saw him as shy and awkward.

The therapist invites parents to show gentle interest in him and adds, when Paul is distant, ask him why? He suggests helping Paul by showing interest and curiosity about his internal world.

When Paul begins his therapy, he provides his verbalizations and ideations as prescribed by the treatment. He tells of his various complaints—injustices, teachers with left wing agendas and fantasies of revenge. No friends.

Parents report improvements in behavior, but when they hear of inconsistencies in Paul's reports to the therapist—"No friends?" they state: "Untrue, therapist—correct the record."

Attempting to gently challenge the parents' thinking, the therapist asked, "Could it be true, from Paul's point of view, that he did have no friends?" The therapist is attempting to help them by offering ideas about how Paul's internal world may be different than their experience of him. This process is resisted by the parents.

What then is Paul's and mother's and father's idea of how this therapist will help Paul and all of them, if there are such differences in their experiences of each other? What was known but not thought about or let alone talked about? Were there other family secrets? How much had mother, and/or father shared with Paul about mother's depression? The parents report "we rarely have time just with him."

How did Paul manage on his own early in his life particularly at night just before sleep? During the initial evaluation, Paul reported scenes from people being hurt "in the worst possible ways," and how "they did help him relax" and he would "think about these scenes at night before sleep."

The preliminary findings from the neuropsychological evaluation reported Paul to look quite "normal," no evidence of thought disorder, prodromal psychosis or autism. This confounds the therapist suggesting to him that Paul's ominous preoccupations may indicate the possibility of a diagnosis of psychopathic personality. The therapist chose not to share these preliminary findings with the parents. A forensic neuropsychologist was engaged for further evaluation. Given the nature of the interactions thus far, and parents difficulty appreciating their son's experience of his internal world, the therapist refraining from sharing this knowledge is on the one hand understandable but seems to leave the therapist with heightened anxiety. Does the experience of the therapist holding this preliminary finding begin to feel like a secret? A key element in the early work with all parties concerned is the development of a therapeutic alliance and a safe space where all parties can feel some level of security. What could have been shared that didn't telegraph the therapist's heightened concerns? Perhaps given how Paul presents there is more to the picture of his internal world that will take time, patience, care, and safety to explore.

In parent consult, the therapist explores Paul's emotional remoteness. Thomas (father) saw Paul navigating a high intensity family and Anna (mother) saw him as resisting being drawn into things he disapproved of, not lowering to the level of his younger brother's loud and defiant ways. The therapist sees this as reflections of each parent's view of Paul in their own image.

189

Also, at this time toward the end of school, his mother began making plans to travel with her youngest son Nick. Paul describes his "hunger" to kill, elaborated to then kill his brother Nick, and, to prevent there being witnesses, the rest of the family.

This sequence is understandably experienced as an escalation of aggressive ideation that needs to be addressed. It's not clear if the therapist has asked Paul if he has communicated this ideation to anyone else—father or mother—if not, is this another instance of tension between maintaining secrecy and privacy/confidentiality? Has the therapist become the messenger in communicating this fratricidal ideation with Paul's father and events follow that lead to Paul's hospitalization?

A parenthetical question and thought: Is the therapist by virtue of being asked to keep this "killing ideation" between therapist and patient in the throes of a secret? The preliminary findings from the neuropsychologist suggested to the therapist that there was something more seriously wrong with Paul, psychopathy that could blow up. One way to look at this dynamic is that Paul has been keeper of this "killing ideation" and perhaps other family secrets for a long time—perhaps years. We can speculate about the "why now—was it less safe than it was before being verbalized?" Mother's departure, Paul's developmental age, unresolved sibling rivalry, father's own history, therapist serious concerns are all significant matters. What we don't have yet is a working psychodynamic formulation of what ails Paul—his primary defensive structure and level of development.

With Paul's escalation of aggressive ideation, hospitalization is recommended and accepted by the father. What was mother's input on this decision? Does she cut her travels short to return and attend to her son? The usual expectations of hospitalization are that not only will it hopefully keep Paul safe but there are many eyes that can take a look at Paul and perhaps aid in understanding from what he may be suffering. This is a way for not only Paul to not be alone with these "killing ideations" but the therapist is not alone either.

More trouble emerges as Paul remains "stony and guarded" towards his therapist while in hospital. Paul also did not speak with his mother who had called during one of his sessions while hospitalized. It's not clear but this seemed to be in keeping with a family pattern of limited communication among everyone. What follows is perhaps an expectable sequence where Paul does not release his therapist to speak with his parents regarding the neuropsychologist's findings on testing and thus the potential for a set-up of experience of betrayal when the neuropsychologist explains that he had explained to Paul that the findings would be shared with his parents prior to having interviewed Paul.

This sequence leads to an opportunity for the findings which were reported as inconclusive to be potentially discarded by not only Paul but his parents. What was seen, particularly by Mother, was reassurance by the absence of conclusive diagnosis.

The therapist proposes, that if safety can be maintained at home, a six-month trial of intensive four-times-a-week therapy may be indicated. The parents accept the treatment recommendation. What's not clear is if there will be regular parent consultation sessions to be continued.

Outpatient treatment is placed on hold while Paul and his family depart for summer travels with intensive therapy to resume in late August. Assurances are made regarding safety and close adult supervision of Paul during this treatment hiatus.

In the interval between hospital discharge and travel, Paul begins to contest the therapist recommendation for hospitalization, in effect, "How could you, knowing me so little?" Paul demands an apology and notes that the therapist is "too stubborn and arrogant to make one." The therapist makes a technical decision to comment, not in the here-and-now transference but instead to a then-and-there comment regarding "Who does this remind you of?" This is not an uncommon approach to anger directed towards a therapist. Paul is appeased by the therapist's eventual acknowledgment that his decision was governed by what he did know at the time and how he might have made a different decision had he known him better. It's not clear how this expression of Paul's anger in session is acknowledged and accepted within the safe confines of the therapeutic space. Anger is likely to be a prominent affect that would emerge in the working phase of treatment should a sufficient therapeutic alliance be formed not only between therapist and analysand but also between therapist and parents.

What follows is a statement by Paul that all he has said to the neuropsychologist is a lie—he has never thought of killing anyone and that unless the therapist forgets everything, he would switch therapists.

One way to interpret Paul's approach at this juncture is to consider his disavowal of "killing ideation" as a way to turn the passive experience of being hospitalized into active attack on the therapist efforts at helping him. Understandably, the therapist "struggles to keep his composure." Is Paul doing to the therapist what he feels has been done to him? Does Paul's "killing ideation" now extend to killing the therapist's memories and perhaps in some way suggesting that it is not safe for Paul to be intimately "known" by his therapist?

An additional idea: Is what Paul has said a lie because there is another "truth?" Unlikely as it may seem given his display of anger, might he also harbor loving feelings? This is conjecture at this point. But it is worth bearing in mind that if there hasn't been sufficient fusion of the drives, libidinal and aggressive impulses remain unintegrated. Integration of loving and unloving feelings are an aim of intensive treatment. There had been some hope on the part of the therapist that all was not lost with Paul given his age and absence of other serious indications in the neuropsychological testing. However, with Paul's challenge to treatment, his parents are also skeptical about what can be accomplished in treatment.

In meeting with the parents, the therapist confronts the resistance to continued treatment, Paul's conditions—"forget about what I have said, or I will get another therapist," and now the therapist finds the parents are also resistant to continued work—"written neuropsychologist's report" has not been provided and with the hiatus from treatment while family travelled over the summer, "how would therapist agree to such a plan if he had so worried about Paul's safety?"

The therapist has lost his alliance with not only Paul but with both parents, all are feeling betrayed and distrustful. Soon Paul's parents make plans to discontinue treatment, using as their rationale the finances that are needed for the other children in the family.

We can reflect on this case and wonder if there may have been a different approach to the consultation that may have led to continued treatment. No doubt clinicians would have been challenged by this case. What is clear is that unless there is an alliance with the child/adolescent and at least one parent during different phases of treatment it is unlikely to be sustainable through significant crises that often accompany treatment of patients with serious "killing ideation."

Some features of this case to consider:

1. There is a natural tension between secrecy and privacy/confidentiality. The experience of secrecy lends itself to aloneness with the potential for significant danger and harm.

By maintaining communications between interested parties, respecting privacy/confidentiality, individuals are less alone.

2.   When it is hard to arrive at a diagnosis, it is helpful to have a psychodynamic formulation of what is going on in the internal mind of a patient, even if it seems to be changing as a consultation progresses. Attending to shifting defenses from more inflexible obsessional to projective identification and/or other more primitive defenses will be necessary as they may challenge the safety of the therapeutic space. If there is significant difficulty arriving at a useful formulation this not knowing can be a signal to help a patient and family understand that there are internal matters at work that need safe exploration. The not knowing can lead to too much anxiety that hopefully can be modulated enough such that families can experience the care taken working towards understanding and aid in the therapeutic alliance among all parties concerned.

3.   There is a need for at least one parent or significant other person to <u>be with</u> a child/adolescent patient who is suffering from internal disruptive ideation and affect at home in a good enough way. Parent consultation is an avenue to help the parent(s) at these difficult moments. Otherwise, the need for higher level of care begins to be sought out as an approach so that a person with "killing ideation" has someone to reach out to in a moment of crisis.

4.   There is no fail-safe approach to the assessment of dangerousness in a patient, it is often fraught with potential countertransference affective responses. Clinicians are often pushed to modify their approaches. When clinicians experience this, it can be an internal signal that can present an opportunity, when not too affectively arousing, to reflect on what is occurring in the here-and-now

transference between patient and clinician. When recognized, this moment can aid in understanding some of the dynamic forces that have led a patient toward achieving a resolution of disruption through ideas of "killing" rather than repair.

5. Patient, parents, and clinician need to feel safe in the therapeutic space. This is an ongoing challenge, the "how" is often governed by a basic trust that if an internal disruptive moment occurs there is a means to reach out to clinician, family member, significant other, friend, and thus, they are not alone with catastrophic thoughts and feelings.

6. Regular parent consultations are helpful when the patient understands that communications with their parents are not an effort to break confidentiality but to assist a parent in the process of <u>being with</u> their child/adolescent. However, if a parent has <u>not been with</u> their child in a good enough way earlier in their life, it presents another set of difficulties to be explored. Again, the need for a safe therapeutic space is paramount. The child/adolescent needs to experience some locus of control that will allow them to explore where they are now and how they got there with the idea that there is more to life than "killing." Disruptions in relationships may not only be repaired but perhaps also begin to flourish in a healthy and loving way.

Editorial Reflections

Most referrals come at a moment of crisis when parents feel helpless. There is tremendous pressure from parents for the therapist to give them an answer, a verdict, a solution, especially in a case where there is a pressing question as to whether the child or adolescent will

195

kill themselves or someone else. The analyst is immediately put in the position of doing a risk assessment and then expected to intervene in such a way that the risk will diminish or disappear.

The reality is that the professional is in some ways as helpless as the parent and the adolescent. The challenges that emerge from this chapter convey the situation in vivid and dramatic terms, but the predicament is there in all cases to some degree. How do we resist defending against our own anxiety and helplessness by invoking a rescue fantasy and accepting the attribution of omniscience? How do we set up instead a collaborative partnership where the therapist offers expertise, experience, and the willingness to explore and learn and the parents bring their broad and deep knowledge of their child and his history?

The commentators for this vignette independently note the importance of establishing a positive working alliance with the parents. They identify the analyst's decision to see the patient after he saw the parents only twice and could not get a picture of the patient as a technical choice point. Do we accede to the parents' presentation of the child as the designated object of attention and see him right away or do we stay longer with exploration of the possible defensive vagueness picked up from the parents? In relation to concurrent parent work, the commentators are implying that the lack of a clear picture of the child was not a deficiency requiring a shift away from parent work, but rather an indication of pathological dynamics within and between parents and child needing continued intensive exploration before deciding on therapeutic goals.

The skill of the therapist allowed for the later emergence of some of these dynamics but it came in the context of changed parental goals. Rather than looking to the analyst as a source of help, the analyst became a person to blame. What one commentator described as a possible "unholy alliance" between mother and son, what has been characterized as a "negative therapeutic motivation" (J. Novick 1980) probably came into play and sabotaged the treatment. This is where the therapist ends up as the humiliated failure and the parents and adolescent are reunited in the blissful fantasy that as bad as the parents may seem, the therapist is worse.

The material of the case offers striking examples of disparity of perspective among everyone involved: what the analyst characterizes as an "extended evaluation" is seen by the parents as "the therapy"; Paul and his parents have very different descriptions of him and his social situation; the mother's departure has a different meaning for everyone, and so forth. Here we might infer as a possible general technical indicator that such disparities need to be explored sooner rather than later, as they offer potential interferences to maintaining treatment.

This case, and others in this volume, underscores the necessity to first establish a positive therapeutic alliance with the parents before coming to and sharing any conclusions. In the context of an emerging partnership with and between the parents, areas can be explored leading to provisional answers to questions about who is the patient, what are the dynamics within and between all family members, what are the distinct roles and responsibilities of parents and therapists, what are the goals for each and what techniques should be employed. A long period of working with parents in an extended evaluation that is understood by all parties to be a time of exploration, getting to know one another, mapping the situation in the present and its history, may also protect against enmeshment in a net of secrets, where everyone is withholding information from everyone else.

CHAPTER NINE

SEVERE ACTING OUT: MAINTAINING MULTIPLE ALLIANCES

Mid-adolescent

Clinical Vignette

At the time of our first meeting, then seventeen-year-old Annie was seventy-five pounds overweight, with over-dyed hair that was breaking and falling out. With glassy eyes and a vacant look, she seemed unaware of how deeply she had fallen. Her parents, who were divorced and both worked full-time, appeared weary and overwhelmed.

During an extended three-week evaluation, I met with parents four times and Annie three. I learned that Annie, until her high school years, had been a gregarious straight A student in classes designed for the highly gifted. She excelled in select and elite sports teams and on occasion appeared irritable with outbursts of anger. By her junior year of high school, Annie typically entered school only to exit through the back door to indulge in drugs and alcohol with wayward friends. Her once-close relationship with her mother

199

had become angry and hostile and her relationship with father was distant.

Through the developmental history form filled out and mailed before the meetings I learned Annie had made her first and near fatal suicide attempt at the age of twelve, subsequent to her father allegedly degrading her and accusing her of the parents' pending divorce. Father, according to mother, had always targeted Annie with scathing remarks. According to Mother, she divorced father to protect Annie from Father's attacks, though mother said she had been targeted by father's attacks as well. Annie had subsequently been hospitalized four times for suicidal thoughts, abuse of alcohol and drugs, and severe anxiety and depression. The last hospitalization occurred immediately before her initial hour with me.

Annie felt degraded by her academically stellar sister, Sarah, four years her senior, and had alienated all but one of the friends she had enjoyed since grade school. Psychological testing and my meetings with Annie revealed fears of intruders entering her basement to murder her and her family, as well as Annie's use of feelings for wallowing and indulgence rather than a source of insightful knowledge. Annie was terrified of crowded concerts and the sporting events she had previously loved, and she had resorted to lying in bed for hours on end, rising only to retrieve food to take back into her bedroom.

I recommended a four-times-a-week psychoanalysis for Annie and concurrent once-a-week parent sessions. I told Annie and her parents in separate meetings of Annie's difficulty regulating her feelings; she was using eating, alcohol and drug abuse to relieve her depression and anxiety. Annie needed to discover thoughts and words for her feelings to contain and make them more useful to her. Annie's approach was not working; it was making her worse. I explained that the parent meetings would support them as they strove to be the best parents possible for Annie. All agreed with my recommendations.

Subsequent to their acceptance, I was aware of feeling apprehensive, frightened and concerned about my ability to help this suffering family. So much had been tried and failed before. Though Annie seemed to be making a positive connection to me, I wondered whether it would be adequate to sustain us through what promised to be a difficult journey.

In the eighteen-month psychoanalysis, Annie revealed, struggled with and worked through entanglement in sadomasochistic entrapment. Though she accepted my interpretations, mixed with her own insight and resulting in a feeling of positive well-being and overwhelming excitement, nevertheless, toxic guilt, resulting in a powerful urge to withdraw and escape would often follow. With each such cycle during our work, Annie moved closer to evolving from an adolescent who expressed herself primarily through her body with destructive action to a young woman capable of insightfully connecting word, thought, and reason in support of constructive action. Concomitantly, her parents evolved from a primarily sadomasochistic dynamic between themselves and with Annie to becoming able to use words compassionately to promote close connection and mutual growth.

Annie immediately embraced her first hour by sobbing over the loss of a beloved boyfriend, a loss that had occurred exactly a year before the evaluation. She spoke of her terror of melting into the thoughts and feelings of others while simultaneously fearing abandonment by them. My interpretation of her fearing feeling close to me, only to lose herself and feel abandoned, resulted in an initial sense of calm and positive feelings that was followed by withdrawal through missing sessions. When she returned, we worked to understand her disappearance as a reaction to the good and exciting feelings followed by guilt. This pattern repeated and intensified when we understood her need to take full responsibility for her sister Sarah's lacerating criticisms as a desire to compensate for feeling unbearably helpless following such an attack.

We came to understand how Annie embraced feeling responsible to feel more powerful and in an effort to heal the relationship through her attempt to rescue it. However, assuming omnipotent control resulted in feelings of toxic guilt followed by an urge to self-cut and descend into a depressive spiral. Annie felt much better after understanding this pattern, only to descend into panic and somaticized darkness manifested in headaches and sleeping at home through two subsequent sessions. With her parents, I urged them to cease the angry outbursts towards Annie, speak calmly to her when she raged, and confront Sarah's inappropriate hostility towards Annie. Annie reacted to her parents' calm response to her angry outbursts by going to her room, returning and apologizing, and then revealing more advanced conscience development than the parents were aware of.

The parents' ability to remain calm and compassionate was reinforced when Annie, panic-stricken and unable to drive herself, pulled mother into a session where Annie spoke of feeling bad after feeling good. When I interpreted the guilt as emanating from feeling responsible for every malady in her family and as if she had murdered someone, Annie screamed in agony, clutching her abdomen saying, "I can't feel anything. I can't feel any pleasure in my life." Mother, shocked by the depth of her daughter's pain, then understood how Annie's angry attacks and outbursts were a smoke screen and protection against unbearable pain. Mother used her understanding to more deeply empathize with Annie and shared her perceptions with father in the next parent meeting. Both parents were able to respond with greater calm and compassion to Annie. Their new calm and understanding enabled me to help them conceptualize Annie's provocations through lying and choices to withdraw from completing chores, as an effort to engage her parents in angrily criticizing her to relieve her guilt.

The parents' new calmness and compassion were invaluable when they discovered Annie's sexual rendezvous with a man in a hotel in a nearby town via the reading of Annie's text messages. The parents had told Annie they would, on occasion, read her text messages to keep her safe from herself and others. With Annie's permission, the parents attended the beginning of her next session and revealed their knowledge of the encounter, by exclusively addressing their concern for Annie's safety and health rather than digressing into moral judgment as they had been inclined to do in the past. Annie accepted their concern with calm and allowed them to accompany her for a pregnancy test and use of more reliable birth control. Previously Annie would have withdrawn emotionally or run away for days in response to such a parental confrontation.

After this session Annie revealed her engagement in unprotected sex with a friend of her previous boyfriend. When I recommended that she inform mother, Annie agreed and brought mother into our next session. When mother left my consultation room, Annie was able to talk in more detail about the encounter. Based on information from previous sessions I suggested Annie felt completely responsible for all of the criticism father had bestowed upon her, leaving her feeling unloved by him. I said, "Annie, I feel you engage in sexual relations to feel love through sex. It's not working. I think it does not feel good and is used as an avenue to destroy yourself to prove your father's criticism is your fault. This belief is a product of a very young mind and is not relevant today." Annie immediately clutched her abdomen and cried out in pain and nodded in affirmation. She said she felt the love briefly during the sex and then felt horrible. I suggested that while she was seeming to seek love, on another level, of which she was not aware, she was seeking through the sex, punishment for the guilt and self-criticism she felt for not having received the love from father. I said her agony over the loss of the boyfriend might be a displacement for feelings of loss of father. Annie agreed.

Subsequent to this session, four months into her analysis, Annie ceased having indiscriminate sex with boys and asked her parents to help her in socializing at home until she felt safe. Mother shared her knowledge from this session with father in the next session. While father was initially judgmental when I told him, with Annie's permission, that the experiences of sex were not pleasurable but were for self-punishment for feeling unloved by him, father wept. Shortly after this session he requested Annie join him in a session where he tearfully apologized for all the times he had criticized her harshly and called her inappropriate names. Annie responded with forgiveness.

What followed was the revelation of masked fears of oedipal strivings manifested in terror of competition. Annie revealed her view of competition and success as a zero-sum game. If she wins, she leaves her opponent bloodied and dying on the ground. We spoke of how in reality this was not the case and discussed how she projects her competitive conflict on public sports events while identifying with the winner. Subsequent to these interpretations she was able to enjoy attending public sports events, something she had not done in a very long time. Annie also relaxed more around Sarah after revealing her fear that, if she moved forward academically, she would destroy her sister, by taking away the only thing Sarah had. Annie and her parents felt she is empathic and caring with other people while Sarah was not, leaving Sarah without relationships. Academics were Sarah's only accomplishment in life.

Annie was convinced that, if she succeeded, her success would detract from Sarah, harming her and potentially the rest of the family. When I told Annie that such extreme "either/or" thinking was from her much younger mind and that, possibly, all members of her family could be successful, she responded by allowing herself to successfully complete her GED. Previously, in a moment of horrible anxiety and in response to father's criticism, she had abandoned the idea of continuing to attend high school. When father regressed after Annie's success and began criticizing Annie and suggesting she had not improved at all, I suggested he might have been responding to Annie's success by fearing her abandonment as she grows. Father calmed and ceased his criticism.

Subsequent to this growth on Annie's part, both interpersonally and in academics, Sarah began criticizing Annie with merciless hostility. Looks of disdain and sarcastic remarks from Sarah occurred without provocation, piercing Annie's fragile sense of self-worth, according to Annie and her parents, who at first failed to respond. When this happened, Annie acted out by leaving after our session to convene with friends when she had been instructed by her parents to return home and help with a party hosted by Sarah. When the parents with my help finally confronted Sarah, Annie calmed only to feel flooded with anxiety. Her response was to run away to a friend's home for several days. Parents responded with masochistic and helpless passivity. For a week I worked with them to take action. I explained again how Annie was convinced she was the poster child for failure in the family and felt she must assume this role or others would suffer and perish. I told them their daughter was fragile and unsafe. Police would come to their aid in bringing Annie home if they employed them to do so. I told the parents to not give Annie money, as she was asking them to do, but instead tell her how they feared for her safety and if she did not return home within twelve hours, they would call the police. They did and Annie returned.

During the time of Annie's disappearance from home, I had also tried to reach out to Annie, emailing her on several occasions. Annie would not respond. When I interpreted the negative therapeutic reaction through mother, Annie responded with, "She [the analyst] is trying to be my mother." Mother responded by telling Annie I was not, and mother asserted her wish for Annie to return. Annie responded immediately by attending her next session and crying out to me saying, "I want you and my parents to scream at me and tell me how horrible I am." This opened up a deepening level of awareness of how far her sadomasochistic strivings had reached. We talked about the depth of her guilt when feeling so much better and healthier. She was convinced if she succeeded, she would become like Sarah and be angry and hateful. I spoke of her wish that this negative persona would provide punishment, relieving her toxic and overwhelming guilt. I said the guilt turned to rage and she became hooked on this rage by becoming pleasurably intoxicated by its power. I said this was to compensate for the helplessness she felt in response to the emptiness resulting from pushing her success out of her awareness. I said all of this was coming from her and not from me, Sarah or her parents. Annie agreed and calmed.

What followed was an outpouring of grief through words and tears over the abandonment of her stellar academic and athletic career. She then exhibited progress by realizing she was the one inhibiting herself by assuming she had to take on the role of failure in the family. Paternal transferences surfaced of feeling "nothing was enough" to satisfy me in her progress in our work. Once this was interpreted, she exhibited the ability to move forward. When Annie experienced sexual excitement when feeling success in her work with me, she wanted to cut back her treatment and mother colluded. When I interpreted mother's support as an act of denial of her guilt over feeling she had not protected Annie from father when Annie was younger, mother understood and encouraged Annie to continue at four times a week. Annie agreed.

Progress followed more rapidly and consistently than regressions for both Annie and her parents. Following Annie's projection of her sense of failure onto the world and on loved ones, and my interpretation of them as an avoidance of intimacy, Annie relaxed with more pleasure in her relationships. Dreams that Annie suggested represented her greater ability to experience sexual feelings and the accompanying guilt as well as her parents' and friends' support of her, confirmed how Annie's mind was organizing her thoughts more effectively to help her face, work through, and contain conflict. Parents' guilt over father's attacks on Annie in the past and mother's difficulty protecting Annie were faced and grieved in parent sessions, resulting in more lively closeness between them and Annie. The parents were spontaneously able to talk of Annie's progress in all areas of her life, including her ability to face and embrace pure feelings of pleasure in her relationships. When oedipal strivings were heightened, Annie discovered she reversed longing and desire into disgust followed by a digression into self-hate projected onto her body in the form of disgust with her own desires. Annie regressed into oral striving, eating copious amounts of food.

These insights helped Annie work toward mastery of her over-eating, which resulted in weight loss. When Annie was able to take charge of interpreting her somatic responses to excitement and anxiety over excitement during our sessions, her insights were followed by guilt. We both cited the need to repeat these reactions to understand them in more depth, making her stronger and more pleasurably integrated as a person.

Annie demonstrated the ability to appropriately confront Sarah and father when they criticized her and when both backed down, she allowed herself to reexperience her beauty through growing her lush hair out naturally. We both agreed Annie's ego boundary disintegration in response to mother's distress was a need to take full responsibility for mother to counteract Annie's helplessness. Following this interpretation, Annie reported feeling much freer in relation to others. After a disruption in her sessions and Annie's and mother's move from the family home, we revisited her delusion of omnipotence in feeling responsible for the divorce, our separation, and the suicide attempt. We talked of the suicide attempt as an act of imagined power, largely over overwhelming feelings of responsibility for the trauma of the divorce and the imagined reuniting of her parents in grief over the loss of their daughter. Annie identified it as misguided power. Mother and Annie responded with wanting to again cut back our sessions. When I interpreted their collusion in pretending "everything is alright" they agreed to continue the four-times-a-week frequency.

In the last six months of her analysis, Annie continued her cycle of pleasure, guilt and withdrawal but with less dramatic acting out. Each time she embraced deeper insight into her behavior and unconscious mind. Catastrophic defenses were identified and explored with Annie and mother in separate meetings subsequent to Annie emptying her mind and shutting down in response to one of Sarah's attacks. Mother revealed that father's irascible temper, along with attacks on mother, Sarah, and eventually targeted toward Annie, intensified significantly subsequent to Annie's birth. Annie agreed when I suggested that mother met Annie with vacant stares in possible reaction to the tension from the attacks. Annie also agreed when I suggested that she responded to the tension by mentally and physically shutting down when she was younger and at times throughout her life into the present.

During this last six months, Annie entered the mid-phase of her analysis as suggested by greater awareness of her catastrophic defenses and more eagerness to explore her internal world. Concurrent parent work evolved into separate parent meetings where father was more comfortable addressing his defensive anger and mother her urge to vacate when Annie withdrew. Real libidinal energy surfaced for Annie as a result of her analysis, according to Annie. As well, she was able to significantly decrease the psychotropic medication prescribed by a psychiatrist prior to the beginning of her analysis.

Annie spontaneously talked of how much gratitude she felt towards me and her analysis for her stronger and clearer thinking and sense of self; her father's mollified temper and greater compassion towards her; and her disbelief that her family, including Sarah, could exude so much warmth and compassion towards her. Yet, she realized she still had much to do. Annie spontaneously felt and expressed remorse for her displaced rage from father onto mother. At that time, Annie enjoyed great success and accolade as a nanny for a family; she spontaneously reported more pleasure in her life and friendships; and she was excited about her enrollment in two college classes that spring.

Subsequent to her eighteen-month analysis, Annie continued for one year in two-times-a week psychotherapy. During that time, she consolidated her gains, performed well in college classes, acquired more satisfying relationships, and began working as a part-time waitress, while continuing to work as a nanny.

Commentary 1

With so many emotional currents, conscious and unconscious, in play at the same time, psychoanalysis with adolescents is particularly complex. As Meltzer and Harris (1973) observed, "… Adolescents live mostly in the external world of adolescents and are not naturally or comfortably in touch with adults" (p.21). For most, if not all, adolescents the parental world of adults is something that they are both attracted to and reject. How then to place and deal with the actuality of the adolescent's parents within this often contradictory context? Should parental participation be included—and if so in what form and to what extent—in the analytic consulting room? Will parental participation facilitate the constitution of the transference-countertransference experience and help maintain the stability of the relationship between the patient and the analyst or does the adolescent patient need to feel the separation and security of a private space away from the parents in order to help consolidate a stronger sense of independence and personal identity?

Whether or not parents are actually present in the treatment room, they are already and inevitably included within the territory of analysis. When we accept an adolescent patient into treatment, we have also, by default, accepted the anxiety, the pain, the confusion and contradictions that most probably emanate from the family. Parents are more than simply points of reference they "… appear above all like a political structure and a class system (Meltzer 1973, p.22)" and, as such, can encourage the analytical process or hinder it.

Every family, as a definable independent group, has its stratifications formed by culture, secrets, trauma, structures of organization and defenses that they use to face unpredictable reality. In characterization of the family, Bleger (1966) says that it is a place for the projection of the most immature and symbiotic parts of the personality and serves to contain and restrain expression of the psychotic parts of the members' personalities so that the most evolved and adaptable parts may be expressed toward the world outside. He describes four types of family organizations. The "conglomerate type" is where people are not separated from one another and the family acts as a totality. The "schizoid type" is where we can observe distance and coldness. Both these organizations are dysfunctional, produce inadequate defenses and do not promote differentiation and separation of the individual. The "hypochondriac type" is where claustrophobic defenses are in place. The "adaptive type" is where all defenses maintain the flexibility needed for the family to address each changing moment.

Independent of whether or not the parents of the adolescent are physically present in the consulting room, our territory, as analysts, will encompass the psychopathological emotional patterns of every family passed on from one generation to another, as well as individual traumatic experiences. These may have a profound impact in blocking or favoring real change and growth in our patients. For example, sexual development in the adolescent's body and mind challenges established relationships and relative positions within the family. When this occurs, hidden or negated experiences originating within the family can suddenly reappear during treatment and parents may be unprepared to face and digest this. Often this happens when adolescents try to release themselves from the belief and moral systems of their parents, while, at the same time, desperately needing their parents' support to face emotional difficulties as they oscillate between an excited sense of omnipotence and a precarious sense of independence.

Often, the favorable position of the analyst is that of creating and helping to preserve a potential space in which the adolescent can oscillate between closeness and separation, autonomy and dependency. At such moments, what effect will the presence of the actual parent in the office during the adolescent's session have on the process? In my experience, I have found that maintaining the separation between patient and parent helps us to develop the "binocular"—both up close and at a distance—which affords the analyst the freedom to see and understand the emotional movement inside and outside the patient and the family group. This position allows the therapist to "cut out the extraneous noise" and listen deeply to the patient. It goes without saying that parents have a seemingly impossible task; to care about and be present in the life of their child while at the same time gently pushing them out of the nest so that they may develop their own autonomy. When the adolescent passage becomes problematic, parents may be doubly traumatized because their child exposes them to criticism or public blame at the very moment that they are straining to loosen, relinquish and rework emotional bonds and ties with them. Thus, when an adolescent is referred for treatment, we may be presented with two sets of traumatized people, adolescents and parents, whose psychic realities may overwhelm the analyst, outstripping the analyst's capacity to deeply listen.

M. Klein (1932) was very sensitive to the possibility of interference by parents in the treatment of their children and adolescents, encouraging the active inclusion of the parents in the adolescent's analysis only during occasions when the adolescent was overtaken by massive acute anxiety and/or violent resistance. She believed that work with parents, "… generally proves not only useless but calculated to increase their [parents'] anxiety and sense of guilt" (p.117) and noted and described the difficulties that can arise between parents and their child's analyst precisely because the psychoanalysis touches closely upon the parents' own complexes. Thus, she advocated maintaining a separation between "education" and analysis and emphatically stated that, "… we bear in mind that the aim of our work is to secure the well-being of the child and not the gratitude of its mother and father" (p.121). Klein's advice was to carefully try to maintain the separation between the analysis of the adolescent and contact with the parents, keeping the latter to a minimum while the analysis of the adolescent is ongoing, perhaps "only enough to maintain their support for the treatment." She did not of course preclude referring the parents for their own separate treatment when that was indicated.

Winnicott (1965), despite his recognition of the importance of the "real" (actual external objects) and the traumatic potential of the quality of *not good enough* parenting, was profoundly aware of the need to keep in mind the strict separation and relation between external and internal reality and the potential impact of the failure to do so on the psychoanalysis. Thus, he cautioned that "… the analyst is prepared to wait till the patient becomes able to present the environmental factors in terms that allow for their interpretation as projections" (p. 37). This implies dealing with the parents in the analysis as *internal* objects and remembering that we are working with the *unconscious phantasy* and attempting to interpret the anguish that emerges from the deeply embedded psyche of the adolescent. Thus, Winnicott advocated waiting to address the issue of parenting until it had entered the analysis as an aspect of the child's omnipotence or transference rather than intervening directly with the "real parents" in external reality. He asserted that "… the reliability of the analyst is the most important factor" (p. 38).

Both Klein and Winnicott agree that the primary goal of analysis remains intrapsychic change rather than environmental restructuring. Their view of the main work of analysis, a view with which I strongly concur, is when the analyst helps the patient to discover and valorize emotional elements that have not yet been digested by their objects and thereby facilitate their metabolization. Similarly, I believe that our primary task is to understand the emotional world of the adolescent, and in that sense, I emphasize the way in which the family has affected and still exists within the adolescent's psyche. Thus, I consider my task is to introduce the adolescent to his or her own emotional truth, which then enables the maturation and growth of his/her mind.

When I work with an adolescent, I work in collaboration with a colleague who treats the parents while I establish a relationship with the adolescent. We decide the conditions and ground rules for the therapeutic setting, including the number of sessions per week, the kind of communication that may take place outside the session, above all respecting the confidentiality of the patient. In order to choose what is significant and what is not; what makes sense and what does not; what would be truth and what is not, I seek to promote intersubjective transformative processes in the service of the adolescent patient, encouraging his/her emotional growth, but never forgetting the differences in role and power between us. As an analyst in the service of an adolescent patient, I consider that trust is essential to the analytical process and that, above and beyond all other considerations, I must work to establish, maintain and protect that trust in order to be able to penetrate the surface noise of the troubled adolescent and wait for the unconscious phantasy to emerge.

The patient under consideration, Annie, has been having a negative therapeutic reaction, possibly because something was either missing or incongruent within the analytical process. And precisely for that reason, we are thinking about and reconsidering the process, particularly the active inclusion of the parents. Annie grew up in a family with high expectations that she had conformed to until she reached adolescence. She came to analysis full of pain and desperation after an emotional breakdown. Annie fluctuated between being a competent "young woman" (false self) and a destructive adolescent when she felt overwhelmed and unable to manage her emotions and live up to the unconscious expectations she had for herself and her family had for her. Feeling oppressed and frustrated, she likely had an unconscious hope of meeting a receptive object, located in time and space, that would understand her contradictions, her turmoil and promote her emotional growth. I believe, through her actions, she was reproducing the inconsistencies within her family, oscillating between adaptation and disorganization which had produced inadequate defenses and did not promote differentiation and separation of her as an individual. Her family was poorly equipped and not sufficiently flexible to contain the emotional turbulence of Annie, who had lost her direction. Quite clearly Annie was in crisis, so too were her parents.

Such a complex situation, with multiple layers of anxiety, conflict, suffering and desperation would be, in my opinion, an overwhelming task for any single analyst to manage and contain, not to mention digest and transform. In this way, I advocate keeping parents physically at arm's length, but emotionally inside the room.

Commentary 2

It is very special to have the opportunity to discuss material and share our experiences. The task of discussing this case may seem, at first sight, simple, but is far from being an obvious one. In preparation for doing so, I have been thinking about my practice with adolescents and their parents in a special way. In order to bounce ideas around, I invited some psychoanalyst friends who also work with adolescents

215

to review our practice during the last twenty-five years. We soon realized that much has changed in our practice in the last decades, but we still have a lot of doubts. I am relieved that we still don't have formulaic solutions to apply to all situations; this is one of the riches of the psychoanalytical thinking that we must preserve, it is the very nature of psychoanalysis.

While psychoanalysis, theory and practice, has its main axis, there are a lot of different psychoanalytic cultures, following the history of each place and the local culture. My colleagues and I started working with children and adolescents in a Kleinian way, with a lot of content interpretations and with direct transference interpretations of every moment of the session. In the past few years, the ideas of post-Kleinian authors, along with those of Bion and Winnicott, have joined our main frame of reference. Nowadays, we include the thinking of a wide range of authors, but we can consider that we work mainly in a line composed by Freud-Klein-Bion, with an increased space for the idea of intersubjective field, first established by Baranger and developed with creativity by Ogden and Ferro, among others.

What does it mean in practice? Mainly, that the focus is on the emotional experience of the session co-constructed by both patient and analyst and that this is our main source of data. The model of Matte-Blanco (1959) about the bi-logic function of the mind is present: we, as analysts, need the symmetric mode, the non-Aristotelian logic (primary process) to perceive the affective climate of the session and we need the asymmetric mode (secondary process) to decide to formulate an interpretation (even a silence). Our feelings are the most important guides, because this is the only way to capture what is not conscious, what cannot be grasped by logical thinking. Intuition, the possibility to know without using reason, becomes a fundamental tool of observation in our work. During a session we don't observe only the patient, but also the various ways that we feel about him. The idea follows quantum physics, where the observer participates and directly influences the experience. There are also changes in the mode of perceiving the psychoanalytic task: more than interpreting content per se is emphasis on the way the psychic apparatus deals with stimuli. The patient needs a mental container able to contain emotions and symbolize them, "think" them out, and this becomes the main purpose of our work. In summary, I realized that we work in a much less deterministic manner, with a broader concept of causality, not searching for causes and explanations, but trying to help the patient to find his way of managing the challenges of life creatively.

Following this line of thinking, (that I provide here in a very brief summary), there are, of course, technical changes in our way of working with patients of all ages. The systematic transference interpretation, as a repetition of old patterns in the here and now of the session, is not the main instrument of work. Along with the traditional concept of transference, we work with the idea of "relations," more or less in the sense used by Freud in the very beginning, when he talked about transferences, in the plural, trying to follow the various ways of relating shown and experienced during a session. The almost obsession with transference interpretation, relating all contents with the analyst is part of our past, at least in great part of our psychoanalysts' group. The kind and the frequency of interpretation must be suitable to the patient's conditions at each moment, and the patient is our best colleague, pointing us to how he feels about our way of working with him, what we say, how and when we say it, our silences, etc. As I said before, more than interpreting contents, it is the ways the patient deals with his feelings/thinking (seen as a continuum) that is emphasized. The concept of neutrality focuses on a reflective, non-judgmental and non-intrusive mental attitude of the analyst, more than the traditional model of the neutral analyst who cannot smile or answer if asked whether he watched a movie or not. It is what we transmit with our attitude, tone of voice, etc., that constitute the frame that will determine the way our words will be understood.

The understanding is constructed together with the patient and not from a position of the one who knows the "truth." This presupposes a humble position of the analyst. We work today with a more flexible technique, which is easier and more difficult at the same time. At the same time that it broadens our resources, and makes it possible to work without a severe psychoanalytic superego controlling us, it also increases our responsibility, demanding an additional psychic work in dealing with our feelings and our desires, to use them to help the patient to find his way, trying not to conduct him or imposing, even unconsciously, our own vision of what would be better for him.

Having described in a very brief summary, my way of understanding the psychoanalytic work, it is time to ask: And what about the work with adolescents and their parents?

All that I said before about the changes in our way of working, is also suitable for adolescents, but there is, of course, some specificity. Working with adolescents requires a much more flexible technique, and a much more spontaneous way of relating during the sessions.

It is important to underline that adolescents were not considered suitable for analysis until relatively recently, for reasons that we all know. It is only when the psychoanalytic theory of technique expands the idea of transference to include, besides the traditional concept, all kinds of patient/analyst relations, that adolescents become more analytic patients. So, we probably still need more experience, observation and discussion about the specificity of adolescents' treatment. We came to perceive that we commonly base our decision about the way to proceed with parents on a case-by-case analysis.

We didn't usually refer the parents to another therapist, as others have done, but this is not a theoretical position; that is to say, we are not against this way of working with parents. While this practice seems to protect the setting with the adolescent, it brings the possibility of increasing dissociation and creates a new "mingle" setting. We don't treat the parents or see them regularly as a rule. It all depends on the severity of the adolescent condition; of the parent's conditions and motivation and the way we feel about the entire situation.

The difficulty, when facing the problem of how to work with parents, is to establish a general rule. In my point of view, it all depends on the situation. The more severe the case, probably we need more working with parents. However, in any of these cases, there are some challenges to face. It is inevitable that we identify ourselves with the parents or with the adolescent and it demands consciousness of these feelings in order not to act them out. In this case, it is remarkable how the therapist speaks with the parents without blaming them. Of course, I'm not talking about doing that in an explicit manner, but the infinite pre-verbal ways of transmitting culpability.

It is also indispensable that we have clearly in mind that we cannot be better parents than the parents. Our narcissistic needs make us vulnerable to this illusion, to know the best way to behave, the best family model for that adolescent, etc. I thought about this when I read in the report that the aim is helping them to be better parents for Annie. Do we really know what is better? The therapist worked with great sensitivity, but I am thinking as a general rule. I miss in the report the presence of the therapist's feelings in such an anxiety-promoting situation. Probably it is the way the report is written; everyone can imagine the suffering and the containing capacity of the analyst to face this case. We can also imagine the amount of doubts the therapist must have had: What to do when Annie left her home? How to speak with the parents about her sexual activity? And, etc., etc. When we write a report, the analyst's feelings are essential. Maybe this is one of our differences; the role that we attribute to the analyst's feelings and thinking during the process, not as accessories, but as essential to understand the analytic process.

It is also essential while talking with parents to have in mind what we expect to achieve and all the limitations of this setting. If it is hard to achieve changes in a setting of high frequency with the assignment of the patient who attributes to the analyst the role of searching for the unknown and, many times, what he doesn't want to know, what can we expect with parents, who are not there to be treated?

Commentary 3

It is always a pleasure to read of skillful work that confirms the value of psychoanalytic interventions. When we hear that it is difficult to get parents to cooperate with treatment, perhaps we need to turn the lens on what is difficult in us, especially when we hear of such assured work in what seemed like very difficult circumstance that brings such fast results. My discussion will be clinical rather than theoretical or technical.

I have focused on the analyst's work without going very wide, but it is important to contextualize the work as of a particular genre not always subscribed to in other orientations round the world where the parents might be seen by another analyst. The Novicks (Novick, K.K. and Novick, J. 2005) have very clearly put their reasons why they believe that involving parents makes child therapy work, and as a supervisor I have seen work by other analysts and candidates that is transformed by involving parents in the way that the Novicks describe. (I also think the increasing direct work with infants in infant-parent therapy, which often extends long after infancy, has indirectly supported this trend.)

The quality of the disturbance the girl presents with is enormously serious with the suicide attempt, drugs, bingeing and body attacks and what I thought of as soul murder which was my initial response in quickly reading of the very difficult relationship with and between her parents.

The analyst achieves extremely impressive results, particularly what almost seems like characterological change in the parents within a very short timeframe. There is the additional problem of separated parents in acrimonious divorce proceedings and the analyst works appropriately to see them together and, later, to see them separately. We get little overt description of how the analyst experiences the parents, what their strengths might be; yet the analyst describes the enacted sadism with a clear eye and still retains the capacity to find some likeability in them, particularly while being able to see the desperateness behind the defenses: Father's attacks, vicious at times, and the parents' collusion, etc. The extraordinary rapidity of the parents' responses to the analyst's interpretations is a tribute to the analyst's clear sightedness as well as the capacity to convey insights in a way that results in them having an almost instantly mutative effect.

We hear how by urging the parents to speak calmly instead of through their angry outbursts, the analyst is again effective, as, soon after, the parents are able to remain relatively calm and compassionate. I presumed the parents' transference to the analyst was ultra-positive and desperate. So, there are early, "honeymoon" changes in the parents stemming from this transference which carries the parent work here.

Annie's enacting her need for parental love in random sexual encounters forces this into the analysis and into the parent work, culminating in the analyst interpreting to the father that Annie's use of sex was not experienced as pleasurable by her but functioned as a punishment. This comes over as a somewhat bald, yet clearly seminal interpretation, and one that leads to a cascade of change. I was reminded of Serge Lebovici's charismatic way of working, as for example when he described making interpretations and relying on his authority to bring about therapeutic change—I don't think Annie's analyst did exactly that but there is a quality of firmness which would bring about a sense of feeling held by this analyst.

Next, we see a tsunami of negative therapeutic reaction in both the father and then the daughter. Father is very vulnerable and volatile yet responds immediately to an interpretation, as though the analyst is an authoritative parent or parent figure from his childhood; certainly, the kind of figure who could bring about instant change that he wished in regard to his attacks on his daughter. Then Annie regresses big-time and disappears and however helpful an enactment it will turn out to be in understanding how she felt as an infant that her parents disappeared for her, the overarching priority is to keep her safe when, in the past, she has played so fast and loose with her own life and safety. Here we see the analyst making really strong recommendations, well outside the usual things we have to do as analysts, such as advising the parents not to give their daughter money and to tell her they will call the police. Whatever hesitation some analysts may have about telling the parents to get the police, it is clearly effective in this case—because it was needed?

Next, mother, as a character, takes center stage. First, the analyst, in the absence of the patient, needs to use mother to interpret; desperate times need desperate means. However, this enables mother to claim her daughter in a more unambivalent way, which then moved into a more collusive, pre-oedipal trying to claim her daughter back from the analyst who then needed to make a quick, bare transference interpretation, at least to the mother, about how denying her guilt had the result of not protecting Annie from her father when she was little. Here a perhaps more powerful interpretation than one usually hears about in parent work is absolutely needed to protect the analysis.

The analyst had to summarize that the parents' guilt was faced and grieved with this seeming to happen with very quick results.

When Annie and her mother work through a sequence of Annie's disintegration when mother is distressed and to counter feeling helpless, Annie, in part, parentified mother, and then attempted to commit suicide, unconsciously to bring the parents together. This new understanding and the relief it brought led to an immediate attempt to castrate the analyst and the work done up until that point, by pretending everything was all right. As usual, a firm and authoritative interpretation brought an immediate response from patient and parents. I guess by this point it was clear to the analyst and also available for the patient and the family's understanding about an almost pseudo-flight to health, bringing in part enormous relief that the self and the parents were not collapsing, and passing the collapsed self onto the analyst.

The analyst was even then able in the parent work to point back to what may have been catastrophizing defenses that both mother and daughter used in Annie's infancy, as well as mother's possible dissociation leading to Annie's difficulties in having a reliably functioning self-reflective mind. This seems to be beyond the usual stuff one hears about in much work in helping parents to become the best parents they can, but I am convinced of the likely helpfulness and probable "rightness" of this interpretive offering. The mother had appeared not to be much in Annie's inner world; the parents may also have "handed over" their daughter to the analyst or the analyst had such personal and moral authority that they "crumbled" before it—the British Independents write about being the analyst that the patient needs; I think that the analyst has shown us about being the analyst for the *parents* that *the parents* need. As discussant, that I have found myself only discussing and not critiquing is, I think, testament to the work.

Editorial Reflections

The commentaries for this chapter depict the range of attitudes often encountered when analysts are asked to opine regarding whether and/or how to work concurrently with the parents of a child or adolescent in treatment. Moreover, the authors of the commentaries also provide insight into the evolution of thinking on this topic as portrayed in the analytic literature.

The first commentator acknowledges the myriad ways that parents are involved when their adolescent child is accepted into treatment, noting "the anxiety, the pain, the confusion and contradictions that most probably emanate from the family." Confronting the analyst are "two sets of traumatized people, adolescents and parents, whose psychic realities may overwhelm the analyst, outstripping the analyst's capacity to listen." Does the adolescent patient need to feel the separation and security of a private space away from the parents in order to help consolidate a stronger sense of independence and personal identity? The attitudes of Klein (1932) and Winnicott (1965) are reviewed to show how both emphasized the role and the quality of the private analytic-patient relationship. It is noted that Klein's advice was "to maintain the separation between the analysis of the adolescent and contact with the parents, keeping the latter to a minimum while the analysis of the adolescent is ongoing, perhaps *only enough to maintain their support for the treatment.*" For this commentator, and indeed for many others, historically and currently the solution has been to "work in collaboration with a colleague who treats the parents while I [the commentator] establish a relationship with the adolescent." This is an excellent summary of a classical Kleinian position.

The second commentator reviews a progression in work with children shared with colleagues that began with being influenced by Klein, then by post-Kleinian authors (including Bion and Winnicott), and by Freud and then by more recent authors writing about the intersubjective field. Having come to a way of working that is "less deterministic," the commentator asks, "What about the work with adolescents and their parents?" The reported answer is, "We commonly base our decision about the way to proceed with parents, on a case-by-case analysis." Regarding the practice of referring the parents to another therapist, the second commentator states, "While this practice seems to protect the setting with the adolescent, it brings the possibility of increasing dissociation and creates a new 'mingle' setting."

So, from a strongly expressed contemporary Kleinian view we come to former Kleinians who have become more flexible, aware too of the dangers of splitting the treatment, and more open to other influences on child and adolescent functioning, like the influence of parents.

Continuing the progression, the third commentator opens with the statement, "When we hear that it is difficult to get parents to cooperate with treatment, perhaps we need to turn the lens on what is difficult in us, especially when we hear of such assured work in what seemed like very difficult circumstance that brings such fast results." The focus here is on the case vignette and the analyst's responses to

Annie's troubles and the parents' needs. After reviewing the myriad interactions reported in the case vignette between the analyst, the patient, and her parents, the commentator concludes, "This seems to be beyond the usual stuff one hears about in much work in helping parents to become the best parents they can, but I am convinced of the likely helpfulness and probable 'rightness' of this interpretive offering."

This chapter lays out for us the areas of perennial tension inherent in our inevitable interactions with the parents of child and adolescent patients. We cannot avoid parents, but should we be trying to? We are challenged by the material of this chapter to estimate the relative costs and gains of regular concurrent parent work in relation to transferences and counter-transferences/reactions in all parties, confidentiality and the nuances of privacy and secrecy, and what we might characterize as the ambivalent feelings of therapists in regard to the balance in our efforts between psychic and external realities.

Additionally, we are challenged by the underlying assumptions regarding the tasks of adolescence and the techniques which follow from such assumptions. Privileging the technique of separation of adolescent and parent work implies continuing to hold the assumption that the main task of adolescence is separation from parents, as conceptualized by many psychoanalysts. If, however, the task is transformation of the parent-child relationship, undertaken from the side of both child and parents, then concurrent parent work is seen as essential. See Novick, K.K. and Novick, J. (2013) for more extended discussion of concurrent work with parents of adolescents.

CHAPTER TEN

RECONFIGURING PARENT WORK

Adolescents

Clinical Vignette

Adolescence brings many challenges, including reframing of the psychic structure, increased drive activation, continuous body modification, mourning for earlier phases, individuation from primary objects, and greater pressure from the alternative virtual world outside the family. What needs to happen in the psychic apparatus in order to go through the latency period and become capable of meeting the demands of adolescence? When we think specifically of the development of girls at this time, we can ask what they need from the primary parent-child relationship, particularly from the mother, where both identification and differentiation are part of the task, to negotiate the adolescent passage.

In adolescence the bodies of both mother and daughter have changed and continue to change. Each reflects herself in the other, joining the past, the present, and the future of their feminine identities. Feelings and conflicts related to the new body image of the girl may be relieved with the presence of an empathic mother who accepts her own bodily changes. But feelings of loss and depression may be intensified if the mother struggles with her own identity and with negotiating new iterations of oedipal rivalry and self-definition.

The analytic task with female adolescents is complex and unpredictable. Classical technique has focused mostly on individual adolescent development, leaving parents out. Given the importance of transforming the mother-daughter relationship for the daughter's future autonomy and identity, it seems necessary to include parents in the therapeutic process. Leaving the mother out breaks the relationship rather than integrating and transforming it.

Creativity is important in structuring the analytic situation so as to offer each patient what they need, sometimes providing something different from what they have received in their lives or in other treatments. In some cases, I suggest a three-party setup, what I call a "binomial treatment model" that respects the individuality of each person but integrates rather than disintegrates. The goal is the bond between parent and child. The organized collective transference allows words to modify the object relationships in this attachment situation.

Here are some examples:

Tita

From the first contact about fifteen-year-old Tita, her mother requested individual sessions for herself, seeming to seek attention and intruding on Tita's therapeutic space. Tita was isolated, without many friends, critical of everyone, overweight, and rebellious with authority figures. The youngest in her family, with siblings ten and twelve years older, the product of an unplanned pregnancy, Tita felt overlooked, as if she had no secure place in the family; indeed, she had never had her own room, always sleeping instead in the study.

Rather than establishing a treatment plan with only separate sessions for Tita, alongside regular concurrent parent sessions, I proposed mother/daughter binomial work, in which I saw Tita by herself twice a week and spent a third session each week with both Tita and her mother. Tita agreed happily to this. This created a therapeutic space where Tita and her mother gradually became able to share their anxieties with each other and used my help to establish more realistic boundaries.

Being in the room with Tita and her mother allowed me to experience anger and frustration with Tita's mother's controlling and overbearing attitude and voice the impact of each on the other in real time. At the same time, I was able to feel the mother's wish to succeed with this youngest child, and to support her in appreciating Tita in her own right.

Early in the treatment, at the twenty-fourth session, Tita's grand-mother appeared as well. She had wanted to attend to talk about the breast reduction surgery she was encouraging for Tita "when she finally lost weight," so that "she would look better." I think she sought to enlist me in this bodily intervention. I was able to identify inter-generational patterns of defense by action and avoidance of inner experience, which Tita and I spent much time on in her own sessions. Tita concluded that she wanted to think about her school exams at this point and not focus on breast surgery.

Once Tita's father appeared at a joint session when the mother was out of town, and shared stories of his childhood that resonated powerfully for Tita. Their sharing of psychic pain, along with their common feeling of annoyance and resistance to mother's domination, brought them closer together, with good effects on Tita's self-esteem. Tita's parents became closer to each other, Tita more secure, and her mother less intrusive.

My conjecture is that the binomial model kept the powerful forces within the containment of the therapeutic space; without my seeing them together, it might have been easier for the mother to undermine Tita's own treatment, setting up an adversarial situation between the treatment and the family, as well as a loyalty conflict for Tita. Her father's participation opened up alternatives for Tita in the safety of the shared sessions, again possibly preventing splitting.

Maria

My phone rang and it was a Skype call from an ex-patient who had moved to a distant city four years ago. We had a two-year psychotherapy that had helped him very much with his severe anxiety, the first half in person, and the second half after his move through Skype. Now his fourteen-year-old daughter was suffering from panic attacks and multiple fears that interfered with her daily life, her friendships, and her activities. He asked, "Could you please work with my daughter? She is having a bad time and you were really helpful to me, so I am sure you can help her. You can work through Skype and she will be fine with that."

I replied that we could give that a try and then evaluate the whole situation. The first Skype appointment included both parents and Maria and her sister. In the next one, I met with Maria and her mother and it became clear that both were struggling with separation anxiety and multiple meanings of autonomous functioning. After that I worked with Maria alone in her room on Skype, interspersed with regular sessions that included her mother. In those her mother was able to express more explicitly her own fears of growing apart from Maria if she allowed her greater autonomy. Through this work, both parents somewhat relaxed their vigilance, and Maria began to tolerate staying home alone in the evening, despite the scary noises that worried her.

Here too it seemed to me that we would be less likely to be effective in addressing the patient's struggles and her mother's role in them unless we could engage them both in a shared effort to examine their entangled transferences and dependencies on each other, while addressing Maria's own reluctance to grow up in her individual sessions. The different ways that each person made use of Skype became a potent metaphor for thinking together about closeness and distance, and closeness over distance and separateness.

Commentary 1

The idea of parent work done concurrently with individual psychoanalytic work with children and adolescents was a radical departure from standard training in both classical and Kleinian-informed training programs (Novick, K.K. and Novick, J. 2005). Gradually concurrent parent work has become more accepted, as seen in the current child analytic literature, but concurrent parent work with parents of adolescents remains a controversial topic. The main objections to concurrent work with parents of adolescents are issues of confidentiality and the fundamental assumption that the main task of adolescence is separation from parents.

This brief methodological and clinical description addresses the major assumption that the goal of adolescence is separation by positing instead the centrality of "transforming" the parent child relationship. An important contribution is the author's focus on the female adolescent.

The analyst notes the complexity and unpredictability of work with female adolescents and adds that classical technique has focused on the individual while leaving the parent out. The author says, "Given the importance of transforming the mother-daughter relationship for the daughter's future autonomy and identity, it seems necessary to include parents in the therapeutic process. Leaving the mother out breaks the relationship rather than integrating and transforming it." The analyst goes on to stress the importance of being creative in order "to structure the analytic situation so as to offer each patient what they need…"

The author seems to be advocating flexibility and sets up a variant on working with parents (binomial treatment model) as an alternative model. The editors of this volume describe concurrent parent work as an evolving technique, emerging in each case from the needs of the particular parents and children, but all resting on the assumption that parents and children are involved in a lifelong complex interaction which is constantly transformed by changing needs and can be a major source of strength or pathology for both.

The analyst describes a form of concurrent parent work in which the adolescent female is seen in private for one or two sessions per week and then seen together with mother (sometimes others) for one session per week. The analyst presents two brief vignettes to illustrate the efficacy of this approach.

In the first one, Tita, a fifteen-year-old, was seen by herself twice a week and she and mother met together with the analyst one time per week. The author notes that Tita "agreed happily" with this arrangement, further evidence that adolescents are not always seeking therapy to separate from their parents. This finding is similar to that made by the Novicks in their paper on concurrent parent work with late adolescents (Novick, K.K. and Novick, J. 2013).

Another validating finding is that the one session Tita had with her father had a galvanizing impact on Tita's self-esteem and on the marital relationship. The role of fathers in psychoanalytic work with adolescents needs further attention and this example of concurrent parent work further underscores the need for increased focus on the importance of fathers to both boys and girls.

The analyst describes how the sessions with mother and Tita gave the analyst firsthand experience of anger and frustration due to mother's controlling and overbearing attitude. At the same time, she began to appreciate the mother's positive feelings for her daughter and her attempts to support her growth. This echoes my experience when I work with the parents of my adolescent patients. They feel confirmed, validated and then willing to accept my positive perceptions of their parents. It also allows me to share negative views and question their need to protect parents from legitimate criticism.

The second case gives us another example of the analyst's flexibility as the "binomial" form of concurrent parent work is done by Skype. The work illustrates how powerful this binomial form of parent work can be. We see here the complex interaction of similar conflicts in mother and child.

What comes across in this brief description of the theory and practice of the "binomial treatment model" is that the analyst is committed to the proposition that children and parents are in a lifelong complex interaction. As Erna Furman said about the parent-child relationship it is, "a complex overdetermined interaction in which two closely interwoven personalities complement each other in various ever-changing unconscious ways" (1995, p. 25). If one is committed to this proposition, as the author of the paper clearly is, then it follows that concurrent parent work, in whatever form, must be part of every child or adolescent treatment.

Commentary 2

At the start of this brief but thought-provoking chapter, the author notes the many challenges of adolescence, "including reframing of the psychic structure, increased drive activation, continuous body modification, mourning for earlier phases, individuation from primary objects, and greater pressure from the alternative virtual world outside the family." It is observed that "Classical technique has focused mostly on individual adolescent development, leaving parents out." While, on the surface, this comment refers to who the "patient" is in the clinical work that ensues, the author alludes to an important developmental parallel process.

Even as adolescents, both boys and girls, are experiencing the challenges noted in the quote above, so too are their parents experiencing and struggling to negotiate their own developmental transitions. While it is mentioned that "the bodies of both mother and daughter have changed and continue to change," we might similarly note how such changes simultaneously occur in fathers and sons, as well. For both the mothers and the fathers of adolescents, they too are dealing with myriad developmental changes, both physical/bodily changes and emotional ones. They are moving into mature, later adulthood with bodies that are becoming less lithe and limber and with thoughts of a life ahead that begins to loom more in terms of the years they have left instead of the boundless future yet to come. (For some, more, but for most, some, there are feelings of jealousy and even resentment as they watch their recently dependent children seem to charge toward adulthood and independence.) This is an important point but perhaps it needs to be expressed more clearly. Perhaps we can say, "All parents react to the child's growth with a mixture of pride, pleasure, anxiety, envy, jealousy and resentment. It may be the balance of these feelings which can interfere or allow progressive transformation of each person in the parent-child system. Concurrent parent work could be an essential factor in changing the balance of feelings and so enabling progressive growth."

I would further assert (and suspect that the author would agree) that, just as it is stressed that, regarding girls, we must consider what they particularly need from their relationship with their mother, this is also true for boys; and for both boys and girls there are particular needs they have in their relationships with their fathers.

Thus, while we often think of the "adolescent transformation" occurring within the child, to the extent to which parents rework and further their own development by virtue of the experiences of parenting their children, they too need to transform their ties to their children, a process for which they might need help.

In support of these mutual processes evolving, the containing presence of an analyst, as in the "binomial treatment model" case vignettes reported, may prove helpful to adolescents and parents alike. The analyst describes the process as one that "respects the individuality of each person but integrates rather than disintegrates. The goal is the bond between parent and child."

In the case of fifteen-year-old Tita, it was her mother who, from the outset, "requested individual sessions for herself, seeming to seek attention and intruding on Tita's therapeutic space," a possible signaling of the mother's awareness of her need for assistance in "transforming" her libidinal ties to her daughter. "A third session each week with both Tita and her mother ... created a therapeutic space where ... (they) gradually became able to share their anxieties with each other and used my help to establish more realistic boundaries." The analyst describes being able to experience, first-hand, "the mother's controlling and overbearing attitude, and voice the impact of each on the other in real time. At the same time, I was able to feel the mother's wish to succeed with this youngest child, and to support her in appreciating Tita in her own right."

The analyst's role as a container was also apparent when Tita's grandmother attended a session to advocate for Tita undergoing breast reduction surgery. "I was able to identify inter-generational patterns of defense by action and avoidance of inner experience, which Tita and I spent much time on in her own sessions. Tita concluded that she wanted to think about her school exams at this point and not focus on breast surgery."

When Tita's father joined a session while her mother was away, the analyst could be present as he shared stories of his childhood and observed how these were poignantly received by Tita. Subsequently, father and daughter grew closer (as did the parents with each other) and Tita's self-esteem improved as she came to feel more secure and her mother less intrusive. In this example in particular, one can see how a reworking of revived oedipal conflicts, perhaps among all three, was supported.

There appears to be another valuable consequence of this intervention model, one that may impact and support a transformation in the quality of the attachment relationship between an adolescent and his or her parents. The analyst states, "The organized collective transference allows words to modify the object relationships in this attachment situation." It has often been observed that an adolescent who has grown up in the milieu of a "non-secure" (or at least, an "insufficiently secure") mutual attachment relationship with a parent (or parents) has greater difficulty attaining an enduring adolescent-to-mature-adulthood transformation, one that may even modulate the future attachment potential of a developing adolescent.

As with the case of Tita, in the second vignette of Maria, a parent—this time the father who had himself been treated by the analyst—reached out for help for his daughter. In the first session the analyst met, via Skype, with not only Maria but with both her parents and her sister as well. Subsequent work continued both individually with Maria and conjointly with her and her mother. Again, in the analyst's view, "we would be less likely to be effective in addressing the patient's struggles and her mother's role in them unless we could engage them both in a shared effort to examine their entangled transferences and dependencies on each other, while addressing Maria's own reluctance to grow up in her individual sessions."

The type of concurrent/conjoint work with adolescent and parent(s) described in this chapter may not be ideal for use in all cases. However, when the analyst can feel comfortable with the model and when the patient and parents can participate, it may provide a very effective way to move toward restoration of progressive development and the disruption of a transgenerational pattern of non-secure based attachments within a family.

Editorial Reflections

An alternative model of including parents as partners in the work on behalf of adolescent patients is described in this brief chapter. What unites the binomial model with forms of concurrent parent work described in other contributions is that it is, as the author states, "A model that integrates rather than disintegrates." This is a fine statement of the aims of all the variations on the theme to be found in this casebook. The analyst's flexibility is evident, "we could give that a try." Analysts working with children, adolescents, and their families may sometimes feel reluctantly forced to give some out-of-the-ordinary thing a try, only to be surprised by unexpected and productive results. The willingness to agree to Skype sessions is one example that shows the potential advantageous uses of the technologies that people of all ages now consider more "ordinary" than some analysts do.

The experiences described by analysts who provide parent-infant psychotherapy may have at some level influenced this analyst to be less worried about trying something new with the families of the two teenaged girls described here, in this instance seeing various family members together with the patient. Those who observe infants in their homes grow accustomed to siblings and grandparents coming in and out, as happened in the case vignettes offered.

Readers of this chapter might ask whether the binomial model discussed herein is more akin to family therapy than to psychoanalysis. It has been said that psychoanalysis happens when there is a psychoanalyst doing the work. A close look at the psychoanalytic thinking behind the model presented is a good illustration of this. The analyst's thinking includes consideration of the body and drives, attachment, and the reworking of oedipal relationships. Ideas about containment, dependency, transferences, and providing what the patient needs are explicitly included as part of the technique in this model, as is the case in more traditional concurrent parent work. We could consider using the criterion of what contributes to accomplishing the dual goals of treatment for assessing the relevance and utility of innovative treatment structures. Does the treatment structure promote the restoration of the child to the path of progressive development and does it contribute to the transformation and strengthening of the parent-child relationship?

Both of those who wrote commentaries for this chapter speak about the "transformations" that affect adolescents, parents of adolescents, and the evolving parent-adolescent relationship. One underscores a fundamental principle of working with parents, that is, the recognition that "children and parents are engaged in a lifelong, complex interaction." Here again we can think about the grandmother who shows up to offer an opinion on what her daughter's daughter ought to do. The other commentator points out that work on attachment in adolescence "may even modulate the future attachment potential" into the next generation.

CHAPTER ELEVEN

THE ADULT ATTACHMENT INTERVIEW: CREATING A THERAPEUTIC ALLIANCE

Adolescent

Clinical Vignette

Assessment in adolescence raises complex and specific challenges, aimed at achieving a reliable and shared view of the previous developmental pathways as well as of the adolescent's vulnerabilities and resources. This reliable and shared view should lead up "naturally" to treatment indications—whenever treatment is deemed necessary—so that such indications are well understood and accepted by the adolescents and their parents.

Parents are essential participants and a fundamental resource during the assessment and treatment of their adolescent child. How parents see their adolescent child—their image of the child—is influenced by the parents' needs, expectations and fears, which may make it difficult for them to recognize their real child. Their image of their child will be influenced by their relational past, particularly by how they experienced and worked through the vicissitudes of their own adolescence.

During the assessment phase, emphasis is placed on elucidating the parents' perceptions of their child's image, as mirrored back to him. This process of consultation with parents, parallel to the adolescent's assessment, makes it possible to lay the basis for a preliminary working alliance with them. This alliance would enable them to better understand and accept the indication for treatment for their child, if necessary. In some instances, assessment may also result in recommending further work with the parents, parallel to the adolescent's treatment, in order to help them cope with changes and support their child's development from a new perspective.

It is therefore extremely important, already in the assessment phase, to build a relationship which may broaden, in the adolescents and their parents, the awareness of their problems, in an intersubjective framework. In other words, it is important that a preliminary working alliance be established. Developing a preliminary working alliance and broadening the adolescent's awareness during assessment are important factors of self-integration. Work should focus on the development of a self-image and on the conflicting issues emerging from the adolescent's use of the individuation processes.

Diana's mother looked for help for her sixteen-year-old daughter, who appeared depressed and helpless to her. Diana had been suffering from a severe eating disorder for two years, with alternating episodes of anorexia and bulimia. Her mother had split up from her husband three years before. Diana regularly witnessed violent rows between her parents and she was sometimes beaten by her father when she tried to defend her mother. After her parents' separation, Diana lived only with her mother (she was an only child) and became more and more aggressive with her. At the same time, she became extremely clinging, holding on to her mother and controlling her.

In the first interview, the mother appeared preoccupied, scared, and also angry at her daughter. From the very start, she gave contradictory accounts of Diana and their relationship. Mother portrayed herself as a helpless victim in her relationship with her husband, whom she described as a "disgusting man," abusive towards her and her daughter. She would comment she had fallen for it again, because in the past she had already had a horrible experience with a physically and even sexually abusive stepfather.

At the end of this first interview, the mother was asked to undertake an assessment process which included administering the Adult Attachment Interview (AAI) to her, in order to understand how her personal problem areas had affected and were affecting her relationship with her daughter and her development. The mother agreed to this plan. In the meantime, we would start consultation with her daughter and, subject to Diana's agreement, we would suggest the AAI to her as well.

The interview with the mother highlighted unresolved/ disorganised mental processes in her account of her past experiences of abuse. When she started talking about herself, her confused narratives filled all the space. The therapist was cornered, found it difficult to follow the thread of her talk. It was almost impossible to understand whom she was talking about and when some episodes had taken place.

Diana came unwillingly to the first interview. She looked in a state of intense pain. At the beginning, she would hardly talk, seemed to be deep in distressful thoughts. Then, crying and increasingly upset, she switched to accusing her mother of "harassing" her. It was not she who needed help, but her mother!

However, when she was offered the interview and told that it had been administered also to her mother and that its results might provide some indication about how to improve their relationship, Diana suddenly appeared intrigued and cooperative. In the first part of the interview, her answers to the questions about her childhood experiences were extremely vague, revealing a dismissing state of mind. That was the defensive style Diana had been using since she was a child to defend herself from potentially overwhelming feelings. However, later in the interview, when the most recent episodes of abuse perpetrated by her father emerged, Diana's answers showed disoriented traits, slips of tongue, failing logic and alteration of coherence, which are typical of individuals classified as "Unresolved/Disorganized."

At the end of the assessment, after duly considering and discussing some of her answers which showed clear analogies between mother and daughter, Diana was referred for analytic treatment. The work already done together had generated a preliminary alliance with Diana and her mother, both empathically and in terms of greater understanding of the meaning of some interactive behaviors.

Diana accepted and treatment was started. Treatment was recommended to her mother too, though with another psychotherapist, in order to help her work through her past traumas and manage the violent feelings aroused by her daughter's adolescence. Moreover, the analyst agreed with Diana that he would see her mother periodically to try and develop a collaborative relationship with her and to reduce the dysfunctional aspects in the mother-daughter relationship. It is worth stressing (as have Novick, K. K. and Novick, K. 2005) that therapeutic work with this type of adolescent is useless if it is not paralleled by an intervention with the parents, who would otherwise continue to threaten the therapeutic process.

With this clinical vignette, I have tried to illustrate how this assessment model implies a focus not only on the adolescent's but also on her parents' mental functioning and, in particular, on how their modalities of functioning are influenced by the internalized relationships of their recent and remote past.

During this assessment process, in analyzing what emerges from the interviews and from the AAI, the therapist may investigate the "relational dispositions" that are enacted in the system and in the setting. It is worth stressing that specific and comprehensive training is required to administer the AAI and to work out its classifications. On the other hand, I also believe that in-depth knowledge of this approach may provide new theoretical perspectives and technical skills to supplement the armamentarium of any psychoanalyst who deals with children in all phases of development and in particular in adolescence.

The assessment model I have outlined here is aimed at developing a preliminary working alliance with the adolescent and his parents, so that all of them can be helped to invest in their own and in the others' potential. In some cases, this preliminary working alliance should at least lead the parents to allow the adolescent to "be with" the therapist, thus making an exchange between minds possible. In general, this model recommends the psychotherapist to provide a new relational experience already in the assessment phase.

The experience offered by the therapist, as a new, kindly disposed object in a safe context, is grounded on the qualities of secure attachment (acceptance, empathy, respect, curiosity, playfulness, coherence) and takes into account the adolescent's interactive modalities which tend to be repeated, while "gently" differentiating from them. In due time, the therapist also supplies his reflective capacity to the adolescent in order for them to make sense—

together—of feelings, thoughts and behaviors, and to try to achieve greater integration.

This model implies deeper and broader parental involvement in the assessment, in comparison with other psychoanalytic models used to assess adolescents. The key role of the parents as advocates for their child, even in adolescence, is thus recognized. This role is characterized by the history of their emotional bonds with their child and by the relational modalities that have developed in the course of time.

The Adult Attachment Interview was developed to investigate the transgenerational dimension of attachment relationships. In other words, as underlined by other authors (Fonagy et al. 1993), the AAI was designed to "measure the ghosts" present in the spaces of these relationships.

Keeping this in mind and considering how important it is to involve parents in the assessment and treatment of their adolescent children, I suggested developing a clinical assessment approach that combines the assessment of the adolescent's and of his parents' attachment styles using the AAI. Realizing that our research on "non-clinical" samples had shown that the Interview was well accepted by the adolescents, we started a study on a clinical sample of anorexic adolescents, proposing the AAI to those young girls and their parents.

It should be noted that, with few exceptions, parents were also very willing to participate and be collaborative in the study. We came to realize that this interview is an extraordinary tool, in a clinical setting as well, to take the patient's history, while bringing into focus the adolescent's and her parents' states of mind and their interactive styles which tend to maintain and recreate the pre-established pattern (in particular, in the here and now of the relationship with the therapist). By merely administering the interview, it is often possible to establish a preliminary working alliance with the adolescent and her parents, who feel like they are being "recruited" in a useful process of reflection that involves reviewing the past, sometimes leading to early insights and early transformations. This attachment-based methodology allows us to explore, during the entire assessment, various aspects of the self, as well as other risk and protection factors unrelated to attachment.

The assessment methodology described above implies a focus on how the attachment relational patterns of the adolescent and of his parents influence and try to "activate," mostly unconsciously, specific types of emotional and behavioral responses in the therapist.

It is therefore important to determine whether there is a way of not responding to such demands coming from the adolescent and his parents and what reaction—i.e., what resistance—to such discrepancy in behaviors and representations is contributed by the therapist. From the beginning of the assessment, Arietta Slade (2008) proposes that therapists adopt an attitude of "sensitive flexibility," testing the possibility of gently countering the adolescent's and his parents' prevailing attachment style. It is also important to bear in mind that the therapist's own attachment organization plays a crucial role in determining whether her or his responses are matched or unmatched to the patient's style.

Commentary 1

From the first contact with parents who have called with concerns about their child, the analyst aims to build an alliance. To understand that all parents, regardless of their difficulties and shortcomings, are parenting their child in the best way they know how, aids in the analyst's empathy towards them and their situation and facilitates this process. The initial appointment with parents is a way to begin to ascertain what their concerns are, to explain the assessment process and what the analyst has to offer, and to convey the belief that analyst and parents are a team working together to help their child.

Obtaining a detailed developmental history is crucial to the assessment process and further fuels the working alliance. A developmental history is far more than a checklist of developmental milestones and significant events, as that in and of itself says very little. Rather, it is a process of gathering information within a context of the relationships within and between family members with the intent of understanding the whole child, not merely the symptoms or current concerns. A developmental history begins at the beginning, with parents sharing their individual histories and the history of the two of them as a couple, then proceeds with the story of the child. The pregnancy and how it came about, parents' hopes and wishes, what the pregnancy itself was like, what the situation in the family was like, how the relationships were at the time, all are part of this initial phase. The parents are then asked to go through, with open-ended questions by the analyst, the child's life, taking special note of various developmental phases and tasks aligned with a certain time of life. Issues such as different caretakers and separations are important to explore, as are the child's ability to tolerate frustration and deal with anxiety. The analyst attempts to comprehend the emotional lives of the child and his parents, and the nature of the relationships between them, which changes during periods of development and environmental circumstances. The way the parents' psychological makeup impacts the child is also important.

The analyst approaches this task with a framework in mind, understanding that what is presented is not usually a straight line, but a back and forth through various periods of life. This framework is based on the analyst's understanding of development, comprising knowledge about the aims and tasks of stages and hierarchies, of watershed points of reorganization, and of the regressions and progressions of the developmental process itself in all of its intricacies. Questions on the Adult Attachment Interview (George et al. 1985) can be helpful in orienting aspects of this framework, and when administered by a trained professional result in an attachment type, which is certainly helpful, but it is not the whole story.

Additional pieces of an evaluation come from the child himself. These diagnostic interviews are different than therapeutic sessions, and at times can be more directive. The analyst is curious about the child's assessment of his difficulties and his relationships, including those with the family and to the analyst. Older children or adolescents can be interviewed directly while, if it is a young child, this diagnostic interview process is done through play. At the same time, the analyst tries to understand the inner workings of the child, his object relationships, his defenses and conflicts, the way he manages or fails to manage his feelings, his level of anxiety and attitude toward it, to name a few areas of exploration. The analyst's framework is that of a Diagnostic Profile where specific categories of development are considered, for example the relationship to objects, internal and external; the development of the self and one's relationship to it, including the bodily self; the development of the ego and its functions; the relationship to affects and anxiety; and the development of the superego. Included are significant environmental factors also important to consider, for example moves, losses, and trauma. The analyst is also interested in assessing how or if the child can utilize the analyst's interventions and the treatment itself.

Once information is gathered, it is useful for the analyst to outline, at least in her own mind, a provisional Diagnostic Profile.

The point of the Profile is to ascertain an emerging complex model of the mind, "conceived of as a multi-modular system designed to manage a wide range of biopsychological motivations" (Green and Joyce 2017, p.139), and to understand the child's psychopathology within a developmental viewpoint. The profile was developed by a research group at the Hampstead Clinic, which eventually led to Anna Freud articulating her own ideas into a formal framework (A. Freud 1965). In 2006 the Diagnostic Profile was revised (Davids et al. 2017), then reconsidered again in 2013 (Green and Joyce 2017). It now took into consideration advances in our understanding of an increasingly complex dynamic system of the mind built out of a series of hierarchies resulting in a multidimensional way of conceptualizing developmental psychopathology. This Profile "allows for the consideration of pathology arising out of different developmental stages; deficits in the foundational structures of the mind for a variety of reasons including biological, and symptoms which arise out of more mature functioning where a good enough mental structure has been established" (p. 146). As a result, the child can be viewed in "a more postmodernist light" not as "an entrenched fixed steady state," but with "the potential for greater fluidity and shifts" (p. 147).

As a result of a Diagnostic Profile the analyst is able to propose a provisional developmental diagnosis, which brings together different aspects of the child's internal and external worlds and provides a formulation of the child's development and psychopathology. The revised 2006 Profile offers three possible areas to include: A dynamic understanding of the child's presenting problems and other psychopathology, a narrative of the various etiological factors, and an understanding of the child's development, both normative and pathological (Davids et al. p.156). The analyst provides an understandable narrative to the parents of the whole child, not only of the child's difficulties, but also of who the child is and how he came to be with ideas about the origins of the developmental disturbance. Parents and analyst can then consider and make an informed decision about the best ways to help the child, whether analysis, psychotherapy, or no intervention for the child, and working with the parents in more defined ways.

Anna Freud and her colleagues believed it was important to work with parents in conjunction with a child's treatment, ideas examined and refined by Kerry Kelly Novick and Jack Novick (Novick, K.K. and Novick, J. 2005). Rose Edgcumbe (2000) concurred. She outlined two fundamental assumptions regarding work with parents during a child's treatment derived from a study group on the topic at the Anna Freud Centre; (1) the "central role" parents have "in promoting the child's development" and "remedying psychological problems," and (2) that they can "best be helped by discussions about the child's emotional needs and development, and about their own experiences of being parents" (p.150).

Proceeding with a psychoanalytic developmental assessment in the ways I have described fulfills a number of aims. It provides a clearer understanding for the analyst and the parents of the child's development and psychopathology leading to an informed recommendation for treatment, it establishes a working alliance with the parents and the child, and readies the child for the ongoing work with the analyst and between the analyst and his parents.

Commentary 2

We all know that diagnostic consultations rarely lead to a "natural" evolution toward "understanding and acceptance" of the recommendation for treatment in the population of adolescents and their parents, however much we wish for such an outcome. Anything that can help the process toward a better result more often is a helpful addition to our professional repertoires.

This chapter brings a welcome combining of research knowledge with clinical challenges. Psychoanalysts have always known that family histories matter, that the experience of prior generations impacts individual development and functioning. There is ample clinical discussion of inter-generational transmission of strengths and pathologies. But we have also had this knowledge confirmed and validated from the extensive research conducted as the AAI was developed and has been used now for many years in various ways.

We hear in this vignette a further extension and application of these ideas, with the pilot use of the AAI as part of diagnostic evaluations of adolescents brought for assessment by their parents. The experiment brings in another central analytic assumption, that is, that the therapeutic alliance is an essential element of treatment. Here we have the additional premise, long familiar to child and adolescent analysts, that the alliance with parents will be critical to establishing a viable treatment with a child or adolescent patient. The author underscores the importance of building a relationship during the assessment.

The example of Diana and her mother illustrates and highlights some particularly interesting issues. Diana herself sounds like a very troubled youngster, with numerous adverse childhood experiences, and an ominous clinical picture of severe eating disorders, anxiety, and depressive symptoms. Forming a workable alliance with her would be challenging enough. But our focus here is on the parent work, and what makes it possible, what impact it has on the treatment. There too we are given a sense of a disturbed mother, confused and angry, needy and wishing for attention. In blaming her child, it sounds unlikely that she would be available to form an alliance with the analyst on behalf of her child. Nevertheless, she does volunteer the connection between her abused childhood and the violence of her relationship with Diana's father.

I was interested to tease out from this vignette and the discussion those elements that seemed to make it possible to create an alliance with Diana, with her mother, and eventually between them. The initial interview with the mother sounds very difficult, both frustrating and puzzling to the therapist. This experience continued into the AAI meeting, with results that confirmed the initial clinical impressions. But I think that the mother received a message through this process that *she* too was important in the situation, that *her* history mattered, and that the therapist cared about knowing the story and knowing her. For someone abused throughout her life to feel of value creates the germ of a collaborative bond and offers hope in what feels to the mother like a desperate predicament.

I think a similar process might have been involved in presenting the idea of the AAI to Diana, which seemed to transform her mood and attitude to the assessment quite markedly. Diana, like many adolescents, sought to externalize blame and pathology on to her mother. When she was taken seriously, that is, when the analyst suggested that her mother was indeed an important factor in the whole situation, rather than interpreting the defense prematurely, Diana became interested and engaged.

Another dimension that is usually part of building an alliance involves some degree of making sense of things during the assessment. From a chaotic, inchoate situation, one seeks to at least begin to construct jointly with patient and parent(s) some formulation, some explanation of what is going on and how it came to be. This calms things down, in the way that naming brings things under the aegis of the ego and points the way to defining treatment goals. I think both the idea and the experience of doing the AAI, as well as the actual content that emerged, crystallized and accelerated that process of making sense.

In turn the shared experience of having done the AAI brought Diana and her mother closer than they had been for a long time, enabling them to embark on their treatments together, rather than as competitors or adversaries. We do not know how the ongoing course of work played out, but the base established in the assessment seems sturdier than might have been predicted from the initial picture of both people.

An additional dimension described in this report speaks to the perennial challenge of therapists' reactions, transferences, and countertransferences to parents. The material derived from the AAI protocols, the findings delineating relationship patterns in child and parent, offers the possibility for a heightened awareness in the therapist of the transferences that are likely to arise. This foreknowledge may serve as a protective factor for therapists, as well as a reminder to therapists always to strive for self-awareness of their own relationship paradigms.

Editorial Reflections

The therapist emphasizes the importance, during the assessment phase, of building a relationship, an intersubjective working alliance, "which may broaden, in the adolescents and their parents, the awareness of their problems." Such awareness is supported and enhanced by the extent to which relatively accurate "self" and "other" observations become available to both parent and child. It is such observations that facilitate reflective functioning (RF), a capacity which research has shown augurs well for success in psychoanalytic psychotherapy and psychoanalysis (Steele H. and Steele, M. 2008).

As noted in the vignette of Diana and her mother, entrenched defensiveness in adolescents and their parents often looms large as an interference at the time of referral to treatment. Mother presented as "preoccupied, scared, and… angry at her daughter," who, for the previous two years, had alternated between episodes of anorexia and bulimia, following the separation and divorce of her mother and abusive father. In a "state of intense pain" and "deep in distressful thoughts," Diana had come reluctantly to her interview and asserted it was, "not she who needed help, but her mother!" However, intrigued by the AAI interview process, she became cooperative and participated. For both mother and daughter, the creative use of the AAI during the assessment phase proved most useful as each gained insight into the meaning of some of their interactive behaviors. In turn, Diana consented to analysis and her mother to work with her own therapist, even as she continued periodic consultations with Diana's analyst.

One commentator noted the value of using the frame of Anna Freud's Developmental Profile in work with adolescents and their parents. In her 1992 text, *Toddlers and Their Mothers: A Study in Early Personality Development*, Erna Furman not only adapted the Developmental Profile to the toddler level of development, she added to the Profile, and emphasized the value of an in-depth assessment of the toddler's parents. In assessing adolescents, the Developmental Profile can be useful in constructing for parents an understandable narrative of their "whole child." Augmenting that process with the parent(s) gaining insight into how the enduring influences of their own childhood experiences have impacted both their parenting of their child and their view of their child can be both personally powerful for the parent(s) and can lead to support for the adolescent's treatment.

Another commentator noted the value of "making sense of things during the assessment" and observed how "both the idea and the experience of doing the AAI, as well as the actual content that emerged, crystallized and accelerated that process of making sense." Such "making sense" provides the beginning of a process of creating for both child and parent(s) alike a "coherent narrative," a process that has been demonstrated as a key to success in working with children and parents engaged in the "transgenerational transmission of trauma" (Liberman and Van Horn 2008).

The use of the AAI with adolescents with symptoms of eating disorders and with their parents may also be particularly useful given emerging research which has highlighted a possible relationship between attachment style to the primary caregiver(s) in childhood, and the development of eating disorders later in childhood or adolescence (Masters 2018). The disordered eating was better understood if looked at as a symptom or a manifestation of an underlying insecure attachment to the primary caregiver(s), rather than a disorder in itself.

This chapter underscores the importance of forming an alliance with both adolescent and parent(s), as early as possible, and offers additional ways to do so. It also reminds us to be open to combining established and new methodologies and incorporating the fruits of research into our knowledge base. One of our findings regarding concurrent parent work is the necessity to extend the initial exploration period long enough to initiate a series of transformations, the most important being the beginnings of a working alliance with parents, with child, between parents, and parents with the child.

This usually conflicts with parental anxiety and their wish to have an immediate diagnosis and therapeutic plan. To accede to parental anxiety often leads to premature withdrawal. The AAI is one of a number of instruments which can be used in a collaborative way to promote an alliance and demonstrate the necessity and value of an initial exploratory period before recommending treatment. The same holds for the Profile. It was originally designed to help formulate a psychoanalytic diagnosis but as presented by the commentators, the Profile can lead to crucial transformations during the long exploratory period, especially the transformation of self-help to a collaborative therapeutic alliance.

CHAPTER TWELVE

SUBSTANCE ABUSE AND CHALLENGES OF PARENT WORK

Older adolescent

Clinical Vignette

Victor ("Vic") entered analysis as an older teenager. For many years, he engaged in a variety of self-destructive behaviors. He described that the sensations involved in his multiple piercings and almost tattoo-covered body brought a blissful detachment. When this more socially acceptable type of dissociation wasn't enough, a variety of more dangerous self-destructive behaviors were relied upon to release intense and overwhelming feelings and aggression from within and onto his body. This way, he wouldn't hurt others as he had been hurt. He asked his mother Kera, unaware of his struggles, to bring him to see me when he began to fear losing control and accidentally killing himself.

His background included physical and emotional abuse at the hands of his father Ivan. Many years prior, Ivan had left the family abruptly after his gambling and other addictive behaviors were exposed publicly. Vic was neglected by his mother, whose denial protected her from her own trauma but left Vic vulnerable and alone to fend for himself. In analysis, Vic's self-destructive defenses softened over time, revealing admirable resilience, love, and hope for his future.

After two years of analysis and several months after Vic's seemingly successful transition to university, he almost died from a fentanyl overdose. He had claimed to have not used drugs since very early in treatment. The stresses of transition and leaving home seem to have activated his old defenses. His near-death experience provided an opportunity to address vulnerabilities and transferences that were previously hidden.

Prior to the overdose, Vic seemed to be in the pre-termination phase of what appeared to be a successful analysis. Kera's absorption with a new relationship (one of many to draw her attention away from Vic) promised to force a premature termination of his analysis, but he and I both felt he was on a good path. She needed the money to plan her upcoming wedding, a "do-over" that in her mind would erase the pain of her marriage to Ivan. Once married, her new husband would no longer house or support Vic, forcing him to leave his support system (and analysis) and fend for himself sooner than would be ideal. Unfortunately, there was no flexibility in this plan, especially after Vic's overdose. Our four-month termination focused on consolidating his successes in the face of his addiction, working through an intense transference neurosis, and saying goodbye in a connected, loving way. The involvement and lack of involvement with each parent both facilitated early treatment and contributed to a less-than-ideal ending. In this short account, I will provide a summary of treatment, focusing on the roles of the parents (Ivan and Kera), followed by a description of and reflection on our untimely goodbye.

During an extended evaluation, Vic provided most information about his family. Kera and Vic focused on the present, reluctant to revisit their painful history. They described "Ivan the terrible" as a deadbeat addicted to substances and poor choices. They believed Ivan would shame Vic if he knew about therapy. Vic claimed he felt only fear of and hatred for Ivan. He sympathized deeply with Kera's perspectives and forgave all when it came to her obvious denial and neglect. He blamed Ivan exclusively for all of his troubles. Kera and Ivan had ended their turbulent marriage when Ivan's addictive tendencies in many arenas became undeniably destructive. The family's language was one of denial. I found it painful to understand the way each parent and child justified massive transgressions, omissions, and lies. In spite of Kera's protest and Vic feeling ashamed of Ivan, I felt I could not work with Vic without knowing each parent. When I reached out to Ivan, I was shocked when this so-called villain burst into tears at hearing of Vic's self-destructiveness. Blaming himself, he felt guilty for having mocked therapy when Vic brought it up. Ivan agreed to be as involved as possible, offered to pay for the lion's share of Vic's treatment, and met with me at least once or twice monthly to talk about how the father-son pair might find a way to find (or re-find) the love they once shared. Vic and Kera privately mocked my efforts. "He's playing you," Vic insisted, even as Ivan followed through on every promise. Sessions with Kera, difficult to schedule and often cancelled, felt guarded, defensive, and superficial. She came once a month at most and seemed to have forgotten the life-threatening trouble Vic was in within a few weeks. She would travel for long periods, leaving Vic alone. Our work together always felt hopeless. She spent sessions assuring me Vic was okay, even when he wasn't. She spoke of Ivan's destructiveness, especially when Ivan and Vic talked more.

In the ways Kera was unavailable to Vic, she was also unavailable to me. When she did show up, she was closed to views outside of her own. For instance, I was never able to help Kera consider Vic's need for both parents, or to help her separate her own hatred for her ex-husband from the love her son needed to experience with him. While I invited her to attend weekly parent sessions in an effort to connect, another part of me hoped she'd decline. My countertransference resistance had to do with my sense that Kera became angry and destructive with even gentle challenges. My avoidance of her aggression (and my own) probably helped Kera to support the treatment initially, but at a high cost that became evident at the end of our work together.

During the first year of the treatment, Vic developed a strong alliance with me, developed loving relationships with friends and a partner, and completely discontinued self-injury and substance use. For the first time, he began to feel proud of himself, recognized how bright he was, and began to envision a hope-filled future for himself. Vic began understanding himself in new ways as he provided a more detailed history on each parent.

Ivan was born into a long line of abusive and addicted fathers and sons. He overcame adversity and through sheer willpower tried to create a different life than the one in which he was raised. In spite of his aspirations to change the family pattern of abuse, Ivan became the abuser he'd sworn off. He then sabotaged his successes with addiction and self-destructive choices. From the time he left the family, he had minimal contact with Vic until our work together.

Over time, Vic began to understand the sadomasochistic relationship he and father shared through understanding Ivan's childhood stories. For instance, Ivan always told of his own father whose narcissistic needs were terrifying. If not gratified with praise and adoration by any member of the family, Ivan's father would beat everyone, including Ivan's mother. Vic began to understand that Ivan re-lived this story. When Vic rejected grand gestures and tearful apologies meant to win him over, Ivan became mean and insulting in spite of his best efforts to connect with his son. It didn't hurt less, but now Vic could feel empathy for Ivan and chose at times to respond differently. Notably, Vic never remembered the warm childhood memories of which Ivan told. Instead, when reminded of such memories, Vic was flooded with traumatic memories of Ivan's abuse.

Kera experienced immense shame about her family's involvement with a violent extremist group. Kera had always felt unwanted and misplaced and was constantly and openly shamed in her family growing up. Vic began noticing and telling me more about Kera's troubles, including extreme dieting and frequent purging. Her extreme "minimalism" in home decor also resulted in purges of even special or sentimental childhood items belonging to Vic. Her purges reflected her need to rid herself of unbearable feelings and memories— eventually even her own son's troubles. We began to understand Vic's self-injury as his iteration of trying to release such unbearable feelings. He found relief as he felt brave enough to learn how to recognize feelings as signals and respond to them in masterful ways.

As Vic began to understand his family history, he developed his own more balanced, adult view of each parent. He would never "betray" Kera, but he was privately angry with how his needs and distress had become part of her emotional "purging." And while he could never "forgive" Ivan, the pair found some common ground talking about shared interests. Here, the shortcomings in the parent work began to play out. Though both parents said they supported treatment, Kera and I did not have a frame through which she could be supported through *what it would feel like* to truly support Vic's growing independent relationships.

From the start of analysis, I urged Ivan, Kera and Vic to consider Vic's deferring college so that he could have the support of his family and avoid putting time pressure on his treatment. When the time came however, they unanimously disagreed, and Vic enrolled in a faraway college. "He knows how to take care of himself," both parents told me. When this transition occurred, Kera stopped coming to see me. Vic had made dramatic improvements. I worried that, like Kera, Vic might not be prepared for how this difficult transition away from his conflicted childhood home would *feel*. I reminded him of his strong reactions to separations during my vacations. Vic's desire to escape his childhood home overrode his ability to consider other possibilities. He was quick to boast of the lengthy absence of self-destructive behaviors. His transference love was evident. At times I worried that he was "too good" a patient, though there were glimpses of negative feelings when he told me how he and Kera mocked therapy like they mocked Ivan. One of the only ways he and Kera felt close was through their shared trauma and hatred of Ivan. If Vic began to have an independent, loving, adult relationship with Ivan, would he lose Kera's love and support?

At this time, I made a conscious decision and an unspoken agreement with Kera to stop meeting. She avoided, cancelled our sessions, and planned her wedding with renewed vigor as if to leave Vic before he could leave her. It appeared that Vic would truly be on his own, as he had rejected Ivan's offer to take him in for a year. The task now seemed to be to help Vic prepare for this separation that verged on parental abandonment.

In the meantime, Ivan continued to reach out regularly. He continued to pay bills and sought reconciliation. Vic and I agreed to work together remotely for a period to assist his transition to college. He appeared to be adjusting phenomenally, in spite of missing his friends back home. He made new friends and realized the potential of his intellect. He connected more with Ivan. He appeared to be in a pre-termination phase of a successful analysis, having consolidated his capacity to manage intense feelings without self-sabotage. We agreed to continue working together remotely until after Kera's wedding, after which her financial support of treatment would end.

Mid-year, I received a shocking call in which I was informed that Vic almost died from a fentanyl overdose. We soon resumed our work in person, alongside intensive substance abuse treatment. In spite of my asking regularly about substance use, leaving Kera's home had activated Vic's old secretive defenses. To deal with this complicated separation, he found a blissful relief in pain medications he had kept after a minor past surgery. He soon discovered that fentanyl provided a quicker, more intense high. Following the pattern of addiction, he hid the problem from himself and from me by focusing on things he thought would make me proud. After all, his other self-destructive behaviors had stopped. His loyalty to the secret addiction reminded me of how he would not betray Kera, and of how Ivan had hidden his own destructive behaviors before his downfall.

At this point, the lacunae in the parent work became more evident when I discovered that Kera had forbidden Vic to tell Ivan about his overdose. The similarity of Vic's troubles to Ivan's troubles seemed to overshadow Kera's maternal protective instincts, leading to her go-to defensive style of constant attempts to minimize/purge Vic's problems, along with passive aggression towards Vic and me. Kera refused to reconsider the timing of her wedding or support of Vic's analysis, which left a few short months to end our work. She refused to support him in any way after her wedding, forcing him to either live with Ivan or to fend for himself before he was ready, ending his analysis and substance abuse treatment prematurely. Vic chose to try being on his own, perhaps his effort to "purge" his failure and prove his independence, though he did not appear to have a plan that promised success.

Within a week of Vic's return home, I set boundaries that Vic agreed to and later raged against. I would not treat him at a frequency less than three to four times weekly, along with intensive substance abuse treatment. Kera's plan for once-weekly therapy and 12-step meetings "as needed" turned a blind eye to the life and death situations Vic faced. Vic had the capacity to appear to be a "model" patient in his darkest moments. Much like Ivan, Vic could say the right things while suffering alone.

I also faced an ethical dilemma—Vic's parents had both been involved in the treatment, but Ivan was unaware of Vic's addiction and overdose. Did they expect me to lie to Ivan? Cut him off? In a very difficult session, I explained my dilemma and told Vic that if we were to continue together, he needed to inform and involve Ivan as we always had in our frame. I would not join Vic and Kera in keeping secrets from Ivan. At the time, Vic was nervous but relieved. He wanted to tell Ivan and asked for my help in coming clean.

As we prepared to speak with Ivan together, Vic immersed himself in rage. He blamed Ivan for his overdose. He had always hated Ivan. He couldn't remember their growing relationship and Ivan's many apologies. Kera felt that involving Ivan was destructive, though Vic left her out of his decision to tell. Vic braced himself to retaliate against Ivan's harsh judgment. When we told Ivan the truth, he was utterly supportive. Ivan spoke of his own treatment, his regrets, his unconditional love and support of Vic, and his desire to support treatment. Vic was enraged, left alone with intolerable feelings that he couldn't project onto Ivan. Vic needed to see Ivan as controlling, manipulative, and a failure as a human being and father. Soon, Vic described me in just these terms.

At first, a major issue we addressed in treatment was Vic's identi-fication with Ivan's pattern of sabotaging success. I was concerned that Vic was avoiding his own recovery by immersing himself in rage. The rage seemed misplaced and not entirely his own, especially given Ivan's support of treatment and Kera's chronic denial/neglect. Vic felt powerful and excited about his hatred for Ivan. Like a drug, anger made him feel good, it made his problems disappear, and made him blameless in the moment. It was also only in moments of shared rage that Vic could feel close to Kera. Their shared excitement mimicked a collusive and destructive mother-son oedipal victory—together, they could kill off "Ivan the terrible."

Outside of these exciting moments, though, Kera had a way of disappearing. Their relationship hadn't grown much beyond the trauma and anger from Vic's childhood. We also began to understand that for Vic, fentanyl and the other self-destructive behaviors had a mother-like effect. They held and comforted him in ways Kera didn't. It reminded me of how Vic told me how heavily he relied on physical contact, seeking it in any relationship even if he wasn't interested—he often joked about his need for a "cuddle bar." Fentanyl was the most efficient route to this infantile experience of bliss, and Vic told himself it had fewer consequences than the isolation his many soured relationships brought. It became particularly appealing when he left home and all his close relationships (including his in-person analysis), during a transition that for most young adults is filled with loneliness.

I began to confront Vic's addiction not just to substances, but to self-destructiveness, failure, and self-sabotage. Like Ivan, Vic successfully navigated his way out of a troubled home and had a bright future ahead of him. At the moment of success and transition, he sabotaged himself. I urged Vic to stop externalizing and to look inward so that he could understand this pattern before it killed him. Since drug treatment focused only on behavioral change, my

267

challenge to focus inward startled Vic, and was easy to reject as "not supporting me."

A few days later, Vic decided he was quitting analysis. His new addictions therapist, along with his new 12-step sponsor, without consulting me, seemed to identify with Kera's desire for less treatment. They suggested that Vic's analysis was "too much" and would cause him to relapse. The counselor was slightly apologetic and curious when I suggested the treatment team was enacting a family pattern but did not change the recommendation to stop analysis immediately.

Vic decided that I, like Ivan, had become toxic to him. He had a litany of complaints against me. I should have known about the addiction. I had coerced him into a relationship with Ivan he never wanted, and he could no longer trust me. Being around me made him want to kill himself. Attempting to use reality to defend myself was futile. Like Ivan, Vic needed to hate me. In response to my one month's notice policy, designed to help him have a proper goodbye, he sneered. "You have a God-complex, you think you're the only one who can help me." He ultimately came for several more months.

I hated Vic during this time. I was angry about his lies and blaming me. As I regained my footing, I could see that an intense transference neurosis had emerged—I had become Ivan. Vic's insults contained both everything Vic endured from Ivan in childhood and everything he wished he could say to Ivan but could not. I told him I had become Ivan, an untrustworthy, controlling villain. I remembered the good work we had done, that his overdose had not "undone." Now we needed to understand what was happening between us. Vic's rage calmed. Frightened by his lability, he took initial steps towards taking care of himself rather than blaming others. Vic stabilized during the following weeks when I advocated for his medical care, demonstrating a responsiveness to his physical needs that created enough distance from his emotions for us to reconnect.

Vic had trouble remembering why he had been so angry, asking me to remind him often. He suggested we use our final weeks to talk about Ivan. We had both now experienced a glimpse of the rage, terror, and shame Vic experienced with Ivan. We were less entangled by enactments. Vic watched me withstand his rage without retaliation, advocate for him, stick up for myself, and through it all discovered that our relationship was different from either of his parents.

Meanwhile, Kera and Ivan continued to put Vic in the middle of their conflicts, using his analysis as a battleground. Kera shifted parental responsibility to me, refusing to meet because I had "let him" get addicted. Vic refused to consent to further meetings with Ivan, feeling that I would try to force an unwanted relationship. Thus, we were only able to address his internal and our shared experience of his family. In reality, he would continue to need both parents' support for years beyond our work together.

In our final few sessions, Vic told me that when he was in trouble, he had wished that I had the omnipotent power to "know" in the way young children believe their parents know everything. He'd always longed to be "seen" by someone like this and had discovered the boundary of our separateness. "People can't read my mind. I need to let them know what's going on with me so they can help me and not wait for them to figure it out." He was thinking about having more adult relationships.

To the end, Vic remained reluctant to explore his protectiveness of Kera. He could see that his destructive solution to the parental conflict was his identification with the worst parts of Ivan, which provided a disguised way for him to love Ivan. This perverse love side-stepped the loyalty conflicts with Kera. He could love Ivan, so long as it looked like strife, hatred, or self-destruction. Kera and Ivan were unable to tolerate any other form of loving.

While Vic stayed longer than "required" by my policy, he left earlier than our original plan. He could no longer handle the loyalty conflict our work created with his parents. They enacted destructive family dynamics to the end, out of reach of the analysis. Having been tempted to leave with his rage covering any feelings of love or loss, Vic chose to stay long enough to understand the rupture between us and the meaning of the powerful father-transference. He let himself remember the good work we'd done together, and poignantly thanked me. To Vic, I no longer represented "Ivan the terrible," but a more complex separate person who had helped him in some ways. He was still a little angry at me, too. At the time of our goodbye, he was able to give himself some due credit for some successes we'd forged together.

This piece of work around his perverse and hidden love for his father Ivan was the culmination and consolidation of our analytic work on self-injury, self-sabotage, and Vic's problems with loving. While his hidden addiction showed us that he had many more years of work to do, our ending showed both of us that his addiction had not undone the significant progress Vic had made in analysis.

I could not say that Kera and Ivan had experienced such growth, and worried that their strife could easily pull Vic back into old ruts, especially so early in recovery and with a less-than-ideal premature termination. I wish we could have ended with a mutual feeling of assurance that Vic will lead a healthy and productive adult life. It seems that the work we did was only the beginning of a long road which Vic will be in charge of navigating.

As the analysis ended, I was left to reflect on my choices throughout treatment to include and exclude each parent, and my avoidance of the aggression each family member presented in order to preserve the continuation of the analysis—until things fell apart. Ultimately, Vic had chosen to hide important information from me, and probably would have done so no matter what. This was a reflection of his family's conflicts. In hindsight, though, should I have worked more intensively with these parents on their conflicts before or while treating Vic? Would Kera and Ivan have been able to support Vic's analysis if I'd insisted on meeting with them more from the start? Or would this have scared them away, ruining Vic's chance to get any help at all?

In treatment, Vic and I focused on his dangerous identifications with Ivan and understanding the hated parts of himself. I hadn't realized the ripple effect this work would have in his family—that identification with Ivan would cause turmoil, loyalty conflicts, threatened rejection from Kera, and increased malignant and life-threatening secrets. The decision to help Vic sort through his family troubles without his parents' full involvement did seem to help Vic in many substantial ways, but will he be able to sustain his progress in spite of his family's strife over time?

Commentary 1

Consulting on a case after the fact is far easier than the live, raw experience of the consulting room and my comments here are intended only as a different perspective one might have taken, not necessarily a better one. That is, for the therapist to have engaged my point of view might not have culminated in a different result, but I think that it is one worth considering as an alternate method of proceeding.

There are two issues in this very difficult treatment—a treatment that the therapist handled admirably and courageously—that I would like to address. What might have happened had the therapist only worked with Vic, and a separate therapist had functioned as an anchor for the parents? By anchor what I mean is someone *without* an agenda to "help" these individuals understand one another, or to "get along better." I will elucidate shortly a different way of enlisting the parents in a therapeutic alliance, especially in light of their extreme psychological disturbances.

One of the potentially hazardous artifacts of concurrent parent work carried out by the same therapist of the adolescent is that the unconscious meanings that hover over the complex synergy between patient and analyst, parents and analyst, and patient and parents, will always have a pervasive influence on the trajectory of the treatment in ways that cannot be predicted. As much as the therapist may attempt to bring such meanings into the open, there is much that will remain unconscious—sealed over, denied, or rationalized. In such instances, the treatment of the adolescent can capsize, as the adolescent may fear that the therapist is privileging his/her own agenda over the adolescent's wishes, or is biased in favor of the parents' views, or will compromise the adolescent's developmental bids for autonomy in favor of what the adolescent believes (correctly or not) is not what the parent wants.

For example, in the case of Vic, his opposition to the therapist's work with his father was not even lightly veiled. Both Kera, Vic's mother, and Vic openly mocked the therapist's efforts to work productively with Ivan, Vic's father, taunting, "He's playing you"— evidence that the therapist's presumed efforts to show Kera and Vic about Ivan's apparent commitment to Vic were not welcomed so early in the treatment. This is true despite the possibility that unconsciously,

Vic might have wanted to see those very caring aspects of his father. Later in the report, the therapist wisely suggests that one of the only ways in which Vic and his mother bonded was through their shared trauma and hatred of Ivan. The therapist's attempts to engage them to observe Ivan more objectively did not fit the mother's nor the son's needs to see him on their terms only. To experience or even imagine Ivan differently threatened the dyadic as well as each one's intra-psychic balance.

This segues into my second point: The serious pathology and underlying traumata of both parents (as well as Vic) resulted in problematic behaviors, such as substance abuse and addictions, violent and abandoning actions and fragile ego functioning, as well as defensive tendencies of splitting, projection and projective identification. Their prominent limitations in tolerating intense affect without resorting to action, i.e. their "thin-skinned-ness" suggest treatment strategies that feature an empathic listening and containing stance, possibly for an extended period of time. The therapist's holding the patient's projections and not returning them with interpretations can be relieving in such cases, as these individuals require an atmospheric sense of enduring patience from the therapist and a steadiness in silent reflection that may act as a source of future identification. In later phases of treatment, the therapist can experiment with helping the parents find ways to take responsibility for their projections without harsh superego censure and to work productively with them.

Thus, to me, the therapist's ambitious attempt to assist each person to see the other as separate individuals in their own right seemed premature and threatening; each participant appeared to have experienced the therapist's interpretations as assaults on the identities that each had long established—e.g. Kera and Vic as victims of "Ivan the Terrible." Sandler's metaphor of a gyroscope to capture how every patient seeks to maintain psychic balance and equilibrium through mechanisms such as unconscious defenses and the maintenance of old relationships with childhood introjects is apt here.[4]

For Kera and Vic to maintain intra-psychic viability as well as their bond with one another, they needed to blame, attack and verbally destroy Ivan. This was central to their psychological stability. Stripping them of these defenses through interpretive work without adequate preparation unleashed terror for both of them. Annihilation anxiety seemed to be the root fear, thus generating fierce attacks on the therapist given the anxious prospect of facing an internal black hole.

Under such siege, the therapist-adolescent relationship concluded in an inevitable breakdown. As the therapist stated: "Vic decided that I, like Ivan, had become toxic to him. He had a litany of complaints against me. I should have known about the addiction. I had coerced him into a relationship with Ivan he never wanted, and he could no longer trust me. Being around me made him want to kill himself. Attempting to use reality to defend myself was futile. Like Ivan, Vic needed to hate me."

I believe, too, that Vic himself was able to think and feel differently about his past and his present life with impressive self-reflection during the course of his therapy, as opposed to the closed system

---

4   "The stabilizing fantasy of the *present unconscious* is like a gyroscope, a spinning wheel in more senses than one. It weaves the raw materials available into formations that may be quite complicated, and sometimes appear very different from the materials from which they were constructed. And, like the spinning wheel of the gyroscope, they have a balancing, stabilizing function for the individual, who is constantly threatened with being pushed off balance by his infantile wishes *and previous childhood* adaptations... Such unconscious fantasies provide 'compensation in fantasy,' to use Anna Freud's term, and in particular bring about stabilization and intrapsychic adaptation through the use of various mechanisms of defence and the creation of dialogues and other interactions with fantasy objects which can be thought of as rooted in childhood introjects..." (Sandler 1989, p. 189).

framework he had adopted previously. In this way, he might have travelled further afield than his parents, particularly his mother, and this in itself may have been, unfortunately, a bridge too far.

Commentary 2

Like most child analysts, I find the description of Vic's analysis and the ways it was disrupted and limited by his parents heart wrenching. Each of us has had cases such as this, wherein one or both of the parents' hostility toward the patient, the analysis, and us has made analytic progress limited, if not impossible. Thus, it is important to stress that my comments are not meant to be critical. I truly believe that nothing would have changed the outcome of this analysis given the parents' pathology and its interaction with and impact on the patient's defensive organization. My subsequent remarks are meant, therefore, to only be heuristic and help to articulate better the difficulties raised by the parents and possible principles to guide us in our work with them.

To begin with, I want to congratulate Vic's analyst on a heroic bit of analytic work. The severity of Vic's pathology, and the complicating factors of his mother's pathology, and the interaction between patient and mother generally prohibit the sorts of analytic process and results achieved in this case. Ironically, the case both highlights the essential nature of concurrent parental work while the failure at that task looms forebodingly with regard to ultimate prognosis. Kera's overt resistance to the analysis, active undermining of her son's attachment to his analyst, and insistence that her son side with her in her hostility toward his father and his analyst illustrate the fallacy of the old-fashioned belief that the adolescent analyst should only focus on the patient's internal world and stay away from the parents. It highlights the developmental and clinical reality that even later adolescent patients are still very involved with their primary objects in the real world, not just in their fantasies. As a result, the primary objects continue to affect their mental functioning, including the ways in which they regard and use the analyst and analytic work.

Had the analyst failed to try to work with Kera or to engage Ivan, it is unlikely that the analytic work would have gotten as far as it did. Engaging Ivan and supporting a relationship between father and son likely made it possible for Vic to reconsider his rigid, closed-system view of his father. To the degree that a key developmental function of the father is affect regulation, particularly the tolerance and expression of aggression, facilitating a rapprochement between father and son probably helped Vic to gain better control of the rage that he was expressing so self-destructively at the time of the initial consultation. Yet, despite all this, Vic seemed tenuously in control of his impulses at the time the analysis came to a premature end.

Clearly, a significant reason for this state of affairs was the analyst's inability to engage Kera in the analysis and supporting her son's progress. The Novicks (Novick, K.K. and Novick, J. 2005) have highlighted the importance of helping the parents to emotionally differentiate themselves from their child before undertaking an analysis. If a parent cannot come to empathize with their child's own individual pain without experiencing it as a statement about them, they will behave in the ways that Kera did. They will sabotage the treatment, place their child in a loyalty conflict about the analyst, and not tolerate their child developing perspectives on the world or the parents that differ from their own. Most of us are familiar with ignoring the Novicks' recommendation because of what seems, at the time, like clinical necessity. It is not uncommon to minimize one parent's hostility toward us when the other parent and the child want the treatment and the child is clearly suffering.

But my experience is that such situations rarely end well. Usually, the treatment frequency drops to a level unable to sustain an analytic process or the hostile parent unilaterally ends the treatment prematurely. Given these usual consequences, Vic's analyst deserves our kudos for maintaining the analysis as long as he or she did. Nonetheless, I want to question whether it was the right thing to do, not to say not to, but to clarify what one is trying to accomplish. Obviously, most of us will ask what the other choice was. Refusing to treat Vic would surely have resulted in more severe, potentially lethal self-destructiveness. I am pretty confident of that. But I question whether that will be avoided anyway. Unfortunately, I am pessimistic that he will avoid a life of addiction and self-destructiveness. It seems unlikely given his failure to truly consider his feelings for his mother or who she actually was. Failing to face and learn to tolerate his hurt, disillusionment, and rage toward her is likely what propelled him to resume drug use; I see no reason to think that this will not continue. None of us have a crystal ball. And the fact that transformation characterizes development leaves open the possibility, likely a slim one, of a better outcome. But he did not seem headed on that path in any kind of solid way at the time of termination.

So, what was the benefit of agreeing to analyze Vic before his mother could differentiate her own self boundary from that of her son? My belief is that the analyst provided Vic with an experience of what a relationship and analysis could offer him. It left him with some awareness that someone can truly care about helping him without needing him to function as a narcissistic object. That awareness can remain latently present and something he might reconsider down the road. If so, perhaps he will find his way back to another analyst, the original analyst, or just a good reality object to help him master his internal devils. The analyst's heroism will have been worth it if that occurs. If not, the case stands as testimony to the heart ache that awaits those who fail to heed the Novicks' recommendation.

Editorial Reflections

"Each of us has had cases such as this, wherein one or both of the parents' hostility toward the patient, the analysis, and us has made analytic progress limited, if not impossible," the second commentator ruefully puts it. Unlike earlier chapters in this casebook that demonstrate how parent work can transcend difficulties, this one acknowledges the hard reality that our best efforts to work with parents sometimes fail. Vic's analyst tells us that through their first analytic work, Vic developed "his own more balanced, adult view of each parent." It is important to underscore that this is a major achievement in any analysis[5] and that parent work can contribute to it, as the analyst has perspectives from both the patient's psychic reality and mental representations, and from direct interactions with the parents.

The first commentator, however, shares a different perspective, cautioning about the possible pitfalls of concurrent parent work conducted by the adolescent's therapist instead of by someone else who can be "an anchor" without any agenda in mind. After Vic's tenuous attempt to venture beyond family and analysis by going away to college ends in a nearly fatal overdose, he returns but, in

---

5   Analysts who treat children and adolescents may be especially attuned to the power of working on this with adult patients.

the end, the analysis is too much of a threat to desperately held-to psychic buoys. His analyst concludes "he would continue to need both parents' support for years beyond our work together." This poignant recognition applies to all child and adolescent patients and, humbling though it may be, it is good to remember it.

As the second commentator cautions, "If parent[s] cannot come to empathize with their child's individual pain without experiencing it as a statement about them … they will sabotage the treatment, place their child in a loyalty conflict about the analyst, and not tolerate their child developing perspectives on the world or the parents that differ from their own." Though pessimistic about Vic's future, this commentator holds out some hope that despite the limitations of the parent work, the analysis itself provided Vic "with an experience of what a relationship and analysis could offer him. It left him with some awareness that someone can truly care about helping him without needing him to function as a narcissistic object."

Recognizing that Vic and his mother needed to vilify and hate the father in order to maintain their pathological attachment and fragile psychological stability, the first commentator offers an alternative technical approach in such a situation that would privilege empathic listening over interpreting, so as to contain annihilating anxiety and hold projections until such time as they might be available for mutual exploration. The analyst in this chapter speaks honestly about just how challenging it can be to maintain empathy for the parents, the patient, and oneself when a case is sinking.

This chapter highlights the difficult clinical choices facing an analyst in determining when empathic listening may constitute an avoidance of the conflicts and when interpretation of defenses and conflicts may be premature and unbearable for the patient, or, more likely, the parents. The parent work demands as much, or more, technical skill and nuance in dynamic understanding and intervention as the individual treatment of the patient.

A big choice as underscored by the first commentator is whether or not to have concurrent parent work at all. But the patient's second round of in-person analysis demonstrated what could happen without parent work. The mother made sure that there was no parent work when the young man returned from university. She stopped any attempt to contact father, who was the one parent who might have been helpful in the patient's recovery. She chose an alternative form of therapy and she promoted the rivalry between the "recovery specialists" and the analyst. The second round of analysis was an analysis without parent work and it ended painfully with the therapist being blamed and hated by the patient, the mother, and the "recovery specialists."

This chapter reinforces some of what we have gleaned from others in this volume, for instance, the obstacles that rear up from parental pathology, the increased difficulty when parents are not working together as a team on behalf of their child, the dilemmas of loyalty and identification that challenge patients at transitional times of identity consolidation, and the technical complexities of structuring parent work when all parties are not fully enlisted. It also underscores the need for therapists to value what can be accomplished, even while regretting what becomes impossible.

CHAPTER THIRTEEN

PSYCHOSIS AND CONCURRENT PARENT WORK

Emerging adult

Clinical Vignette

James was twenty-five years old when we first met. A young man in his emerging adulthood years who was still living with his mother and was without meaningful outside relationships or a capacity to sustain employment, he appeared to have suffered a "failure to launch." He had also been given a diagnosis of schizophrenia and a prescription for haloperidol. James was enrolled in a hospital-based outpatient clinic, and therein our work together unfolded.

James was an only child of a father who worked in the service sector and a professional mother who worked with children. James's mother and father had met in their early twenties and married shortly thereafter. The pregnancy with James was expected and came soon after the marriage. His mother described the thought of motherhood as filling her with hope, enthusiasm, and purpose. The pregnancy was uncomplicated, and the birth was routine. Developmental delays emerged in James's toddler years, which James's mother identified and for which she effected early intervention and support. Strains developed within the parents' marriage around this time and when he was six, they separated.

James's father initially moved into an apartment just down the block and remained involved in his son's upbringing. In James's pre-adolescence his father moved to a distant state. James's father remained distantly in touch with James by phone through short conversations. James's mother prided herself on providing both parental roles to James with the support of her mother and two sisters. James's mother helped James to complete high school and matriculate to university at eighteen.

James and his mother described James's initial transition to college with departures and goodbyes as strikingly effortless. Yet, problems emerged already in the first semester and included poor grades, missed classes and coursework, increasing use of alcohol, and difficulty socializing. James began to experience auditory hallucinations, which he initially kept to himself.

Early in the second semester of his first year and while intoxicated at a party, James became hostile and physically menacing towards a female peer whom he had been pursuing romantically but who had not responded reciprocally. Another male peer intervened and campus security was involved. James responded erratically, leading to a mental health evaluation and hospitalization.

James was found to be psychotic, placed on medications, and returned to live with his mother through a leave of absence. An attempt at returning to his college was unsuccessful, and James withdrew from his school. A trial enrollment at a community college more geographically near to his mother resulted in similar difficulties and a second hospitalization, followed by his enrollment into the hospital-based clinic where we met.

At the time of his referral to the clinic, James had been noted to have enjoyed few gains in individual work. He continued to live with his mother despite his stated goals of gaining employment and living independently. James' mother was noted to be organized and a responsible asset to his recovery; her low mental health literacy and potential to benefit from the treatment was also noted. The clinic found that James would benefit from concurrent family work in addition to individual sessions, and James and his mother accepted the offer of care.

James's and his mother's first year of family work entailed primarily psychoeducation and problem solving. Treatment maintained a focus upon James's significant disruptive and endangering behaviors, including his frequent telling of mistruths and medication nonadherence. In his second year of therapy, a greater range of issues was enjoyed. These included a structured focus upon appropriate boundaries in the house, feelings surrounding his entry into community-provided occupational training, and new developments with James's tentative steps towards making more substantial peer relationships. The focus mainly remained on James's functional impairment; his mother served primarily as a facilitator of his progress and treatment adherence.

James and I met at the start of his third year of work. I began working with James and his mother in dyadic family work, and ultimately assumed the care of James's individual psychotherapy with medication management as well.

In my first session with James and his mother, things felt emotionally distant and rote. Introductions were made and treatment goals discussed. James understood treatment goals to be "to continue my recovery from schizophrenia," and for his mother, "to better support James." James presented a compliant posture and an uncomplicated, untextured portrayal in his unequivocal acceptance of his identity as "the patient" in the family and in his agreement to move forward with the treatment. James's mother portrayed an attitude of openness to explorations of all subject matters, while subtly expressing the intent to retain the therapeutic focus upon James. I felt an unfortunate foreclosure afforded by these stances on opportunities to understand James's subjectivity. I met the family where they were and presented my own stance of belief in promoting change through understanding rather than influence. We set about our work.

Both certain and uncertain how to proceed after that first visit, James almost immediately solved my dilemma. In his second session James reported a significant sexual trauma from his school age years that had been perpetrated by an older familiar male from the neighborhood. James had not shared this history with either of his two prior female family therapy providers nor with his individual therapy providers. Both mother and son had not spoken of this event in years. A heated mother-son argument ensued. Immediately, in contrast to the descriptions of the controlled and educative movements of the prior work, things seemed wild, alive, and powerful.

I felt overpowered by the intensity of the mother-son argument and by the rawness of James's description of the trauma. I felt pulled into James' life just as much as I felt I had intruded, in parallel with the story of the trauma. I grew almost motionless; I became silent as the mother and son fought. On reflection, my deadening reflected an enactment. At the time of the trauma James was a pre-adolescent, on the cusp of potential entry into a new understanding of the self, marked by renewed feelings of sexuality and new opportunities for individuation and autonomy. The sexual trauma, which was initially actively and mutually initiated in a physical setting hidden from the mother, became passively experienced and traumatic. He expressed anger at his mother both for not protecting him from the trauma and for what he perceived as her subdued response when she learned of it. The intensity of the anger suggested some defensive functioning; was James's anger serving to distance himself from any feelings of sadness? Was James aware that this traumatic narrative had realized one wherein wishes to separate from his mother to explore sexual curiosities would yield to violence and victimization? Did he want his mother's protection, and did he believe that his mother could protect him effectively and in his own best interest? Did he want his father's presence, which may have prevented the trauma but may have meant a different relationship with his mother? Did my presence as male provider reopen these confusions in a violent way? Just like James, with so many questions in my head, I too became quiet and passive in that session, yet a more cemented motivation to work with James and his mother developed.

Reorienting towards continuity with the preceding therapists' work and maintaining a more experientially near engagement, over the next few months a gentle focus on James's problem behaviors through a new lens of listening to their meanings and functions was sustained. These were brought into our sessions by report and then through progressive action. For example, James mother would at first report on how she had confronted James when she learned on a given day that James had skipped his vocational rehabilitation services program. James would show submissiveness and passivity to her confrontation, along with shame, and, potentially, some satisfaction that his mother had "caught" him and "kept" him in check.

With time James's mother began to withhold from him her awareness of his skipping and then proceed to unveil her awareness in the session. I, like James, would feel caught off guard. Yet, I, too, felt somewhat reassured by mother "keeping track" of James's outward functioning, even when I began to see that his increasing autonomy would require his mother to allow these responsibilities to shift to himself.

We tried to move away from action to discussion of how James's behaviors provoked his mother into checking in on him. We discussed how this kept James dependent on and restrained by his mother's vigilance, and how we could in session discuss this "trapping," both in terms of not allowing him to get away with truancy at work, as well as simultaneously in developing his own self-monitoring and proscriptions for good conduct.

When James's mother abided with the closure of action in the session, James began to bring his action into our work. James would often attend sessions late, or not attend at all. When James was present, we worked to neutrally note these interactions rather than to comment on them in a way that would worsen James's shame. A figure who would not praise "good" behavior or punish "bad" was felt to be needed for his development, freeing him as a young adult to self-observe and to consider and to make decisions for himself. Modeling calm responses to the no-shows helped James to internalize a more benign set of proscriptions in our individual work, while in our family work James's mother too learned to recognize another mode of relating. As we would talk about privileging discussion of the meanings of actions, a space opened up for him to talk about things rather than act, and to determine what things he wished to speak about in individual session and what things in session with his mother, engendering a sense of privacy, personhood, and agency.

With time, we moved towards a discussion of the intensity of James's mother's reactions to James, reactions to which he often reacted with shame and took as a motivator to further avoidance and nonattendance. This made the first space for James's mother to move in our work away from her role as a bystander and support in James's recovery towards one in which the family would grow alongside James.

We did struggle with this forward movement. James would continue to skip both our individual and family work for some time until this behavior fully resolved, or he would show up very late. Often my own frustration or concern as we waited for him to arrive, or not to arrive, appeared to be the sole expression of these feelings that James was not experiencing. In sessions when James's mother and I met alone, I privately also wondered what function his unpredictable attendance served to introduce his mother to a father substitute in the absence of the son.

Over time in these sessions James's mother began to experience awareness of concerns regarding her own choices both related to and unrelated to James' immediate needs. Some of these thoughts loomed larger on account of the specter of psychosis often in the room—was James taking his medications? Was he organized and on his way both concretely to session and abstractly to his recovery, or was he lost to reason and at risk for violence towards himself or to others?

Alongside this work, one moment of meaning entailed the discussion of transitioning James's oral medications to a long acting injectable formulation, a recommendation made by an alternate medical provider. Such a change in his medication regimen would entail James to submit to a monthly intramuscular injection of an antipsychotic to reduce the risk of problems should James fail to sustain his own adherence to his oral agent regimen, and to take his mother out of the position of having to administer them. Despite the plan's rationality, ambivalence and resistance were felt within me and within James and his mother as well. James could discuss themes of intrusiveness and a loss of autonomy regarding the plan. He could link his feelings to considerations with his relationship to his mother, as well as to concrete elements of his prior sexual trauma in relation to the "forcing of the point" by the alternate medical provider. Trouble navigating these multiple competing lenses led to a passive and ineffective rejection of this plan by James, who ultimately received the injection. James subsequently enacted a complete rejection of his oral antipsychotic medication doses following the injection during a cross-over period when adherence to his oral regimen would remain important to maintain serum levels of his antipsychotic. Consequently, James again experienced severe psychotic symptoms resulting in his third hospitalization.

At the same time as this setback, James's mother deepened her commitment to the process via exploring the meanings of her own passivity and its effects on her stated goals. James's mother became able to date again, and to navigate her own sustenance of intimacy and closeness with a partner, alongside her relatedness to her son. She reflected upon the role her closeness with her son had played in her life, both in promoting a sense of wholeness, as well as how it had at times facilitated avoidances of other personal anxieties. She became more comfortable exploring anxieties that were unconnected to those surrounding the recovery of her son. James's mother no longer felt the need to hold so tightly to the singular image of herself as protective mother, and together as a group we processed her finding of self-identities that could complement her role towards her adult son. In the process she found a means to better understand her son as a real person contextualized in current realities.

A pivotal session in this process occurred when James and his mother revealed in unison one session that James had appeared as a child on a popular children's television show in which he played the role of a model child. James's mother asked if we could all watch the recording together. We reflected on the wish to do so, with James's mother receptive to tentative explorations of the fantasy for us all to be a family adoring James, as well as of her pull to buttress self-esteem through idealizations of James's achievements. The ultimate decision to watch the video was in the service of gaining historical information, to model a focus of reflection prior to action, to continue to model a flexible relatedness, and to increase their autonomy to direct the discourse of the sessions.

I recall an immediate awareness upon viewing the video of a major disconnect between James's and his mother's reactions to the video. James showed hesitancy and mild discomfort in watching both the video and his mother's reaction to it. James's mother showed exuberant joy and pride. I myself felt a sadness, not only for the demonstration of the failures of James's mother to be available to him at times of high emotional salience, but also for the clear exposition of developmental delays present in James as a young child that the video captured. It became clear that these observable delays had been previously underreported, at best, and misconstrued at worst. My reactions permitted an entry into directly exploring James's and his mother's reactions to his deficits.

Over many sessions, James's mother was helped to experience warm feelings for her son as he was while we worked on parallels in the present of recognizing James's real deficits. We validated the unrealistic and even damaging wish to personally correct them, while not respecting the autonomy of James's path in finding his own way through his personhood. Increasingly, we moved towards guiding James and his mother to make decisions that fit his actual functioning and that addressed his family's current needs. Privately, I reflected on how my own evolution from sustaining a primary investment in the wish to effectively care for all James's problems towards a more truly neutral stance paralleled that of James' mother's growth.

289

My work with James and his family ended when James and his mother made a decision for James to transition to a residential setting for occupational training. James had done the work of identifying and exploring the meanings of this wish for himself, and James's mother in parallel looked at her own nuanced and textured feelings about this plan, replete with loss of her idealizations, yet with a newfound pride in his autonomy. This was maintained alongside their combined ability to connect with one another as they were in reality. We together saw how this pride could take the place of primacy over strivings for previously held-to and wished-for accomplishments. Both James and his mother were open to further individual work alongside family work, with the differentiations between individuality and family better distinguished and developed, and a strong commitment to further work.

Commentary 1

I found this clinical vignette extremely interesting. It is very far from much of the current psychiatric approach to schizophrenia. The patient was treated as if he has both a mind and a brain. Yes, he required medication for his brain disease. But he also required an approach that recognized the fact that he still had a mind, that meaning and intent were still essential to him and to understanding him as a person. James needed to understand himself as a person. He needed an approach that understood that the quality and nature of his close relationships were worth exploring. The therapeutic effort was designed to communicate to him that he was not simply a helpless victim of his condition, that his thoughts and behavior had an effect on those around him. An amputee could feel that he was simply a helpless victim of his situation or he could find a way to not let this define him, that there is more to him than the missing limb. Schizophrenia is not the sum and substance of James and this was recognized by the therapist. He was fortunate to have had such a doctor.

James's early development was not completely smooth. He seems to have had a confident and competent mother who was devoted to him. Perhaps she was overly devoted to her role as a mother. But that does not cause schizophrenia. I would be curious as to what those mentioned early developmental delays were. Could they have been related to his later mental illness? (The evidence provided by the later-revealed video seems to point toward that.) The marital strains that develop around his developmental delays must have caused stress, but marital problems are not the cause of mental illness. His father's growing distance from James was unfortunate, probably would have led to some emotional problems, but again does not cause schizophrenia.

I would have liked hearing more about his adolescence. This is the time when surging drives and developmental changes challenge the ego. The strikingly effortless transition to college seems to speak for rigid, brittle defenses which soon broke down. He was unable to meet the social and intellectual demands of college and began experiencing symptoms of psychosis. Inevitably, he returned home. He began individual therapy and later joint therapy with his mother was added. Initially therapy with his mother focused on James's functional impairment and his mother's role as facilitator.

When James brought up the early sexual trauma, the sessions with mother and son became "wild, alive and powerful." This particular therapist was able to see this as an opportunity rather than try to tamp down the rawness and intensity of the sessions. I think many therapists would have been frightened by this and try to tamp it down. Instead, he was able to think about the countertransference and use it

291

in a productive way. He continued to try to understand the meaning of these experiences for James's development. The complicated countertransference feelings increased the therapist's motivation to work with this couple.

A therapeutic environment was created in which all three parties, all at different points in the process, got the idea of what might ultimately prove helpful to this young man in his attempts to navigate his way through his life. Yes, the schizophrenia would continue to play a role. Perhaps that would be ameliorated by the medication. And James would play a role in deciding if he was going to accept that assistance of the medication.

Despite the looming threat of psychosis and violence, the therapist was able to maintain his stance of inquiry, looking for meaning, and non-intrusiveness. Everyone seems to have grown due to this approach. Mother found a role for herself that included being responsible for James, but in a way that allowed for his emerging adulthood. She also began focusing more on her own individual needs so that she might have sources of gratification and meaning, other than being in charge of her son's life. This could ultimately aid in James's efforts to become a person in his own right.

In summation, I think that the key point in this therapy was the therapist's ability to not be carried away by his own anxiety and take charge of everything so that he might feel in control. This is what the mother did. And that is completely understandable because she wanted to save her son. But that allowed for no growth in James. The therapist, through his self-understanding, was able to allow a space to open up where growth by all parties could occur.

Commentary 2

The case of James and his mother is not a typical case for the discussion of parent work with a child in treatment. This child is an adult and he is schizophrenic. What I hope to do is to discuss the work with James's mother and consider how it exemplifies work with parents of children in treatment and also something of how it differs from that work.

As a child and adolescent analyst, I have not had the experience of working with the parent of an adult patient very frequently, but it is clear that this mother and adult son dyad needed this therapist. It is also clear that the mother herself needed help with this developmental stage of parenting. Throughout his childhood James had needed more help than many children because of his early developmental delays, and his mother had been willing to provide that extra assistance; but now she needed assistance to find a new way of being with her son as an adult.

We are told that the father was only distantly available to the child, and the mother was apparently able to get support for her task from her own mother and sisters. Of course, it is often hard for parents to know how much direct help their child needs at each stage, and how much they need to step back and remain available for guidance that their child might want. This child's mental health problems were found to be quite severe when he was seen to be psychotic and was unable to return to college.

We are told by James's current therapist, who is a man, that James's first two years of treatment with other therapists, who were women, had focused on psychoeducation and problem solving because of dangerous behaviors, lying, and noncompliance with medication. Then they were able to work on occupational training and beginning steps toward developing friendships. His mother's task was mainly to keep James involved in treatment.

The current therapist took a different position with the child's treatment and with the mother's role in it. Instead of keeping the focus on influencing the patient's behavior, the therapist wanted to help James through understanding. James seemed eager to be heard; and for the first time in therapy, in a session which included his mother, he reported his childhood experience of sexual trauma. This led to a very intense exchange between mother and son which initially stunned the therapist into passivity.

As the therapist seemed to find his footing again, James's difficult behaviors were recast in the new framework of past victimization. James's inappropriate behaviors outside the treatment began to be seen in the mother-son therapy sessions as having current interpersonal meanings. Mother would catch him misbehaving—arriving late or missing sessions—and try to keep him in check. This shamed him but also seemed to give him a certain satisfaction. The three of them began to discuss how James provoked mother to remain vigilant so that she would end up regulating him by "trapping" him and not letting him "get away with" misbehavior. This kept mother entangled with James in a way that interfered with James's developing his own self-monitoring. The therapist found a way to interrupt that kind of ongoing interaction between mother and son. He would note James's behaviors in a non-judgmental way, rather than shaming or praising behaviors. This helped James to think about and make his own decisions.

Of particular note was how his mother learned a new way to relate to her son with openness to understanding, rather than the praise and punishment more appropriate for a much younger child. The therapist was also able to help mother notice that her intense emotional reactions to her son in sessions motivated him to avoid his sessions. She was helped to shift from her role as behavior modifier to one of actively growing in her role of mother of an adult son.

This developing awareness of James's passive victimization in childhood and his fear of continuing that in his current treatment, when he was offered medication via intramuscular injection, seemed to lead James and his mother both to become more aware of their passivity in other situations. Mother became able to be more active in her own life regarding her wishes for a partner instead of having her whole life focused on James.

Finally, an experience in a therapy session of watching a video from James's childhood revealed how his mother had found it so difficult to notice his early deficits, and how sad that had been for James. This also led the therapist to recognize his own difficulty in respecting James's own finding of his pathway to personhood. Therapist and mother were able to grow in a parallel way.

This treatment demonstrates a number of ways that therapists work with parents in general, and some of the work in this treatment resembled a kind of "couple therapy" more than more typical parent work. In one example of typical parent work, the therapist described how mother, seeming to be open to everything that would come up in the work, in a more hidden way insisted that the focus of the work was to be only on James. Parents are narcissistically so vulnerable when they bring their child for treatment. We recognize the fear that they have harmed their child, and that they will be blamed by us. We recognize the wish for exoneration by the expert—"It's not your fault." It can seem as if it would be easier if we adults could all just agree that the child is the problem to be fixed, rather than do the painful work of helping the parent recognize her or his role in the child's difficulties.

In another example more typical of work with couples, when mother and son became involved in an intense, very disturbing argument in a session after James revealed to the analyst his having been sexually abused as a child, James's therapist at first seemed to be excited and then to become struck into passivity. The therapist was able to witness and to let himself feel actively pulled into the family action, and then to let himself consider the many wishes and fears being enacted in this family, including contemplating his being placed in the role of the missing father who might be able to protect the child. He also began to consider how he could provide a chance for mother and son to have a different kind of relationship—a relationship that was part of a triad, not simply a preoedipal dyad. In less problematic development, the presence of a third person (often a father) mediates the intensity of the mother-child relationship and its regressive pull.

We are often pulled into such roles in the families we're trying to help. We can feel invited to participate in a variety of roles in the family drama. In a case with an absent parent, we can find ourselves coerced into filling the role of that missing person. Or we can feel invited to join in criticizing the missing one as the present parent's resentments look for gratification. If both parents are present, we can be asked to take sides in chronic marital battles. Such old battles often find new battlegrounds in arguments over the best way to handle a child's difficult behavior.

James seemed inclined to take a passive stance toward his life, and the therapist too became quiet and passive at times. We are told that the father's involvement with the boy changed three times: at ages three, six and twelve. These should be times of intense passions of the oedipal phase, of turning outward to the world at the beginning of latency, and of both increasing affects and facing the world at puberty.

Coincident with father's leaving when James was twelve, James had a frightening sexual experience. Finally, his psychosis appeared upon his leaving home for college, another time of intense change when his father again was probably not available.

I wondered if the therapist's passivity was an identification with the patient in the face of an apparently powerful mother with no father to act as a buffer. Was this mother seen as able to get rid of males who did not go along with her wishes and views? Did a wish to grow up and leave her mean something frightening to James? It can be frightening for us to delve into such dynamics when one parent comes across as very strong, maybe even dangerous. The analyst's capacity to think about his passive reaction made it possible for him to brave this challenge and become firmer in his motivation to work with both James and his mother.

Modeling new ways of handling a child's problematic behavior is fairly common for analysts with young children. We hear so many ways of dealing with children that I find myself, for better or worse, suggesting to parents possible alternative ways to handle specific challenging moments. Some parents find this useful and feel helped. Others manage to defeat even what I think are simple innocuous suggestions.

However, it is tricky to make suggestions because it can take us away from the objective of understanding the meanings of the child's actions. James's therapist was able to bring focus onto how James seemed to provoke mother into continuing to check on him. When the therapist caught on to this enactment and he helped mother to stop her overt "catching" of James in bad behavior, the therapist could also then show another way of handling these behaviors—not taking on the role of identifying the badness, but letting James take on the responsibility, helping him to develop his own capacity for self-regulation.

Finally, as children grow up, it can be hard for parents to recognize that their roles change. Realizing that the child has begun to need different things from us as therapists, and allowing ourselves to think about this and to change what we offer the child, is another way of modeling alternative ways for a parent to react, as James's therapist did.

A well-written description of a case, as this case of James is, always leaves us wanting to know more about the people involved, and we're also left wishing we could have more details about the interactions. I wanted to know if the therapist scheduled separate appointments with the mother, or only saw her alone when James failed their joint meetings, which might have been more appropriate for a disturbed adult son. We can infer that, whatever the particulars of how the therapist worked with her, James's mother learned things about her own conflicts and possibly about her guilt regarding her psychotic child. The therapist seemed to be able to help her to take these difficulties seriously and to receive help with them.

Commentary 3

The sequence and course of emotional development in humans is one of the major advances in the past century in coming to understand the mind. Empirical evidence regarding children's growth has been a powerful navigational tool by which to understand our clinical work. However, few authors besides Erik Erikson (1980) have considered development beyond adolescence. And yet there are a number of developmental stages beyond adolescence, including parenthood (Benedek, 1959).

Parenthood is preceded by young adulthood in which the individual learns to care for themselves and develop an intimacy with another. The challenge of parenthood is not only to have the capacity to obtain the psychological and physical resources to adequately care and take responsibility for oneself and negotiate a partnership; it is also the capacity to take responsibility and care for the development of an other, a child, usually beginning with pregnancy and infancy. The developmental challenge of parenthood is not a once-and-done thing. It involves the incremental adjustment to supporting the child at each stage of the child's development. When all goes well, the parent grows emotionally in tandem, yoked to the child's development. Of course, if there are other children, the leading edge of the parent's development will be with that child who is furthest along in development and the younger children will benefit from a more experienced parent.

Just as with child development, parent development is encoded in a kind of genetics. The child's development is encoded in physical genetics, presumably DNA, as well as experience. The parent's development is perhaps much more encoded in an "emotional genetics." This emotional genetics is encoded in the personality accumulated through the parents' early childhood experiences with their own parents. An example of this emotional transcription and translation can be seen in the spoken language, the mother tongue, which is transmitted from parent to child through environment rather than DNA. Children speak the language of their parents which is transmitted intergenerationally. Greenspan and Shanker (2004) have examined this emotional transcription and translation process which transmits the personality from one generation to the next. Another vivid example of this intergenerational transmission is George Engel's Monica (Engel et al. 1979).

That is not to say that the emotional genetic code is invariable, just as DNA is not the sole determinant of the physical body, i.e. genotype is not necessarily phenotype. In emotional development, parents do not have to do what was done to them as children. However, for a parent to do something different usually requires a conscious decision to do something different. Otherwise, the transcription and translation from parent to child is automatic. There are, however, many circumstances in which the parent faces a situation in the child's development that they themselves did not face in their own development, and therefore do not have any coding as to how to proceed.

For example, consider the deaf child with a hearing parent. In this case, the parent has no experience what it is like growing up as a deaf child. In order to provide healthy growth-promoting parenting, to begin, the parent must learn to speak a different language and then transmit that language to the child. But the novel challenges do not end there. Deafness in the child will drive the trajectory of development in directions never faced by the hearing parent, challenging the parent to develop in novel, unanticipated ways as the child's development unfolds.

Now let us consider the vignette of James and his mother. Normative development challenges the parent of an adolescent to provide a steady foundation as the adolescent pushes off into young adulthood. "Yet problems emerged [for James and he] returned to live with his mother…" With a child who is unable to establish meaningful relationships outside the home and no capacity to sustain himself, what is a mother to do? Just as with a deaf child of a hearing parent, there is no emotionally encoded genetics to guide James's mother here (although a careful history from the mother of her own childhood and adolescence may reveal that there may have been experiences the mother had that may be having influences here). With James's return home, the entire trajectory of development of both the mother and James is off a normative developmental course.

One can consider all of the possible contributions leading up to the "failure to launch," as it has been called. For example, we might consider mother's deficits in being able to clearly "see" her child, as revealed by her lack of recognition of James's deficits as an early child when she watched the videotape. The truth as I know it in clinical work is that most parents are not what we might consider "good" parents, but they are good enough. Just as most childhoods are not necessarily "good" childhoods, but they are good enough. We can perhaps say the same for clinicians, that we are not necessarily "good," but we are usually good enough.

In any case, whatever was provided to James was not good enough and likely deficits were seen on both sides of the parent/child equation. The question at this moment in the case is, "What are the strengths and resources available to attempt to address the challenges faced by James?" We also want to include consideration for how we can best support mother's supporting role. I find it useful to remind myself as I begin a case that we are in unknown territory. In this case the territory is unknown for adult child, unknown for parent and unknown for clinician. One thing that most clinicians seem to use to begin to navigate this unknown territory is to consider the narrative that each person brings with them into the office. Embedded in each person's narrative are models of themselves, the world and how they fit together.

In my experience working with such parent-child dyads (or more correctly triads, including myself), there are cases in which the parent's misplaced anxiety and reluctance to let go holds the child back. There are also cases in which the parent's reluctance to let go is from the parents' realistic anxiety that the child is not ready to grow to a higher level of maturity, and if the parent lets go, the child collapses, or worse. It is only after sometimes working in the triad for a long time, with a trust that everyone is doing their best, even if it is not good enough, that a "feathering" back and forth, holding on/letting go a tiny bit at a time, can one come to perhaps feel, more than understand, the capacities and incapacities of each of the triad. Even then, after a decade I have been faced, for example, with a twenty-five-year-old adult child of normal cognitive intelligence biting into her mother's thigh and only letting go when the police arrived to take the child away—all of this provoked in the child because I suggested that the mother more clearly represent reality while the daughter could not tolerate her mother not confirming for her that death only happens in fairy tales. Each misstep brings more understanding to the situation. And if the missteps are not too traumatizing, it is through all of these kinds of experiences that development happens… if it is ever going to happen.

In the case of James, it certainly is a disadvantage that self-reflection is limited in the mother and almost completely absent in James. Perhaps that is the major challenge in this case, as it is in so many cases. The goal in this case is to help both mother and child to be able to bring to their conscious mind and hold in their conscious mind their own states and reflect on the influence these states have on themselves and on the other, mother to child and child to mother.

Technically, one can ask, who is it best to work with, the adult child, the mother, or the dyad? I have found that the matter of practicality usually wins. Who is available to do the work? I once struggled over how to bring into the office the mother of a forty-five-year-old dependent son. The mother would send her son on his own while she stayed home to watch her soap operas. After working with this man for some time and struggling to understand the complete history, he and I decided that it might be worth a try to lower his high dose of anti-psychotic medication after he had been on it for almost thirty years without adjustment. Within fifteen minutes of his arrival back at home, the mother was in my office, ready to work... or fight— both she and I were not sure. But there she was and so we forged an alliance to work to help her son and the case moved forward.

Our patients and their families get in trouble with the world. They come into our offices and of course they get in trouble with us in the same way, living out their narrative, their model of the world that does not work for them. This enactment, in action, happens at all levels. For example, Roy Shafer (1980) calls attention to this in his exploration of "action language." From another perspective, we call this transference.

Our clinical work is to meet this phenomenon patiently and provide a safe and good enough foil, allowing a "clinical transmission of good enough development" perhaps using the same mechanism as parents do when they transmit personhood to the next generation. The therapy becomes a lived experience for both parent and child, supporting development in both. We clinicians provide a transitional space for them to develop a more robust narrative, a model that is a little more closely aligned with reality. That is the stuff of maturation, of development. In the case of James, for example, the clinician "models calm responses to the no-shows [that help] James to internalize a more benign set of proscriptions... while in our family work, James's mother too learned to recognize another mode of relating."

Winnicott (1969) talks about a holding environment. We can see in this case how the clinician is holding intense reactions. Little by little, each in the triad moves toward self-reflection and in that self-reflection, begins to see their role in this yoked development of parent and child. As viewed by Kanner (1949) and Bettleheim (1967), it was a mother's non-responsiveness that created the autistic child. But a closer look shows us that in many cases, it was the other way around—it is the child's non-responsiveness to the mother that leads to the "refrigerator mother."

In the case of James, as described toward the end of the case presentation, it is likely that mother's self-reflection helps her see the nature of the yoke and who is pulling who. This clarity is what helps the mother un-yoke some of those aspects of the mother-child connection that are not supporting healthy growth-promoting development, and in some cases may even be interfering with development, both James's child to adult development as well as mother's own development as she transitions from parenthood toward a parent who no longer provides for the day-to-day dependency needs such as we normatively see in parents of dependent children.

Generally, adolescent development pushes toward un-yoking the parent and child. Most of the time with a good enough working dyad or triad, the child can reasonably stand on their own. I have had occasions in which I have been able to work with a child or adolescent such as James intensively in a psychoanalytic setting and have been able to help move development along. However, many times, either because the resources are not available or because of the denseness of the delay, the child is not able to emotionally move into young adulthood and stand on their own. Sometimes it takes years to figure out which.

My experience suggests that the child will usually do best with their parent involved, even if the parent is not that good at parenting, as long as the parent is not sadistic (or masochistic) with the child. And with steady reasonable support, the delayed child, such as James, may continue to develop, albeit slowly. But the child may never reach even emotional autonomy, let alone physical resource autonomy. The parent may feel, and it may really be the case, that the parent becomes exhausted and is spent, and only one of them is going to make it out emotionally alive. For the sake of the parent's survival, the child ends up having dependency needs met by an entity other than the parent. Otherwise, they both may fail to move on in life.

This alternative care not provided by the parent usually involves some kind of organization or institution (such as a "residential setting for occupational training") since dependency needs of an adult child like James can rarely be managed by an individual. This difficulty for a single individual to provide for the bulk of the care is demonstrated by the parent who was providing the care and has the greatest investment in the child not being able to manage the child. It is therefore unlikely that any other single individual with less investment could manage the adult child.

The disadvantage of such institutional care has been demonstrated by Spitz (1945). Although orphanages caring for infants such as Spitz was studying seem a far cry from an adult in a group home or residential setting, I would suggest that it is not. Institutionalization is usually the last desperate push for the child to stand on their own; occasionally it works and the child makes attachments with the institutional staff. However, in my experience the child usually does not do as well in an institution as they did with the parent, but at least the child is kept safe physically, as he slowly emotionally withers away.

In the case of James, I wonder if the "recommendation made by an alternative medical provider" was a desperate penultimate push to do something to make it right for James, not wanting to give up hope for James and say good-bye. The events that unfold when James is transitioning from an oral to long-acting injectable anti-psychotic, perhaps stand as a warning that much of the clinician's work is not with formulations and devising narratives for their charges, but is done in a quiet feeling state which we might want to try to explain with a narrative after the fact. Outside interference from clinicians who have not experienced the triad clumsily make recommendations that usually end up being destructive.

Sometimes, second opinions and pontificating supervisors can provide useful alternative perspectives. However, I see the more important role of second opinions and supervisors as helping the primary clinician explore the quiet feeling state, just as it is the role of the clinician to help the patient self-reflect. On the other hand, if there is a challenge to the trust and attachment of the clinician, and the clinician cannot address it within the triad, then I feel that the clinician discharging his duties to the clinician providing the second opinion, rather than carry through with what does not feel right, is the best course. The clinician is expendable, and in any case, life, and not the clinician, is the ultimate teacher.

In retrospect in the case of James, perhaps we can see how the tandem development of James and his mother delayed mother's normative development as a parent. Parents of newborns serve as slaves, responding to every whimper and wish as an imperative, and yet taking great joy in every burp, fart and grimace. For James's mother, by necessity, this imperative continued into James's twenties, at the cost of seeing clearly James's deficits. It is to the great credit of James's clinician, and perhaps as a final un-yoking of the mother/child development, that both James and his mother were able to see and reflect on James's very real deficits and limitations (watching the historic videotapes). At that point, mother let go as James went off to an institution. For mother, this likely turned neurotic misery into ordinary human unhappiness. I would anticipate that for James, his development would slow or cease as he becomes an institutional fixture.

In conclusion, this case of delayed development in the adolescent child gives us a demonstration of the tandem, yoked development of parent and child. For the sake of the child, the parent's parenthood development is delayed. The benefit of the parent delaying the parenthood development is to the child in the continued, albeit slow, development in the child. In other words, the mother's view of her child even as she first watched the video of her delayed, struggling toddler was of the parent of an infant, and it was not until the clinician was able to help the mother see James's real deficits did the mother's development progress to that of the parent of an older child/ young adult. At that point, the mother likely felt (rightly or wrongly, although I think in the mind of the clinician, rightly) the futility of continuing to be the mother of a dependent and significantly developmentally delayed child in an adult body.

In the numerous cases such as James's that I have worked with, at some point, either because of the parent's exhaustion, push for the adolescent's own development, assistance from a clinician or death, the parent's and child's development is unyoked. As an epilogue, in my experience once this tandem parent/child development is unyoked, unless an emotional attachment is made between caretakers and (adult) child, the adult child's emotional development ceases. With this observation, we can observe what has been observed in other circumstances—development is contingent on attachment to another. In some cases, we as clinicians can work with staff of these institutions and support healthy attachments. In other cases, these institutions, such as criminal justice systems, are mostly heartless, although I have seen exceptions.

For some, this may raise an ethical dilemma as to whether or not we as clinicians should be working toward unyoking the parent/ child tandem development. In my experience, the ethical question is moot when we consider what is possible. The limitations of what is possible usually eliminate alternatives that might beg an ethical question. In other words, in a case such as James's, if the mother continues as the parent of a dependent child, both the mother and child expire psychologically. Consider, for example, the movie *Gray Gardens*. In any case, the answer should be left up to the parent and child. As clinicians, I see our job as helping the parent and the child to see more clearly the situation before them. Our job in the triad is to work to see more clearly what is.

Editorial Reflections

The final chapters of this casebook demonstrate the usefulness of thinking about work with parents as a potentially "ageless" endeavor that does not end at some chronologically or situationally determined moment. The parent-child relationship continues to evolve and transform throughout life; while the cases included here do not go beyond early adulthood, it is quite possible that there are clinicians who are doing versions of parent work when treating even older patients in certain circumstances. The work with James and his mother serves to also widen our thinking about the applicability—indeed the critical importance—of parent work when the patient suffers from severe mental illness. As one commentator sagely points out, "schizophrenia is not the sum and substance of James." We could say that having a schizophrenic son is no more the sum and substance of his mother either. The analyst helped the mother move forward from an identity that constricted both her and James—as mother of a child with out-of-the-ordinary needs—to one that allowed them both greater freedom over their life choices. She came to see herself as the "mother of an emergent adult with a special set of challenges to face with the appropriate supports," and as someone who could have her own fulfilling life as an adult woman.

The analyst states that he worked with the mother-son pair "with the aim of promoting change through understanding," as opposed to the psychoeducation and problem solving offered by previous therapists. He identifies elements of his approach such as modeling calm responses to James's provocations and demonstrating a belief that James could internalize responsibility for his functioning. As one commentator observes, he saw James as having a brain *and* a mind (and an ego?). A great deal more was going on in the work beyond these attitudes and techniques. One commentator highlights the analyst's perhaps unconscious falling in with this "couple's" characteristic passivity, letting himself "feel actively pulled into the family action"… and to participate in taking "a role in the family" drama. The analyst himself articulates something that more often goes unstated: "Privately I reflected on how my own evolution from sustaining a primary investment in the wish to effectively care for all James's problems towards a more truly neutral stance paralleled that of James's mother's growth." He changed too (!) as do we all when we engage fully with both parents and children.

Erna Furman (1992) closely observed the mutually unfolding development of mothers and toddlers. She described the maternal task of shifting from a narcissistic investment in her child (as a part of herself) to an object investment in him or her as a person in his or her own right. The case of James and his mother shows that parent work, even with the mother of a young adult, can help this shift occur. In fact, there may be some work on this developmental transformation in every case we treat, whether explicitly or implicitly. A third commentator concludes with the intriguing thought that our job as clinicians is to "see more clearly what is." This job encompasses many things and in parent work it becomes even more complicated as we try to see "what is" from multiple, confusing, and often conflicting points of view, while maintaining our investment in our patients and their caregivers as they are and as they may become. We are challenged by the commentators to consider the analyst's dual role in fostering development in both the emerging adult and the parent, while addressing the therapeutic needs of the patient.

CHAPTER FOURTEEN

BECOMING PSYCHOLOGICAL PARENTS: EMERGING PARENTHOOD

Emerging adults

Clinical Vignette

I chose "Emerging Parenthood" as the title for this case contribution because I wanted to call to mind the developmental phase now termed "emerging adulthood" (Arnett 2014). The young mother and father to be described here were in this transitional period of their lives when their child was conceived—no longer adolescents but not yet really functioning as independent adults. Their story may highlight some of the particular challenges for young persons who are faced with the task of becoming parents while still undergoing developmental transformations internally and in their relationships with their own mothers and fathers that continue well into their twenties. Their story also provides the opportunity to pay attention to the place of grandparents in such a situation and how they can affect the "emerging parenthood" of their not-yet-fully-grown-up sons and daughters.

The child of these parents was a worried and upset four-and-a-half-year-old who was having great difficulty in daycare when his mother first sought help for him. Carson's behaviors in the classroom looked aggressive and out-of-control and he was unresponsive to teachers' efforts to help him. He was frequently sent to the director's office where he would settle down easily, once he had an adult's exclusive attention. He plaintively asked her to help him keep his promises to be good. One strategy to deal with his difficulties was to shorten the length of his days at the center, or to have his mother come to pick him up early when he could not make use of the supports in place.

His mother was also worried and upset and sought the advice of her trusted pediatrician, who referred her for guidance and support. At the time, Sharon was a single mother in her early twenties who was still living with her own mother while she attended community college. She was highly invested in her child but felt helpless in the face of his difficulties. She was embarrassed by his behavior, believing it reflected badly on her, and she was angry and conflicted about having to miss class in order to come pick him up early. In her distress she could become harsh and punitive with him, or cast blame on others, including his father who was unreliably available.

The father, Carl, was a bit older, also in his early twenties. He, too, was still living with his parents when Carson was unexpectedly conceived. He and Sharon were friends in high school but not romantically involved; the pregnancy later on was the surprise result of a causal sexual encounter. Sharon viewed Carl and his family members as unsuccessful and lacking in ambition. Carl aspired to a career as a professional athlete but had no secure future prospects. Despite their situation, the two made the decision to try to make a go of it, hoping to raise their baby together. Thus, to one degree or another and for whatever complicated reasons they may have each had, they wanted and chose to become parents. Carl moved into the duplex that Sharon shared with her mother and her teenaged cousin.

Mrs. Lane, the maternal grandmother, was already raising her nephew because his parents were unable to do so. She herself had brought up her own children as a single parent, although their father remained involved and supportive. Even though Mr. and Mrs. Lane were not together as a couple, they managed to find a way to function well as partners in parenting and grandparenting. Mrs. Lane had many regrets that her younger sister had problems that required her to step in and take over the care of her nephew, but she resigned herself to the role and carried it out with love. She had pinned her hopes on Sharon, her youngest child, whom she believed had the potential to graduate from college with specialized skills that would secure her a well-paying job. She was sorely disappointed by Sharon's unplanned pregnancy, but she offered acceptance and to help in any way she could.

Within a few weeks of Carson's birth, the hard realities of becoming a family proved too great for Carl and Sharon to overcome. Carl felt that he was left out by Sharon and her mother as they shared in tending to Carson's needs and he responded angrily. After one of their frequent quarrels became violent, Sharon insisted that Carl move out. When I met her four years later, she confirmed his marginalization, saying that she and her mother had always been partners in caring for Carson, "like a husband and wife." Carl's parents encouraged him to step up and be a responsible father and keep regular contact with Carson, but he never consistently provided financial or emotional support, nor did his development into the phase of parenthood progress at this point.

Although there were problems due to the grandmother's close involvement, she also deserves credit for investing in her daughter becoming a parent. She supported her choice to breastfeed and in this way provided early reinforcement for the fact that Sharon was the mother and *she* was the helpmate. She became the "third," a containing presence as a father is in other families. Sharon was able to be at home fulltime with Carson during his first year, only resuming her college studies when he was a toddler. When she did start school again, her mother babysat when she had to be in class.

When Carson was three, his father had a sudden change of fortune. He was a participant in a nationally televised sporting event and briefly became a local celebrity. During this time of public attention, he used Carson as a PR prop to promote his image as a devout and devoted father. He began to take him to his parents' home for weekend visits and exposed him to large, overwhelming crowds. Sharon was swept up in the excitement of all of this, even imagining they might get back together, but she also felt that Carl was not thinking about Carson's needs nor protecting him adequately. She was stunned and furious to learn that Carl had suddenly married without informing her or Carson in advance. Soon afterward he and his wife moved to a distant city and he again was only in intermittent contact with Carson.

This was the way things were when I began working with Sharon on Carson's behalf in the model described as "treatment via the parent" (R. Furman and Katan, 1969). The aim of this work was to support and help Sharon understand the underlying reasons for Carson's behavioral difficulties so that she could be the one to help him herself. By this time, she was a fulltime student again and had enrolled Carson in the daycare where he was having such a hard time. She would often have her mother pick him up on the days when the school called to say his behavior was unmanageable. The task in the beginning of our work was to help her recognize how much Carson still needed her and her alone. However much she and her mother might believe they were interchangeable at this point, Carson was begging for her time and attention. Sharon went along with a plan to make herself more available to him by reducing her course load so that she could accompany him to school and remain in the building to support him emotionally until he felt safe and able to stay on his own. Her presence had a calming effect and Carson began to improve noticeably.

Sharon and I met weekly in an effort to understand what was troubling Carson and how to help him. In our sessions Sharon began to open up about what it had been like for her to try to become a mother. She reported that her pregnancy was complicated both physically and emotionally. She was plagued by thoughts that she was carrying an alien baby who would resemble Carl's side of the family, not hers. She felt extremely guilty that she had let her mother down and believed that her out-of-wedlock sexual activity was a sin for which she deserved punishment. When it appeared that she might go into labor prematurely, she was terrified that she had caused damage to her baby and might lose him. Carson's newborn squalling convinced her he was "born angry." She imagined he would grow up to be a murderer. By projecting her own intolerable aggression and anger, she spared herself, at the expense of her relationship with Carson. Luckily there were other ways in which she delighted in his appearance and his curious nature that tempered this somewhat, but she continued to view any sign of distress as anger and recrimination. As one example, when Carson expressed frustration by banging his head when confined to his crib, Sharon again felt he was somehow demonic—failing to put together that he might be missing her and wanting to be with her, or to simply use his growing mobility to explore his world.

Our work began to focus on their mutual ambivalence. When Sharon felt overburdened and angry, she easily lashed out at Carson or withdrew from him. This heightened both his anxiety and his aggressive behaviors, leading to a downward spiral neither knew how to escape. Mrs. Lane's remedy was to try to take over, but this only helped temporarily and actually made things worse as Sharon then felt rejected and incompetent. What we were learning in our work helped Sharon to feel her importance, but it also increased her guilt. In addition, Carson's improvements meant that he seemed to be moving away from her at the very time she was beginning to like being with him. In response, when a new school semester began, she signed up for more classes again and asked that her mother be allowed to come for him at the daycare center if necessary.

Mrs. Lane then approached me to see whether she could be the one to attend parent sessions when her daughter could not make it. I decided to have a meeting with her and to clarify directly how I thought she could be most helpful. I expressed my admiration for her support and involvement that had been so important to Carson and his mother his whole life. We talked about the many practical ways she assisted them, but I said that Carson really still needed Sharon to remain consistently invested in being his mother, rather than withdrawing from him. Mrs. Lane had been pressuring Sharon to let her take over Carson's care so that she could finish school more quickly. In this way she was functioning herself as a mother who wanted her own child to move ahead developmentally. Fortunately, however, she could recognize that an opportunity for Carson and Sharon to consolidate their gains might be lost. From that time on she helped out by transporting Carson to sessions on occasion and we had regular contact, but the prior double-mothering underwent a shift.

When Carson entered kindergarten, his behaviors worsened again. At this point it no longer seemed that he was experiencing anxiety related to separations, but rather that his longstanding problems with self-esteem were interfering with learning and relationships with peers. He would act out in order to avoid the conflicts aroused by comparing himself with others or when he was feeling left out. Sharon also wisely observed that she thought he was "thirsty for a father"[6] and it seemed possible that he was identifying with the picture conveyed to him of Carl as an aggressive and unsuccessful man. Early on I had told Sharon that at some point it would be important for Carl to be involved in the work we were doing and she agreed. She consciously tried not to speak ill of him to Carson but her disappointment in him was no secret. She also began to tell me that she felt that her efforts with Carson were not enough to help him overcome his difficulties. I was aware of the risks of "taking over" as I had warned Mrs. Lane not to do, but I was sufficiently concerned about Carson's development that I recommended a five-times-a-week analysis at a much reduced fee. Sharon accepted the recommendation and Carson and I began our work together as he was turning six. The beginning work allowed Carson to work on the loyalty conflict he had always experienced between his mother and his grandmother and the ongoing weekly concurrent meetings with Sharon provided the chance for her to rework some her own feelings about this as well.

Early on I learned just how much Carson's wishes for a strong, protective father were disappointed in reality. He asked me to show him on an office globe where his father had moved. He said, "My father has trouble with his temper." He introduced a Lego story in which there was

---

6   Her comment brought to mind James Herzog's work on "father hunger" (2004) and the important role fathers play in helping boys in particular to tame aggression.

a father, a grandfather, and a son who was having a birthday party. He had the father say in a gentle voice, "Hi kids, are you having a nice party?" He said the father had a six-pack from eating healthy food and had the characters do snowboard and bicycle stunts—the father bought the son a bike helmet for safety. He built a second house next door for the father's brother, commenting that the uncle took good care of it and it had flowers.

When I met with Carson's mother for our regular appointment, I heard a very different story. Carl had been in town for Carson's sixth birthday but did not buy him a gift. He and his brother got into a physical fight over this hurtful neglect. Carson ignored his father's warning not to tell his mother, but he did not want her to tell me. (I think it was just too humiliating.) Sharon encouraged him to tell me anything and said he had her permission to do so. After I let Carson know what his mother had told me, his mood and the content of the play changed from skills to fights. He began to talk about a boy in his classroom who had recently gone on a trip with his father and could say he was jealous when he heard the boy talk about the fun they had.

About six months into the analysis, Carl reached out to Sharon to say that he would like Carson to come stay with him for the entire summer. Carson was clear that he did not want to go so far away, for so long—but he wanted his father to come visit him. I used this opening to ask Sharon and Carson whether I might contact Carl myself, a request to which they both agreed. When I called him, Carl expressed surprise to hear that Carson was having difficulty in school but he did not object to the analysis. He wanted to know my opinion about his wish to have Carson visit him in the summer and said he would go along with whatever I recommended. I shared Carson's feelings about the plan and suggested that we begin to have regular phone conversations so that he could feel more involved and aware of what Carson was struggling with. Despite agreeing to this, he did not follow through. He did, however, begin to call Carson regularly and to come to visit more often. Carson would spend occasional overnights with his father at the paternal grandparents' home again when he was in town. Carl seemed to function more like an uncle than a father and his involvement was based more on his parents' urging than on his own initiative. In his analytic hours after these visits, Carson would pretend to play video games and ignore me, leaving me feeling desolate and alone. I began to interpret the emptiness between him and his dad, along with the anger and sorrow Carson felt about this.

One morning Carson arrived early for a session and I had to ask him to wait a minute. When I went to get him he said, correctly, "That was more than a minute." I said maybe my making him wait was something that made him angry. At this point he tried very hard to preserve his analysis as a place where only good feelings were tolerated, while he still acted out at school. He said he wanted to go get a drink of water and was pleased when I said he'd make me be the waiter. He came back and said he'd been gone for three minutes. "You made me have to wait, like you had to wait for me," I said. I went on to add that I'd had a phone conversation with his father the day before and his dad had told me that Carson was making him wait by not coming to the phone. I said he also told me he'd be coming to town in a week. "That's a long time I'll have to wait," Carson responded. He left for another drink and returned asking how long he'd been gone this time. I asked if he noticed what we had been talking about when he left. "My dad." I said he had to wait for his dad a lot and wondered whether he could let him know that this made him angry instead of taking his angry feeling with him to school.

During the period of time when Carl was out-of-town and not a regular participant in the work, I believe it was essential to keep him in mind and be ready to respond to both clear and disguised references to him in Carson's material.

When Carson was in second grade, Carl moved back home when his career stalled and his marriage failed. He began to have regular visit times with Carson and to bring him to his analytic sessions on days when the two were together. He met with me every few weeks and I was surprised by his growing investment in his son. His parents' support for him being a father and their positive regard for Sharon seemed to be important elements in him taking new developmental steps toward fatherhood. He started to attend school functions and contributed financially for the first time. Carson asked his father for and received a backgammon game as a birthday present—a game they now enjoyed playing together in contrast to the distant parallel video-game play of the past (and in stark contrast to Carson's narcissistic wound the year Carl neglected to buy a gift at all).

Carson began to ask his mother lots of questions about why she and his father "got divorced" and she explained that they had never been married. She and Carl were getting along better at this point and were able to agree about visits without arguing as they had in the past. A turning point in their ability to work together as parents on Carson's behalf came one Halloween. Instead of overriding Sharon's objections about a scary costume as he would have done in the past, Carl called her to consult about whether the one Carson was requesting was appropriate. Carson asked his father to practice sports skills with him—and to buy him protective gear so he wouldn't have to worry so much about getting hurt. Carson confided to me that he used to think his parents would get engaged but said that he now knew that wouldn't happen. He thought his mother and her boyfriend might get married, but hoped they'd soon get divorced so that his parents could be together. Sharon valued the new closeness between Carson and Carl and even called Carl one time to come and get Carson when he was misbehaving with her. He was able to step into this role that is so useful for any father to take when things between a mother and son get too heated.

A new level of integrating his past was evident when Carson introduced aliens in his material. I commented that he used to call himself an alien, but I was thinking of his mother's fantasy during her pregnancy that she was carrying an alien. The next day Carson said his mother wanted to bring a book about aliens for me to see. "She thinks other seven-year-olds don't notice as much as me." I took this opening to say that he seemed to know that his mother had felt surprised by him and thought he was somehow different than other kids. He then asked for a legal pad and wrote out a detailed account of an argument between his mother and grandmother. He said of himself, "That anger I used to have, I can control it now." His thoughts turned to his father and he said, "My dad used to get angry, but he doesn't anymore." Later I could offer a reconstruction when I told him that all babies get into rages, but it's harder for some mothers to know how to help. When he was little he used to bang his head on his crib rail and this had seemed weird and scared his mom. Now that he was seven, he and his mother could both know that anger didn't have to be so scary or mean that there was something wrong with him.

Meanwhile, Sharon's dating represented a new step for her, too. She was staying out late at night which caused more arguments between her and her mother. She seemed to be taking some steps toward independent functioning and sexuality that she had never accomplished in adolescence. She and Carson moved to the upstairs apartment in the house they shared with Mrs. Lane, a small but significant sign of movement into adulthood. Carson was very troubled by the angry fights between his mother and grandmother but he could observe their troubles and still keep the loving parts of them in his mind. He said he did not want to be like that when he grew up—perhaps imagining by then how he would be as a man, a husband, and a father.

*In his analysis, Carson began to complain about his mother's dates and said she was spending too much time with one man in particular. In a parent session, Sharon told me Carson was acting like he himself was "her man" and would ask her boyfriend disrespectfully, "Why are you here?" He arrived for one session with red-rimmed eyes. He didn't want to talk but then complained bitterly, "She no longer makes me her first priority... and I'm not just repeating what my grandma said." I interpreted his experience by saying that other boys who have always lived with their mother and father together have to work it out that they have a separate grownup relationship. He had his mom to himself for a long time and now it was especially hard to share her. "That's what she's been saying," he said. Sharon and I had, indeed, talked about this in our ongoing parent work and in this way a shared understanding among the three of us could be talked about both at home and in his analysis. In addition, Carson and I could talk about his observations of my husband, since he came to my home office, and the ways in which he felt that **I** did not make him **my** first priority.*

When I first met Carson at four-and-a-half he often wore a t-shirt with the words "Parents for sale, cheap." In choosing and allowing her son to wear this shirt, Sharon seemed to advertise to the world how poorly she felt she and Carl were doing as parents. It was a privilege to work with them both through the time when their development into parenthood went from "emerging" to solid and became a source of pride. In his work, Carson was able to use the transference and his parents' greater availability and understanding to move into an oedipal phase for the first time. Mrs. Lane also grew as Sharon's mother and Carson's grandmother during the time I knew them. I did not have contact with Carl's parents, but their steadfast efforts toward maintaining the relationship between their son and his son were invaluable. By the time Carson's analysis came to an end he had a mother and a father who had taken great strides in their functioning as his parents.

Commentary 1

I was honored to be asked to comment on this project, and to think of it being available as a lens to view parent work in the therapeutic community. On the one hand the case had personal meaning to me as it was a reminder of work via the parent introduced by Erna Furman during her visits to our local institute. On the other hand, the case presents an ongoing conflict of how emerging parents can present a disorganized attachment to the early relationship between the child and the mother. My commentary will take the focus of affect regulation in the emerging parental role of the mother, Sharon. The parent work is full of imagery and important content that allows the reader to explore many layers presented. The analyst begins with providing the systems outline of the family. In doing so it created a stage for the reader to travel the developmental timeline not only with Carson, but with the parental conception and development of his parents, Carl and Sharon.

In preparation for writing this commentary, I reread Ruth Hall's article "Working with Parents" (1993), and Erna Furman's *Toddlers and Their Mothers* (1992). Hall's article describes how the parent work becomes a learning experience for both parent(s) and analyst, along with the parent's wish for the analyst to magically have all the answers. It may be important to question how much the parent(s) feel independently sufficient or wish for the care of the

323

analyst to convey a step-by-step system to developmentally master parenthood. In *Toddlers and Their Mothers*, Furman's chapter on "Coping with Aggression" explores not only the fear of aggression, but also aggression towards and of the mother. Furman reminds us that the toddler's aggression is an essential part of daily life and coping with aggression is an important developmental task in the toddler's personality growth. She continues to explain age-appropriate difficulty in differentiating between self and other, so anyone's anger could be one's own. This can be extended to the love-hate impulses of the mother-child relationship. Furman stated this often manifested itself in the form of a loyalty conflict. When exploring the parent's aggression Furman reminded the reader that moms and dads came into parenting with their own varied measure of difficulties in coping with anger, and when the child's behavior threatened or weakened their self-control, they sometimes acted like their children themselves.

Regardless of one's clinical view about working with parents, it would be important to consider the following tasks. First, explaining the meaning and significance of parent work, and how it may be met with some resistance from the parent(s). I wondered in this case how much of the resistance was the confusion of the mother and maternal grandmother sharing the parental role. Secondly, how the analyst approaches the family dynamics. This would include recognizing the importance of patriarchal-matriarchal dominance within the family and how it relates to the life of the child. Third, establishing the roles within the parent work and if and how other helpers can be recognized. This allows for the parent work to identify where the power is positioned within the family in order to form an alliance in support of any recommended treatment. In this case it was clear how the maternal grandmother, Mrs. Lane, was a powerful voice within the family, and having her participation was important. Meeting with the mother weekly was essential in the analyst-parent dyad to creating a space for Sharon to think and begin understanding her challenges and emotional experiences. This was such an essential step in affective validation for the mother. In the parent helper process the analyst seemed sensitive to the mother's insecurities as she so carefully helped Sharon gain an awareness of her importance to Carson and slowly transition to mother from mother substitute.

Emerging into awareness seemed to be a strong thread in steps to securing the attachment. Early in the work the mother seemed to struggle with deciding to parent versus letting her mother and/or the analyst take on the parenting role. The analyst addressed the mother's ambivalence with owning her role, but also owning her own aggression and guilt. It was recognized that her anger towards Carson only contributed to his increased anxiety and aggressive choices. Furman (1995) brought to analysts' attention that parental aggression accentuates the child's aggression. It was suggested that as one gets bigger their anger gets bigger and more dangerous. At the same time there is the implied loss of love, from the parent and for the parent, and the interference with loving self-investment of one's body. This seemed to parallel the triadic aggressive pattern between Sharon, Carson, and Mrs. Lane. The parent work assisted the mother in understanding how her aggression unknowingly rendered a splitting of two sides, desperation and weakness. In Sharon's desperation emerged thoughts of why she doesn't put herself into what she believes in. On the end of weakness are the thoughts she's not of much value and needs to be cuddled and taken care of. Perhaps this is where Mrs. Lane gains control of the parenting of Carson, but in doing so takes care of Sharon's weakness as well. In their efforts both sides of the split needed to be simultaneously held in mind to gain an understanding. The description given was a beautiful illustration of the delicate work of the analyst and the mother to explore Sharon's difficulty with resolution of conflicts, but a willingness to move into a place of affective tolerance. It seemed finally Sharon was being heard and, being aware of more confidence, could establish a workable dyad. In doing so Sharon was able to explore the similarities of her own and Carson's wish to have more of an available mother. The parent work was creating a useable space for Sharon to explore the reality of being a mother.

What I find most compelling in this case is how the analyst presents the father's near, but distant presence. During kindergarten Carson began to become less dependent upon his mother, his use of aggression seemed easier for Sharon to listen to and interpret, rather than reactively joining her son. The analyst allowed an unfolding action and discussion to shape the process in which Sharon became more aware of Carson's needs and wishes. The analyst reminded the mother she was not alone in this journey and perhaps Carl could now be more available. The mother agreed. Again this was an example how the analyst recognized the emergence of emotional growth of Sharon, and perhaps that of Carl as well. Carson began to communicate how he was thinking and how he was organizing cognitive content. This seemed to occur when the analyst discussed how the father continued to struggle to regulate his anger effectively, and Carson was able to self-activate boundaries, and still engage with his father. Carson would visit with his father but choose not to have overnight visits unless they were at the home of his paternal grandparents. His approach to his father's aggression was a beautiful indication of how Carson was balancing and regulating his own aggressive concerns and confronting the triangular oedipal conflicts.

In conclusion, the parent work allowed the analyst to assist the mother in how to be affectively available to her child and therefore through internal conflict resolution resolve the conflict in the parent-child dyad. As the analyst and the mother worked together, Sharon began to recognize how she was aggressively externalizing her helplessness and later regretting her primitive impulses invoked by Carl. I found it specifically skillful how the parent work assisted in eventually helping both parents with how their aggression externally and internally could affect their son. This case is a wonderful example of emerging parenthood and how such a collaboration is not confined to working with the dominant parent, but slowly and patiently creating a strong alliance that developmentally matures into a co-parenting partnership.

Commentary 2

I am a clinician who makes emergency psychiatric evaluations of people in crisis. As part of my job, which takes place in the emergency department of an urban hospital, I see children and adolescents. As minors, they are connected to one or more adults. Most of my patients belong to the working class or poor. Reading the case, "Becoming Psychological Parents," I was struck with its erasure of race as a marker. There is a value structure in the case presented. But it is ambiguous as to whether its origins lie in culture, class or the evidence accruing to the practitioners of psychoanalysis. The extent to which these values are structured by the ensuing assumptions, possibilities and limitations of these origins is also ambiguous.

As a white, male practitioner with psychoanalytic training, yet one who is neither sociologist nor cultural anthropologist nor researcher, I am thrown back upon my intellect and sensibilities. Although one might consider that stance one of presumption and white privilege, I

327

embrace it as positioning me toward the expectations of transference and symptom relief that I encounter as a clinician.

The paper itself is presented with a simplicity, directness and focus that is both beguiling and appropriate. These qualities are born of the demands of a brief case that it be clear about its argument; it is also a spinoff, it seems to me, of a research model which seeks to eliminate variables. The result, though, is that the case shimmers with the ambiguities mentioned above and is not explicit in addressing realities which this reader experiences in his work or the assumptions which inform him and blind him. Although embossing specificity as this response intends might seem an unneeded excess, I hope rather to bring front and center problems of concept and of policy.

The terms of effective parenting are implicit in the case discussion. In a key comment, the author states, "The task in the beginning of our work was to help [Sharon] recognize how much Carson still needed her and her alone." The centrality of the mother-child dyad in early childhood is a core tenet of contemporary psychoanalysis. Its disruption by any of various causes has complex sequelae for the child. In this case, Carl has early on been excluded by the mother/grandmother dyad. And the grandmother is sidelined by the analyst—adding to the singularity of the attachment between Sharon and Carson. The author here discusses the challenges to that dyad when emerging parenthood overlaps emerging adulthood.

Variations on the Eurocentric theme that the individual is to be prized over the community are also played throughout the paper. Individuation and separation become central tenets of the psychotherapeutic encounter: Carson's attachment to his mother must be protected, paradoxically, to facilitate his separation from her; Sharon's attachment to Carson is encouraged in part to facilitate her separation from her mother. This is the context for the author's applause for Sharon and Carson's move to live alone in the second-floor apartment in the grandmother's home. It is also the context for the author's applause for Sharon's "independent functioning and sexuality that she had never accomplished as an adolescent."

It is not the purpose of this commentary to deride or undermine these choices as accomplishments. Nor is it my intent to throw stones at developmental psychology within a psychoanalytic framework. For each individual is unique and must create compromises between the individual and the community along developmental lines. But looking around the world, one observes significant cultural differences in how an individual, a dyad, a family or a community negotiates these values and structures.

My work in an urban emergency room shines a light on differences relevant to a conceptual understanding of this case. Children and adolescents in crisis are brought in for psychiatric evaluations to my pediatric ER by grandmothers, aunts, great-grandmothers, foster mothers, biological mothers and, at times, fathers. The nurturing tie for the patient may be to the grandmother; it may be to the aunt who is raising the child—and that person called "aunt" may or may not be a blood relative. In fact, the child may have been raised, even outside the foster care system, at different times by several different members of this extended family. I have worked in the ER with children and adolescents who have wished—with reason—to live with any of various biological and non-biological relatives. The result makes complicated the idea that a child "still needs her and her alone." To what extent is the analyst, because of a Eurocentric cultural model apparent in this text creating the solution to the need?

Given the cultural paradigm I am questioning—and the one I am positing as an alternate overlap to the developmental structure—it is curious that beyond one mention no attention is paid to the role of the analyst in this "family structure." And that one mention is, I argue, in defense of a Eurocentric model of individualism over community. For the analyst fears that they will, in fact, play the role that they are seeking to deny the grandmother in Carson's life.

Yet the significant role the analyst does play is elided. Carson does not wish to be away for the summer. Is it the analyst, at least in part, from whom Carson does not wish to separate? Is the analyst, even if not replacing the grandmother, playing the role, as a new object and in the transference, of the alternate maternal figure—aunt, biological or not, grandmother, older sister from a previous sexual encounter—so prevalent in the African American community I serve? If so, what are the implications for the family and community models which the analyst has the option to advance?

I would now like to shift directions to a consideration of aggression. To do so, I would like to propose a verbal Venn diagram overlapping, for the light they shed on each other, my emergency room work with children and adolescents, the history of the African American community, and the case under discussion.

As I remarked at the beginning, the case does not have racial markings. What it does have is enough ambiguity that the reader's assumptions and stereotypes are called into play. I initially felt drawn to reading the case as being about a white family, due to the range of opportunities—day care, seeming uncomplicated access to community college, access to analytic therapy—while an African American colleague of mine assumed initially that, because the father was absent and there was a strong grandmother, the family was black. She and I discussed any number of other "markers" and concluded that we simply did not know the racial identity of the family.

I bring this up in expression of the core value within psychoanalysis of respect for the culture, experiences and choices of the patient.

What my colleague and I each independently perceived as the bias toward individualism may not have been a bias if that were the culture and desires of those being treated. But, if those being treated were African American, she and I both felt that there could have been a subtle dissonance or a collaboration with what W.E.B Dubois famously called "double consciousness." That is, the experiences, desires and expectations of the family being treated might well have been culturally different from those of the therapist which, I would argue, shade toward those of the dominant white culture. An African American family will have learned to at times suppress its cultural expression and code shift to the communication and cultural modalities of the dominant white culture. But there is a psychic cost.

That said, I return to the consideration of aggression. There is a dispute I have with my non-analytically oriented ER colleagues as to how to frame not the diagnosis but the problem and the solution of our "acting out" patients. Is the problem "behavioral"—that is, requiring clear, no-nonsense parenting—or psychological—that is, conducive to modification by medication, inpatient containment and talk.

Once the year passes Labor Day, school social workers, mothers, great-grandmothers, aunts and sometimes fathers, bring in their charges for misbehaving in the classroom, and, less frequently, at home. Objects and curse words may be thrown, desks overturned; a child may run out of the classroom or out of the school; suicide may be threatened, an attempt may be made, a child in school may punch a teacher or another child or, at home, a parent, a cousin, a sibling. Of Carson, it was said, there were "days his behavior was unmanageable." Frequently, he had to be picked up early, unable to tolerate the communal requirements of his preschool day.

The dyadic relationship between an inner city mother, battered into hurt, anger and aggression by the inner city deprivations, griefs, microaggressions and violence, which contribute to this sequelae in the classroom, and her child are too often misunderstood as incompatibility, argument, violence—poor parenting and poor behavior—and not as psychological conflicts and dynamics.

Contrarily, the interpretations around aggression of the case before us are often acute. For one, the author notes of Sharon: "In her distress, she could become harsh and punitive with him or cast blame on others;" "Carson's newborn squalling convinced her he was born angry;" and, "By projecting her own intolerable aggression and anger, she spared herself, at the expense of her relationship with Carson."

But, *as presented,* cultural and historical elements are absent. Should the case have been of an African American family, for example, a different light would be cast on Sharon having been "embarrassed by [Carson's] behavior, believing it reflected badly on her." Black parents swim in a culture in which it is important to "control" your children and of being embarrassed when a child is "out of control." The historical root is crucial: if children, under slavery or Jim Crow, crossed a sometimes clear, sometimes obscure line, they could be in grave risk of harm, including being "sold down the river" or murdered like Emmett Till.

Carson was fortunate. He had a mother, grandmother and, it turned out, father who supported therapy and—this is key—had the social and economic resources to get themselves and the child to therapy (a marker of class). If a child and a mother and a family unit, nuclear or extended, has at hand a therapist as dedicated, sensitive and capable as the one evident here, their opportunities to resolve their conflicts and create internal, family and community structures as nuanced as these will be greatly enhanced. However, as a matter of social policy, when more commonly such is not an option, might the best policy for many be to encourage options that provide "good enough" parenting within alternate cultural paradigms?

Commentary 3

In this beautiful presentation, the analyst tells us of the work with Carson, his mother Sharon, his grandmother, Mrs. Lane, and his father Carl. We hear how she established working relationships with all of these people and in so doing we are invited to join the discussion of emerging parenthood.

The work exemplifies respectful listening, thoughtful inquiry and careful guidance exquisitely timed. Given that there will be multiple responses in this chapter, I shall focus on expectant fatherhood and the options available to endorse and facilitate paternal participation when fathers do not follow the more conventional time course of continuous co-participation in the development of the parental couple and the development of a family.

Some years ago, I reported on a study conducted in the Neonatal Intensive Care Unit at a children's hospital and in the Follow Up Clinic we established to follow its graduates, both infants and parents.[7] The gist of this work was that in married couples expecting a baby, men traversed a path of stages and phases which recapitulated aspects of what others and I came to call the developmental pathway to fatherhood. Our focus in this work was clinically tutored. We were trying to understand serious marital tensions which sometimes declared themselves with the premature arrival of the baby and ways in which the new father seemed to be competitive

---

7   References to these studies may be found in the references section of this volume.

rather than co-operative and supportive of his spouse. We were also interested in the ways in which the new father experienced the nurse who took care of his infant. He was often more beneficent toward her than toward his wife. Our conclusions centered around the data which suggested that men needed to make a transformation from more maternal identification in their caretaking to paternal ones and that this did not usually occur until close to term. Departing from the marital partner, at least affectively, and making a new alliance with the nurse appeared to be associated with a premature interruption in the man's parentogenic development.

In our follow up with these families, it became apparent that concepts like the caretaking line of development, which are nomothetic, are always more fully understood when one focuses on the idiographic. Much more was going on in the individual men who became competitive with and blaming of their wives after a premature delivery which could be related to their own boyhoods and their own father's behavior. A history of leaving a relationship when there was stress was a prominent feature, and there also appeared to have been many unresolved issues in the parental couple before the early arrival of their child. There was also some suggestion that depression in the mother may have been a feature of some of these pregnancies.

In another study, I described work conducted with groups of adolescent boys on sexuality and intimacy in a public school. Again, in an effort to establish commonalities, we articulated descriptions of these adolescents' sexual activities which were described as declarative, recreative-interactive, procreative, parentogenic, and integrative. Getting adolescent boys to share their fantasies and thoughts about sex in a group is not an easy matter but we tried very hard to make this possible. It was often facilitated by what happened outside of the group, unexpected pregnancies, abortions, an abortion thought to have happened and then the response to learning that it had not, one member of the group bringing in a two-year-old whom he had fathered and then disciplining him, one member of the group shyly revealing that his unmarried sister had a child and that he and the child were very close and how he felt about that and toward the little boy, interactions that each of the boys had with their own parents.

Each of these events elicited much commentary from our group members and this proved very fecund in terms of thinking about their thinking about sexual activity. The most important aspect of these varieties of sexual activity which emerged was the difference between what we called procreative and parentogenic. Very often these boys thought about making a baby, but it was very rare that this included the thought of taking care of the baby or of the baby's mother. It was more declarative, to show that he was fertile, or even simply representing the cost of having pleasure. "You play, you pay, unless she gets rid of it or you walk away," said one group member. Many of the others concurred, although there was a range of accompanying affect. The conversation was almost never centered on morals, ethics, or religious tenets, but rather matter-of-factly about this seeming paradox: It was cool to make a baby, but entirely another story to want to be an actual father. We called this set of attitudes procreative intercourse and differentiated it from parentogenic intercourse which we did not find in our study except in one group member involved in a relationship with significant plans for a future which involved children at a faraway time.

These boys were in casual relationships. With only one exception, none of them thought about marriage or about beginning a family. It seemed that libidinal and aggressive drives and affects were anything but integrated and somewhat chaotically deployed in their sexual activities. As the earlier work on the caretaking line of development in men had been derived from a sample of fathers of premature infants and had involved the hypothesis that sexual, aggressive, and narcissistic constituents were all being sorted out to try and achieve a coherent whole during the pregnancy, it was not surprising to encounter this still earlier array of similar forces.

Following these two pieces of work and our subsequent efforts in the Clinic for the Development of Children, Parents and Families, also at the children's hospital, we articulated the hypothesis that fathering, with all of its individual antecedents, predispositions and impediments, optimally develops in a triadic setting in which there are two parents with a relationship with each other and a relationship with the child. In such a setting, impulse and defense, style and vulnerability can be viewed, monitored and titrated by both parents and the child can optimally be regarded as the individual he or she is and thus grow with the least possible pathogenic skewing. We also observed that fathering (and mothering) evolved over time in each of our families. In some way practice had the potential for making better and experience of what worked and what did not could also be considered. All of these observations were accrued in a large sample of two-parent families. In our initial sample, all of these families were composed of a mother and a father.

In later work, conducted in families consisting of two parents and at first one child and then two, we reported on different modalities available to each parent in the presence of the other which also may optimize the experiential world of the child and impart greater play capacity in the internal representational world. This work which emphasized the father's play style and its role in gear shifting, and the modulation and organization of aggressive behavior and associated affective states has been widely replicated. It has also been criticized as pertinent perhaps to role divisions in any family constellation and not particular to fathering in the presence of mothering. This important distinction was meant to counter our hypothesis that there were gender specific components to the differing preferred repertoires of mothers and fathers when both were present. So far, no studies have appeared which demonstrate this axiom but there is abundant clinical reporting which does.

Finally, in the response, I would like to mention that in my analytic experience and in that of close colleagues, we have observed multiple examples of what the analyst reports in the work with Carson. As a child's analysis begins, he or she or, more accurately, the analysis, facilitates the absent father's return to a more active role. This phenomenon is evident in multiple other reports of child analytic work. It is almost as if the child and analyst, as the analytic couple, provide a dyad which can function in an inviting way to the father. This almost always features the child's prescient observations on the ways in which life with his mother are relevant to his father's return and in what ways. Carson's early problems with aggression prompted the initial referral. Patiently and skillfully the analyst helped his mother to be there, his grandmother to understand his need for his mother, and ultimately for Carson to begin an analysis. Carson also needed his father's help with this. In the way that these forces optimally arise both analyst and analysand welcomed the more active involvement of the father and he, in fact, became the father Carson needed.

Editorial Reflections

This chapter highlights several significant dimensions of the developmental phase of parenthood. We learn of the importance of honoring the parental role, no matter how little or uncomfortably a parent has initially embraced it. Therapists are also faced with the challenge of dealing with aggression toward the child and among the grownups in his life. This can have a powerful impact on the therapist who may react with rage at the parent or defensively siding with the parents and focusing only on the child's provocative behavior. Anger in any family member can set off a self-perpetuating cycle of increasing anger which can end only by some violent action. Analysts must first contain their own anger and then help the adults and child contain theirs.

"Containment" is a concept that needs unpacking—this case and the commentaries point us toward a more complex understanding of the multiple functions of anger within and between family members. We learn also that analysts have to face multiple directions simultaneously in this realm, helping parents to accept and contain their child's aggression and their own, and additionally working to perceive and accept the aggression of multiple people. Therapists then have to deal with their own reactions to hostility and its effects among family members. Commentators felt that the family's values and the therapist's values were significant as people in each generation of this family developed and changed; the intersection of aspirations and supported growth could be tracked in the changes in how each person dealt with anger.

We are also offered an important distinction between procreation and parenting, between childbearing and child rearing, in both fathers and mothers (Herzog 1979, 1984; K. Novick 1988). The story of Sharon, Carl, and Carson exemplifies the need for these strands to be merged and integrated for consolidation in the phase of parenthood and effective functioning as a parent for a child to thrive. This brings us to the parents' developmental experience of a child's treatment.

Technically, we see anew the importance of flexibility in meeting the needs of each and all important people in the child's world in the context of working toward the therapeutic aims. This helps us redefine "parent work" in a broad spectrum of methodologies, including whomever matters in the situation, while always keeping in mind the central focus of restoring the child to progressive development and the parent-child relationship to its most transformative possibilities. Carson's individual analysis was necessary for his growth. What this chapter also brings home again, however, is that we need dual goals for treatment. The child's progressive development cannot take place in a vacuum but depends on fostering capacities in caregivers and parents to support open-system functioning, with understanding of maladaptive patterns and their deep roots, acceptance of reality, containment and modulation of aggression, and engagement with primary parental love. Carson's parents learned how important they were and were helped to rise to the occasion.

This chapter also raises, perhaps the most vividly of any in this volume, questions about the impact of culture and background of all the protagonists on goals, values, expectations, relationship patterns and dynamics. When we involve parents and other family members in a treatment, we move well beyond a traditional or theoretical focus on only the psychic representational landscape of the child and have to take into account other psychological universes. This is a challenge to therapists and represents one of the potential pitfalls of parent work.

The focus on parenthood as a phase of development allows us to follow the movement of both parents through the sub phases of parenthood. In fulfilling the tasks of the therapeutic alliance, we facilitate the parents' movement through the phases of parenthood from the capacity to parent oneself to accepting one's role as the psychological parent to retaining a positive tie with one's own parents while living a physically and psychologically separate life.

CHAPTER FIFTEEN

CONCLUSIONS AND FUTURE DIRECTIONS

In the introductory chapter, we said that our goal in this volume was to collect examples of actual work with parents. As we invited colleagues to share their clinical work, we ended up gathering an unexpectedly broad sample. Demographically, the patients' ages ranged from four to twenty-six, with roughly half boys and half girls, and adolescents well-represented; there were many family configurations (single parents, divorced parents, adoptive parents, same-sex parents, very young parents, immigrant parents, and so forth); the children fell into many diagnostic categories, and most of the parents seemed to manifest as more troubled than the population of individual adults who present themselves for treatment. Contributors of both vignettes and commentaries work in a wide variety of settings and bring experience in many realms of clinical work, as well as heterogeneous training backgrounds and theoretical orientations.

We set out to demonstrate the reality of doing parent work, how hard it is, what the challenges are, how people try to meet them, what sometimes succeeds in making the efforts effective and rewarding, what doesn't work even with massive effort, pitfalls, techniques and their rationales, and the impact on analysts, patients, and parents when they do or don't work together. We hoped to use this material to challenge, refine, and further elaborate an evolving model of parent work.

In this chapter, we will think about particular elements of the parent work model that has been developing over the past twenty years and see how the work described in this book refines, elaborates, refutes, redirects, or challenges assumptions and findings.

What have we learned?

First, we may address the fundamental question—should child and adolescent treatment include work with parents?

Most child treatment cases end prematurely, with adolescent cases even more precarious (Novick, J. and Novick, K.K. 2006). The bulk of those premature terminations occur very early in the process, often at the point of treatment planning and recommendation (Novick, K.K. and Novick, J. 2005).

In our sample in this volume, despite the manifest disturbances in most of the parents, only one of the cases ended early; that one case was an adolescent who had to be hospitalized. While some others terminated sooner than the analyst might have wished, the remaining fourteen stayed in treatment for substantial periods and they made significant gains. If one of the reasons to include parent work is the pragmatic support of the child's individual treatment, we think the basic question is answered affirmatively—working with parents *does* make therapy work.

Even when parent work with child patients is accepted, many colleagues see work with the parents of adolescent patients in a different light, citing developmental and dynamic considerations.

One of the most articulated concerns about parent work has been the belief that the adolescent would experience the analyst as an agent of the parents, material would not be kept confidential, and so the transference would be contaminated.

The experiences described in this book, however, provide no evidence of the children or adolescents feeling anxious that therapists would betray them. Both parents and adolescents felt reassured by the distinction drawn between secrecy and privacy and relieved that analysts would be meeting regularly with their parents to "help them as parents." This finding validates an earlier study with late adolescents who experienced relief and trust that therapists would prioritize their therapeutic needs (Novick, K.K. and Novick, J. 2013).

What else have we learned from the collective experiences and commentaries in this volume, and where do we go from here? We have a more detailed description of what it's actually like to do parent work, what it evokes in therapists and how it challenges them. What emerges is that there are internal obstacles within therapists to engaging fully with the practical implications of the model even if the analyst is theoretically on board.

Rosenbaum (1994) was one of the first to describe the necessity of assessing parents when evaluating a child for treatment, to try to anticipate difficulties in parental functioning that could interfere with their understanding and accepting a recommendation for treatment that could be worked on and worked through. Robert and Erna Furman and their colleagues at The Hanna Perkins Center,[8] Altman (2004), Edgcumbe (2000) and others have contributed to the sparse literature on parent work. In a series of seminal papers and a book,

---

8   See *Child Analysis: Clinical, Theoretical, and Applied,* available through the Hanna Perkins Center, as well as numerous papers by Erna Furman and Robert Furman.

Kerry and Jack Novick looked in detail at this idea and elaborated a model that forms a significant background to this volume.[9]

All these authors also look to aspects of therapists' motivations, mindset, reactions and feelings as potential impediments to beginning and sustaining a treatment of a child or adolescent. One of the internal resistances all child analysts bring to parent work is our tendency to focus only on the child or adolescent as the patient. If one thinks that psychoanalysis deals only with the intrapsychic, then the patient is singular, and our restricted attention isolates the child from the environment of people, community and culture. If the child is the only patient with whom we ally ourselves, many feelings about parents can come into play. We can feel competitive, critical, judgmental.

But if we see the parent-child relationship as a legitimate object of therapeutic effort, shifting ourselves to thinking of parents in their parenting functions the same way we think of individual adult patients, we come to a different stance. We invoke neutrality and the suspension of judgment, feeling respect, sympathy, empathy, and tolerance for troubles and pathology. This in turn affects the techniques we then access, mandating use of all the same repertoire of interventions we use with individual adult patients.

What we learn from the contributors to this book is how hard it is for analysts to stay equidistant from all family members, as Anna Freud often advised, when they do stay involved with parents. All the clinical contributors, at one point or another, registered their intense feelings, their frustration, their rage, their sadness, their helplessness, their rescue fantasies, their ignorance, their hopelessness, and sometimes their fear for themselves or the child. Even while

---

9   Novick, J. and Novick, K.K. 2000, 2002; Novick, K.K. and Novick, J. 2000a, 2002a, 2005, 2013, 2014; Dowling, S. et al 2013.

celebrating the moments of collaboration and change, clinical authors and commentators alike reflect ruefully on the inevitable pull to enmeshment in transference/countertransference enactments.

Just as the therapeutic relationship in general does not consist solely of transferences and countertransferences, there are also forces at work between parents and therapists that are operating closer to current reality. Much more than in individual adult work, parents seeking to entrust their child to us are making judgments about us as real people. Their mistrust may have pathological origins or eventuate in grave difficulties in the treatment, as we saw in several cases described, but it can also be evidence of appropriate care and concern for their child's wellbeing. We are as vulnerable in our self-esteem as anyone else, and it is hard to be assessed, just as it is hard for parents to feel that we are evaluating them. Several of our contributors spoke to their surprise or dismay when parents unexpectedly turned on them. It hurts to be blindsided or disregarded or denigrated. We have been impressed anew with the strength, the emotional muscle and stamina, demanded by child and adolescent treatments that include parent work.

One of the main manifestations of therapists' internal obstacles is not taking sufficient time in the initial exploratory phase to establish a sturdy therapeutic alliance with parents. In each chapter of this book we hear variations on the theme of challenges in building an alliance with parents. That comes through loud and clear. Perhaps the strongest message of this volume is a clarion call for paying attention to this vital element, which means resisting the pressure of parents and referrers for instant answers, for rescue from acute distress. Analyst and parents will not be able to weather the inevitable rough patches of a child's treatment unless they have a collaborative working relationship; they need a therapeutic alliance built upon a foundation of knowledge and transformation, that fosters trust over time, includes experiences of mastery and relief from understanding and insight, and encompasses joint work.

We know from earlier experience that this takes time. Relationships are not established in one or two meetings. Building an alliance is accomplished only in the context of a relationship, by sharing experiences of achieving insight, by initiating various transformations, with the fundamental one probably being to access primary parental love. This starts the long work of helping parents restructure their relationship with their child from one of using the child for their own psychological needs to seeing the child as a separate person, invested realistically with their love and care. These beginning efforts have to take place in the initial exploratory period, before the recommendation for treatment can be made and therapy begun. Parents and therapist have to agree about the dual goals of treatment.

A radical contribution of the parent work model we brought into this project was the notion of *dual goals* for any child or adolescent treatment:

- ❖ restoration of the child to the path of progressive development, and
- ❖ restoration of the parent-child relationship to a lifelong resource for all.

The dual goals are basic to establishing a therapeutic alliance, motivating the parent to work together with the analyst and giving the analyst the permission to use the full repertoire of techniques. A commitment to dual goals for all treatments pushes us to think with greater focus about what is going on between parents and children, dynamically and practically.

It may advance our understanding and handling of controversial and difficult issues, such as confidentiality in the treatment situation. Respecting the intrinsic privacy of thoughts and feelings, while analyzing secrecy in an active way becomes more straightforward with the insights achieved in thinking about these matters in relation to the material of this volume. The *content* of secrets can be usefully separated from the *effects* of the secret.

Sometimes therapists act as if they don't have the right to say anything to the parent since the parent is not the patient. Often there is a conscious fear that the parent will be upset and end the child's treatment. As one therapist reported, this could be a transference to the mother of the pregendered Ur-mother who has total life and death power over everyone including the therapist. The therapist is then alone with the burden of a secret or something the therapist can see, like the mother's severe breakdown, but feels unable to share it with the other parent or deal directly and therapeutically with the emotionally disturbed parent. Equally it may be important to confirm a child's perception of something "weird" about one or the other parent or take up the child's defense against what they are seeing and sensing especially when it emerges as a displacement to the therapy. This may be even more true in work with adolescents where what may be taken as a transference is actually a displacement to the therapeutic situation of being the powerful perpetrator of the mother's upset and panic that the therapist will send them away into the cold.

When we fully embrace the idea of dual goals, we realize that working with the parents of adolescents is predicated on the idea that the aim is for teenagers and parents to transform their relationship into one that will continue to be a resource for all. That also means including fathers in the work, actually whenever possible, and keeping them actively in mind when there are impediments. This was important in all the cases in this volume.

The material of this volume reconfigures the idea of dual goals, bringing it into the context of life-cycle psychoanalysis in a new way. In the book we reference parent-infant psychotherapy and look at patients from preschool to emerging adulthood. This has pushed us to think about the role of parent work throughout the life cycle, to consider whether and how we might raise our clinical awareness of the operation of internal parent representations, internalized parenting functions, and the role of actual parents for our patients of all ages. The effective concurrent parent work with late adolescents and emerging adults illustrated in this book leads us to think about the application of these techniques and ideas to work with adults. This would be a further step in establishing life-cycle analysis, implemented in integrated programs, as a possible future in psychoanalytic training and practice.

The Novicks' earlier book on parent work ended with a chapter on the application of parent work to therapy with adults (Novick, K.K. and Novick, J. 2005). In that chapter, among other parallels, they wrote about keeping the partner of the adult patient in mind when treating an adult. As with the parent of the child or adolescent patient, the significant other may become jealous, rivalrous and, in general, create obstacles to continued treatment. The adult patient may act out a sibling situation and make the partner feel excluded, criticized and judged by the analyst, and the patient then "has to quit" because the partner is so angry.

An achievement of work in analysis is seeing one's own parents realistically as whole people with strengths and weaknesses, moving to a less need-satisfying stance, a more fully articulated investment in the actual people, in contrast to only transferences issuing from internal imagoes or phantasy constructions. This developmental pathway is not restricted to child and adolescent patients; it operates powerfully in successful adult treatments. Similarly, we look for growth in the strength of a patient's significant relationships beyond the treatment, the bonds that will sustain them and help them meet their legitimate human needs throughout life. That progressive momentum is a criterion for beginning termination in patients of all ages and stems directly from the analyst's attention to the patient's important relationships. Doing parent work with child and adolescent patients affects how we work with adult patients, raising our awareness of the parental dimension in all domains of their lives, including bringing their own functioning as parents into their treatments.

There is a powerful lesson that emerges for us from the experiences described by our contributors. When we do concurrent parent work along with our individual therapeutic engagement with a child or adolescent, we too are changed. Our ideas and theories are challenged; our emotional range is stretched and expanded; our technical repertoire becomes perforce more flexible and responsive to dynamic changes in patients and their parents. We too have a developmental experience.

However the work is configured, we conclude with having learned anew that the crucial issue is keeping the parents in the clinical landscape. We hope that the experiences of the many generous contributors to this volume inspire other colleagues and students to include parent work in their treatment plans, to share with each other the joys and tribulations of such work to further refine techniques and ideas, and to establish the legitimate place of parent work in our clinical repertoires.

REFERENCES

Ainsworth, M. (1985). Patterns of attachment. *Journal of Clinical Psychology* 38(2): 27–29.

Ainsworth, M. (1991). Attachments and other affectional bonds across the life cycle. In *Attachment Across the Life Cycle*, ed. C. M. Parkes & J. Stevenson. New York: Tavistock/Routledge.

Ainsworth, M., Bell, S. M., & Stayton, D. J. (1991). Infant–mother attachment and social development: "Socialisation" as a product of reciprocal responsiveness to signals. In *Becoming a Person: Child Development in Social Context 1*, ed. M. Woodhead & R. Carr. Florence: Taylor & Francis/Routledge.

Altman, N. (2004). Child psychotherapy: Converging traditions. *Journal of Child Psychotherapy* 30(2): 189–206.

Altman, N., Briggs, R., Frankel, J., Gensler, D., & Pantone, P. (2002). *Relational Child Psychotherapy*. New York: Other Press.

Arnett, J. (2014). *Emerging Adulthood: The Winding Road from Late Teens Through the Twenties*. 2nd ed. Oxford: Oxford University Press.

Benedek, T. (1959). Parenthood as a developmental phase—A contribution to the libido theory. *Journal of the American Psychoanalytic Association* 7: 389-417.

Bettelheim, B. (1967). *The empty fortress: Infantile Autism and the Birth of the Self*. Oxford: Free Press of Glencoe.

Bion, W. R. (1970). *Attention and Interpretation*. London: Tavistock.

Blake, P. (2008). *Child and Adolescent Psychotherapy*. London: Karnac Books.

Bleger J. (1966). *Psicoigiene e psicologia istituzionale. Psicoanalisi applicata agli individui, ai gruppi e alle istituzioni*. Trad. it., Molfetta: La Meridiana, 2011

Bowlby, J. (1969). *Attachment and Loss*. London: Pimlico.

Bründl, P. & Kogan, I. (2005): *Kindheit jenseits von Trauma und Fremdheit: Psychoanalytische Erkundigungen von Migrations-schicksalen im Kindes- und Jugendalter*. Frankfurt am Main: Brandes & Apsel.

Davids, J., Green, V., Joyce, A., & McLean, D. (2017). Revised provisional Diagnostic Profile: 2006. *Journal of Infant, Child, and Adolescent Psychotherapy* 16: 149–157.

Dowling, S., Lament, C., Novick, K.K., & Novick, J. (2013). Dialogue with the Novicks. *Psychoanalytic Study of the Child* 67: 137–145.

Edgcumbe, R. (2000). *Anna Freud: A View of Development, Disturbance, and Therapeutic Techniques*. London and Philadelphia: Routledge.

Engel, G. L., Reichsman, F.K., & Viederman, M. (1979). Monica: A 25-year longitudinal study of the consequences of trauma in infancy. *Journal of the American Psychoanalytic Association* 27(1): 107–126.

Erikson, E. H. (1980). On the generational cycle, an Address. *International Journal of Psycho-Analysis* 61: 213–223.

Evans-Pritchard, E. E. (1940). *The Nuer, A Description of the Modes, Livelihood and Political Institutions of a Nilotic People*. Oxford: Clarendon Press.

Ferenczi, S. (1949). Confusion of the tongues between the adults and the child—(the language of tenderness and of passion). *International Journal of Psycho-Analysis* 30: 225–230.

Fischer, G. & Riederesser, P. (1998). *Lehrbuch der Traumatologie*. München: UTB.

Fonagy, P., Moran, G.S., Edgcumbe, R., Kennedy, H., & Target, M. (1993). The roles of mental representations and mental processes in therapeutic action. *Psychoanalytic Study of the Child* 48: 9–48.

Fonagy, P., & Target, M. (1996). Playing with reality: I. Theory of mind and the normal development of psychic reality. *International Journal of Psychoanalysis* 77: 217–233.

Fonagy, P., & Target, M. (1997). Attachment and reflective function: Their role in self-organization. *Developmental Psychopathology* 9: 679–900.

Freud, A. (1965). *Normality and Pathology in Childhood: Assessments of Development. Writings* 6. New York: International Universities Press.

Freud, A. (1970). Problems of termination in child analysis. *Writings* 7. New York: International Universities Press: 3–21.

Freud, S. (1892). Letter from Freud to Fliess, December 18, 1892. In *The Complete Letters of Sigmund Freud to Wilhelm Fliess, 1887–1904*, ed. J. M. Masson. Cambridge, MA: Belknap Press, pp. 36–37.

Freud, S. (1895). Project for a scientific psychology. *Standard Edition* 1.

Freud, S. (1901). The Psychopathology of Everyday Life. Standard Edition 6.

Freud, S. (1905). Three essays on the theory of sexuality. *Standard Edition* 7: 130–243.

Furman, E. (1969). Treatment via the mother. In *The Therapeutic Nursery School*, ed. R. Furman, & A. Katan. New York: International Universities Press, pp. 64–123.

Furman, E. (1982). Mothers have to be there to be left. *Psychoanalytic Study of the Child* 37: 15–28.

Furman, E. (1992). *Toddlers and Their Mothers*. New Haven, CT: Yale University Press.

Furman, E. (1995). On working with and through the parents in child therapy. *Child Analysis: Clinical, Theoretical, and Applied* 6: 21–42.

Furman, R. (1995). Some aspects of the analyst-analysand relationship. *Child Analysis:Clinical, Theoretical, and Applied* 6: 106–127.

Furman, R. & Katan, A. (1969). *The Therapeutic Nursery School*. New York: International Universities Press.

George, C., Kaplan, N., & Main, M. (1985). The Adult Attachment Interview. Unpublished manuscript, University of California at Berkeley. www.psychology.sunysb.edu/attachment/measures/content/aai_interview.pdf

Green, A. (1973). The negative capability—A critical review. *International Journal of Psycho-Analysis* 54: 115–119

Green, V. and Joyce, A. (2017). Revised Diagnostic Profile 2006: Revisions, rationale, and further thoughts. *Journal of Infant, Child, and Adolescent Psychotherapy* 16: 138–148.

Greenspan, S.I., & Shanker, S.G. (2004). *The First Idea: How Symbols, Language and Intelligence Evolved from Our Primate Ancestors to Modern Humans*. Cambridge MA: Da Capo Press.

Hall, R. (1993). Working with parents. *Child Analysis: Clinical, Theoretical, and Applied* 4: 62–74.

Hart, O., & Horst, R. (1989). The dissociation theory of Pierre Janet. *Journal of Traumatic Stress* 2: 397–412.

Herzog, J. M. (1979). Patterns of expectant fatherhood. *Dialogue: A Journal of Psychoanalytic Perspectives* 301: 55–67.

Herzog, J.M. (1984). Boys who make babies. In *Adolescent Parenthood Spectrum*, ed. M. Sugar. New York: Wiley, pp. 65–77.

Herzog, J.M. (2004). Father hunger: Explorations with adults and children. Hillsdale, NJ: Analytic Press.

Jacobs, L. (2006). Parent-centered work: A relational shift in child treatment. *Journal of Infant, Child, and Adolescent Psychotherapy* 5 (2): 226–239.

Kanner, L. (1949). Problems of nosology and psychodynamics in early childhood autism. *American Journal of Orthopsychiatry* 19 (3): 416–23.

Klein, M. (1932). *The Psycho-Analysis of Children*. London: The Hogarth Press

Klein, M. (1937). Love, guilt and reparation. In *Love, Guilt, Reparation and Other Works*. London: Hogarth, 1975, pp. 306–343.

Lane R.D. (2018). From reconstruction to construction: The power of corrective emotional experiences in memory reconsolidation and enduring change. *Journal of the American Psychoanalytic Association* 66: 507–516.

Lane R.D., Ryan, L., Nadel, L., & Greenberg L. (2015). Memory reconsolidation, emotional arousal and the process of change in psychotherapy: New insights from brain science. *Behavioral and Brain Sciences* 38:1–19.

Laplanche, J. (1997). The theory of seduction and the problem of the other. *International Journal of Psycho-Analysis* 78: 653–666.

Levy-Warren, M.H. (2005). To weep, to laugh, to mourn, to dance: Key factors for therapeutic change in the clinical exchange with an adolescent girl. *Journal of Infant, Child, and Adolescent Psychotherapy* 4(4): 351–372.

Levy-Warren, M.H. (2018). What does it mean to think developmentally in doing clinical work? *Journal of Child and Adolescent Psychotherapy* 17 (2): 84–89.

Liberman, A. F., & Van Horn, P. J. (2008). *Psychotherapy with Infants and Young Children: Repairing the Effects of Stress and Trauma on Early Attachment*. New York: Guilford Press.

Main, M., Kaplan, N., & Cassidy, J. (1985). Security in infancy, childhood, and adulthood: A move to the level of representation. *Monographs of the Society for Research in Child Development, 50* (1–2), 66–104. http://dx.doi.org/10.2307/3333827

Malinowski, B. (1929). *The Sexual Life of Savages in North-western Melanesia: An Ethnographic Account of Courtship, Marriage and Family Life Among the Natives of the Trobriand Islands, British New Guinea*. New York: Halcyon House.

Marquardt, E. (2005). *Between Two Worlds: The Inner Lives of Children of Divorce*. New York: Crown Publishing Group/Random House.

Matte-Blanco, I. (1959). Expression in symbolic logic of the characteristics of the system ucs or the logic of the system ucs. *International Journal of Psycho-Analysis* 40: 1–5.

Master, J. (2018). Eating Disorders: A Manifestation of Insecure Attachments to Primary Caregiver(s) in Early Childhood. PsyD dissertation, The Chicago School of Professional Psychology.

Mead, M. (1928). *Coming of Age in Samoa: A Psychological Study of Primitive Youth for Western Civilization*. New York: William Morrow & Co.

Meltzer D. (1973). Adolescent psychoanalytical theory. In *Adolescence by M. Harris-D. Meltzer*. London: Melanie Klein Trust.

Morgan, M. (2010). Unconscious beliefs about being a couple. *Fort Da* 16(1): 36–55.

Novick, J. (1980). Negative therapeutic motivation and negative therapeutic alliance. *Psychoanalytic Study of the Child* 35: 299–320.

Novick, J. & Novick, K.K. (2000). Parent work in analysis: Children, adolescents, and adults. Part One: The evaluation phase. *Journal of Infant, Child and Adolescent Psychotherapy* 1 (4): 55–77.

Novick, J. & Novick, K.K. (2002a). Parent work in analysis: Children, adolescents, and adults. Part Three: Middle and pretermination phases. *Journal of Infant, Child and Adolescent Psychotherapy* 2 (2): 17–41.

Novick, J. and Novick, K.K. (2006). *Good Goodbyes: Knowing How to End in Psychoanalysis and Psychotherapy*. Lanham MD: Aronson, Rowman and Littlefield.

Novick, J. & Novick, K.K. (2008). Expanding the domain: Privacy, secrecy and confidentiality. *Annual of Psychoanalysis* 36/37: 145–160.

Novick, J. & Novick, K.K. (2012). Emotional muscle in therapists—A strengths-based learning model for treatment. *Bulletin of the Michigan Psychoanalytic Council* 8: 3–23.

Novick, J. & Novick, K. K. (2016) *Freedom to Choose: Two Systems of Self-Regulation*. Astoria, NY: International Psychoanalytic Books.

Novick, K.K. & Novick, J. (2002). Parent work in analysis. Children, adolescents, and adults. Part Two: Recommendation, beginning, and middle phases of treatment. *Journal of Infant, Child and Adolescent Psychotherapy* 2 (1): 1–27.

Novick, K.K. & Novick, J. (2005). *Working with Parents Makes Therapy Work*. Lanham MD: Rowman & Littlefield.

Novick, K.K. & Novick, J. (2013). Concurrent Work with Parents of Adolescent Patients. *Psychoanalytic Study of the Child* 67: 103–136.

Novick, K.K. and Novick, J. (2014). Psychoanalysis and child rearing. *Psychoanalytic Inquiry* 34: 440–451.

Novick, K.K. (1988). Childbearing and child-rearing. *Psychoanalytic Inquiry* 8 (2): 252–260.

Rizzolo, G.S. (2019). The life cycle (without regression). *Psychoanalytic Study of the Child* 72: 207–227.

Rosenbaum, A.L. (1994). The assessment of parental functioning: A critical process in the evaluation of children for psychoanalysis. *Psychoanalytic Quarterly* 63: 466–490.

Rustin, M.E. (1998). Dialogues with parents. *Journal of Child Psychotherapy* 24(2): 233–252.

Sandler, J. (1986). Reality and the stabilizing function of unconscious fantasy. *Bulletin of the Anna Freud Centre* 3: 177–194.

Sandler, J. (1989). Guilt and Internal Object Relationships. *Bulletin of the Anna Freud Centre* 12(4): 297–307.

Schafer, R. (1980). Action language and the psychology of the self. *Annual of Psychoanalysis* 8: 83–92.

Scharff, D. E., Losso, R., & Setton, L. (2017). Pichon Rivière's psychoanalytic contributions: Some comparisons with object relations and modern developments in psychoanalysis. *International Journal of Psycho-Analysis* 98(1): 129–143.

Schmukler, A., Atkeson, P., Keable, H., Dahl, K. (2012). *Ethical Practice in Child and Adolescent Analysis and Psychotherapy.* New York: Aronson.

Slade, A. (2008). The move from categories to process: Attachment phenomena and clinical evaluation. *New Directions in Psychotherapy and Relational Psychoanalysis* 2 (1): 89–105.

Spitz, R.A. (1945). Hospitalism—An inquiry into the genesis of psychiatric conditions in early childhood. *Psychoanalytic Study of the Child* 1: 53–74.

Steele, H., & Steele, M. (2008). On the origins of reflective functioning. In *Mentalization: Theoretical Considerations, Research Findings, and Clinical Implications,* ed. F. Busch. New York: Analytic Press, pp. 133–156.

Stern, D. (1985): *The Interpersonal World of The Infant. A View from Psychoanalysis and Developmental Psychology.* New York: Basic Books.

Whitefield, C., & Midgley, N. (2015). 'And when you were a child?': How therapists working with parents alongside individual child psychotherapy bring the past into their work. *Journal of Child Psychotherapy* 41(3): 272–292.

Winnicott, D.W. (1958). *Collected Papers: Through Pediatrics to Psycho-Analysis.* New York: Basic Books.

Winnicott, D.W. (1965). *The Maturational Processes and the Facilitating Environment. Studies in the Theory of Emotional Development.* New York: International Universities Press.

Winnicott, D.W. (1969). The use of an object. *International Journal of Psycho-Analysis* 50: 711–716.

Winnicott, D.W. (1971). *Playing and Reality.* London: Routledge.

www.ingramcontent.com/pod-product-compliance
Lightning Source LLC
Chambersburg PA
CBHW051710020426
42333CB00014B/916